2.00

Praise for *Walking Taylor Home*

"In these times, each and every one of us, regardless of faith or background, needs a guide for transcending tragedy. *Walking Taylor Home* is a personal and inspiring story that will resonate with every reader who has known sadness."

RABBI DANIEL LAPIN
President, Toward Tradition, Seattle

"Rarely does courage leap off a page and hook your heart, but in *Walking Taylor Home,* this little guy, this man-warrior, reeled me in with each paragraph. For anyone wrenching their way through a family illness, this book will encourage you hook, line, and sinker!"

JONI EARECKSON TADA
President, Joni and Friends

"*Walking Taylor Home* is a gutsy, honest account of a father's walk with his son through the valley of the shadow of death. The long obedience and triumphant ending of Taylor's life are shown to rely on one thing: Y'shua walked with them. We highly recommend this book."

MICHAEL W. AND DEBBIE SMITH

"Taylor's story will inspire many, but it will also explain what cancer does to an everyday family. In their journey you will see an almost inconceivable but very authentic weave of hope and tragedy in the midst of chaos. This is a truly honest, stirring and unforgettable story that ends with joy and hope for every reader who finishes walking Taylor home."

DAVE DRAVECKY
President, Outreach of Hope cancer ministry and former major league pitcher

"If you dare to journey into this story, be prepared to have your heart broken while at the same time being filled to overflowing with the profound hope of the Gospel."

STEVEN CURTIS CHAPMAN

"*Walking Taylor Home* is an unflinchingly honest journey into the very heart of every parent's darkest nightmare—the death of a child. And yet, miraculously, it is also a journey filled with humor, hope and redemption . . . A heartbreaking, uplifting, extraordinary story that will make you hold your children a little closer tonight."

RUSS AND TORI TAFF

"Man's greatest strength and most vulnerable frailty is the basic need to control and explain his surroundings. What does one do when no earthly knowledge can explain human calamity? It is the interplay of these themes, so insightfully and eloquently expressed by the grief-stricken father of *Walking Taylor Home*, that personalizes this true struggle between a boy and a cancer. Reading this will result in a broader understanding of ourselves. Life is precious. Despite triumphs of medicine, death remains an enigma. Allow yourself to join Taylorman's journey into the "mutha-land." As the story touches you, glean its wisdom spoken with childhood honesty through love, humor, peace, and worship."

HERBERT S. SCHWARTZ, M.D.
Chief of Orthopaedic Surgery and Rehabilitation, Vanderbilt Medical Center

"This is a story that will touch the heart of anyone who has suffered the loss of a loved one....Throughout this story, the love of a father for his son, and of a son for his father, and of a family for each other, is what shines through and makes this a story worth hearing. I would recommend it for anyone involved in treating children with life-threatening illnesses."

LEE J. HELMAN, M.D.
Pediatric Oncologist, Bethesda, Maryland

"In *Walking Taylor Home* Brian lets us inside one family's hearts as they walk through agonizing, glorious hours of agony and ecstasy, the horror of disease and death, and the marvel of love, hope, joy, and faith. Let Taylor's story hold you and draw you closer to this Unfathomable God/Father Who has His own—to us sometimes strange—ways of releasing us into eternal joy."

DON FINTO
Author of Your People Shall Be My People

"THANK YOU for publishing this most powerful book! . . . Taylor IS NOT defeated. Cancer DOES NOT have the last word. This amazing book offered me the rarest experience of extravagant grace. Knowing Taylor, and his Christ."

BONNIE KEEN
First Call

"*Walking Taylor Home* is written for those who exclaim, 'I don't know how a parent can do that!' . . . and for those of us who have."

JAN WHEELER
Founder, Project Joy and Hope for Texas

WALKING TAYLOR HOME

A TRUE STORY

BRIAN SCHRAUGER

W PUBLISHING GROUP™

www.wpublishinggroup.com

A Division of Thomas Nelson, Inc.
www.ThomasNelson.com

Published by W Publishing Group, a Division of Thomas Nelson, Inc., P.O. Box 141000, Nashville, Tennessee, 37214.

Scripture quotations used in this book are either the author's personal translation or have been taken from:

The Holy Bible, New International Version (NIV). Copyright © 1973, 1978, 1984, International Bible Society. Used by permission of Zondervan Bible Publishers.

The Holy Bible, New International Readers Version™, Copyright © 1995, 1996, 1998 by International Bible Society. Used by permission of Zondervan Publishing House. All rights reserved.

"Friends," words and music by Deborah D. Smith and Michael W. Smith © 1982 by Meadowgreen Music Co. (Administered by Tree Pub. Co. Inc.) (ASCAP). Used by permission.

Library of Congress Cataloging-in-Publication Data

Schrauger, Brian, 1955–
    Walking Taylor home / by Brian Schrauger.
      p. cm.
    ISBN 0-8499-1703-4
    1. Schrauger, Taylor, 1988—Health. 2. Cancer in children—Patients—United States—Biography. I. Title.

RC281.C4 S377 2001
362.1'9892994'0092—dc21
[B]   2001045578

TAYLOR, BUDDY, MY LACK OF SKILL COMBINED WITH limited space made it impossible for me to properly develop the crucial roles of your mom and brothers in this book—even though they too are central to your story . . . especially Mom, who nursed and fought and prayed with all her might every single day. Although it still falls far too short in expressing their heroic love, let's dedicate the telling of our pilgrimage as father-son to them:

To my wife, Debbie, who never gives up, even on me. To Christopher, who with a specially tuned heart heard the angels sing. To Jonathan, a boy, a man, who knows God's love and grace.

And Taylorman, let's also give highest honors to just a few of your fellow heroes—gallant peers who, just like you, were mighty warriors masked as children . . .

CAMILLE ROSE ANTONELLI • ROBERT GROSS

SOPHIE SPEAKMAN • MATTHEW TAIT

LIZZY LEMKY • HOPE LAUREN GUTHRIE

VALERIE WHEELER • BRIANNA CADMAN

TRAVIS THORNE • PAUL SYSWERDA

AMANDA PELFREY

Moriturite salutamus

Landmarks Along The Way

FOREWORD

I REMEMBER THE FIRST TIME I SAW BRIAN AND TAYLOR Schrauger. It was on a Sunday morning in our congregation in Nashville. I was late for the service. It had taken me longer than usual to peel my son off my suit and deposit him in the nursery. As I slipped into a seat near the back of the sanctuary, Brian and Taylor were making their way to the platform. The first thing I noticed was that Taylor had only one leg. The second thing I noticed was that this father and son were both bald. As they began to tell their story of a fierce battle against the merciless enemy of cancer, they unwrapped both of those mysteries. Their story was heartbreaking, and yet the fragrance of God's Son filled the sanctuary. It was a holy moment.

A few days later I bumped into them in a store. We talked for a few moments, and as they turned to leave, I saw something in Brian's eyes that I will never forget. They were the eyes of a drowning man. There was an ocean of pain and questions there until the sunlight of Taylor's presence calmed the sea for a moment. He hopped toward us like a jumping bean full of energy and life, whispering, "C'mon, Dad. Let's go!"

I began to pray for them every day. A few weeks later I invited the

Schrauger family to our house for a barbeque. I told my three-year-old son, Christian, that one of our guests had just one leg.

"Where is his other one?" he asked.

"Why don't you ask him?" I suggested. After they had been there for a few moments, Christian decided to broach the subject.

"Do you know that you only have one leg?" he asked.

"Yes, I noticed that," Taylor said.

"Where's the other one?"

"God is keeping it for me," he said.

"That's cool," Christian answered. "He's a good guy."

That's the Taylor I came to know and love: honest with those who were straight with him, tolerant of a pain level that would have crushed five men, full of joy and mischief, enormously alive in the shadow of death.

Throughout Taylor's battle I had the profound privilege of being added to the list of those who received Brian's e-mail updates. From the first letter several things were clear to me. Brian is a gifted writer who can put words to the unspeakable. He is brutally honest at a level that would terrify most of us. His faith is secure enough to wrestle with God until he is exhausted, and then bury his head in the mane of the Lion of Judah.

Many nights I sat at my computer weeping as I read, wrestling with God myself as this merciless dragon decimated his son's body. Taylor's ruthless enemy attacked the whole family. Sometimes Taylor's mom, Debbie, seemed like a fragile leaf on a cold winter's day. Other times she was a tower of strength. His brothers, Christopher and Jonathan, gathered around him, loved him, willed him to beat this thing. If pure courage and the ability to get up one more time had been enough Taylor would have won every battle he fought. But they were not enough. Neither were drugs, surgeries, or an ocean of tears. But in the end and in the truest sense Taylor didn't lose. He won the final battle.

On the day when along with countless others we celebrated that final victory, Christian asked me if Taylor had his leg back now. I told him that he did.

This story will change your life if you will let it. It will take you places you have never been before and let you see that even those with broken wings can fly if God is underneath them. You are invited now to walk beside a father and son on the most profound journey of life, into the very arms of God. As you read you will discover that you too are walking Taylor home. You will laugh and cry; you will want to share this story with those who suffer in silence, wrestling with a God they do not understand, a God who says he loves them and yet allows unspeakable atrocities, suffering that cannot be put into words. The Bible tells us that those who have been forgiven much love much. It seems that those who have suffered much love much too. Taylor Schrauger changed my life forever: a child warrior who never gave up. I believe he is one of God's true heroes.

Who will sing the suffering song
Down to the depths where few have gone?
And let the light shine through their pain
For God is found on earth again.

—SHEILA WALSH

PROLOGUE

ALMOST ALWAYS, ESPECIALLY EARLY ON, I TOLD EACH OF my three sons, "I can tell. Someday you are going be an awesome dad."

Then, almost every night after hugs and kisses, I turned off the lights and said, "Good night! I love you! See you in the morning."

Each repeated back the words exactly as I said them. Except for Taylor, who with dyslexic echo said, "See you in the morning! Good night! I love you!"

Curious twist, I thought.

All throughout their younger years there was a quiet voice inside my mind, my heart, whispering but clear, *Be sure to say this every night. Because it is a promise from both of us. No matter what life brings, you and your sons will always and forever see each other in the morning.*

When I heard the voice, I shuddered, then quenched it with the thought, *This is nothing more than what all parents fear. Of course the worst is possible. But we are careful. The worst is far from likely. Stuff like that only happens to people who are not careful or to the unlucky few. And after all, worst-case odds are very, very slim.*

And so my mind, confident in the odds, told the worry in my heart to just shut up.

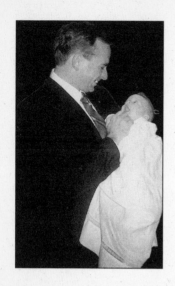

PART I

THE DAM ROAD

 **1 HARD NEWS**

HARD NEWS: AN UPDATE ON TAYLOR

Thursday, June 3rd, 1999

Hi. This is Brian, Taylor's dad. I'm using Taylor's e-mail because his address book is more up-to-date than mine.

After Taylor finished chemotherapy last February, he was given a battery of tests, including an MRI and CT scan. Since then he's had monthly x-rays of his chest.

Two days ago he was given a second round of scans.

Yesterday, at about three in the afternoon, one of Taylor's doctors called. He told us that new scans show four nodules on the left lung and another on the right.

The cancer is back.

The Tumor Board at Vanderbilt Children's Hospital is meeting as I write. They are mapping out a strategy for the renewed battle that lies ahead. Immediately after yesterday's call I went home, cried with Debbie, then exercised and showered.

I also shaved my head. Again.

And all the while I wept and raged, shamelessly pleading with God.

About an hour later, while Debbie worked the phone calling friends and family, recruiting prayers, I went to find Taylor.

He was at his best friend's house just down the block. The two of them were playing on Nintendo 64. Standing at the front door of our neighbor's house I said, "Hey, buddy. I need to talk with you. Would you walk home with me?"

"Well . . . okay, sure! See ya later, Trey." He was as happy as a lark.

Skipping at my side down the middle of the street, he suddenly noticed. "Hey, Dad, you shaved your head again! How come?"

Silently I prayed for help. "Yeah. Kinda felt I had to."

Unfazed by my elusive answer, Taylor chose to tease.

"So why're you out here? Shouldn't you be doing something with Mom? After all, today *is* your twentieth wedding anniversary!" His question was full of impish innuendo. And he seemed to sense a need to make me smile. I tried to comply, but knowing his skill at reading my heart, I quickly changed the subject.

While we walked I made an impromptu promise. "Guess what? Just today I made a decision. We're gonna get you a brand-new, state-of-the-art laptop, one with all the bells and whistles—like tons of memory and a DVD drive!"

The laptop he's used for a year doesn't belong to us. And at the ancient age of four, it's a technological dinosaur.

Taylor was thrilled with the news.

"Yes, yes, *yes!* So when're we gonna get it? Huh? Huh?"

I chuckled, pleased with his euphoria.

"Pretty soon. Prob'ly in the next two or three weeks."

"Yahoo!"

When we reached our house, instead of going in, I directed him to a seat in the front yard. Underneath a large shade tree we sat atop a green metallic box shielding an electrical transformer for our neighborhood. Still excited by the promise of a new computer, Taylor looked at me, curious by my silence, by the dissonance he felt. Finally I spoke.

"Well, buddy, I've got news. Good news and bad news. The good news is what I just toldja about the new laptop . . ."

O God! Help me do this . . .

"The bad news is that one of your doctors called this afternoon . . ." I paused and said no more. I didn't have to.

His jaw dropped. "It's back, isn't it?" he whispered.

I didn't say a word. Instead I just moved closer and put my arms around him. Taylor buried his face in my chest and bawled while I baptized his head with large, hot drops falling from my eyes.

Taylor's birthday is tomorrow, on Friday, June 4. He turns eleven. A huge party is planned.

On Saturday and Sunday Taylor is supposed to be on TV, helping host a telethon in a local effort to raise money for the Children's Miracle Network. And for at least a month he's counted down the days until his Hickman catheter will come out. He's had these tubes dangling from his chest for a year.

With the Hickman gone and treatment over, Taylor's summer is full of plans: uninhibited swimming, three camps, and a nostalgic visit with old friends in Dallas—a school-free time when they can *really* play. Then after summer ends, he's thrilled about going to a new school where he knows the work will be harder.

Now, at best, these things are uncertain. Most are dreams destroyed. And all in less than sixty seconds.

As our tears subsided, still sitting in the front yard underneath a tree, Taylor started asking questions. "Will I still be able to go to camps?"

"Don't know. Prob'ly not all of 'em, anyway."

"What about school this fall?"

"Don't know. We'll just have to see what happens."

"What will the doctors do now?"

"I have a few guesses, but . . . I don't know. We should find out tomorrow."

We prayed, then went inside the house and cried with Mom. Taylor's older brother, Christopher, is in Michigan this week, visiting grandparents, aunts, uncles, and cousins. And while I spoke with Taylor underneath a tree, his younger brother, Jonathan, was at a friend's house, carefree, playing and swimming in their pool.

As Debbie hit the phones, dialing for defenders who would pray, Taylor and I went inside upstairs and lay down on his bed. I put my hand on his chest and sometimes stroked his new blond hair. I knew his too would soon be gone. Again.

Brian

✂

While Taylor and I stretched out on his bed, mostly we just linked our hearts, sharing thoughts and feelings for which we knew no words. But now and then we punctuated our fellowship of silence in the room. When we did, we talked about our top-secret topic, my favorite subject—heaven. Things like . . .

"All of us adopted in God's family are called 'coheirs' with his Messiah, Taylor," I told him. "At the very least that means we're gonna inherit the universe we see. Scientists think there could be other universes than our own. But just this one has about a hundred *billion* galaxies! And that's *galaxies,* not stars!

"No way we could inherit even one universe with these defective, earthbound bodies. We're gonna need that brand-new resurrection suit, a kind of body that teleports and goes through walls and is stronger than gravity.

"With a body like that, who knows? I think that if we want, we'll be able to watch a nova from the inside out, the explosion of a sun a hundred million light-years away from our home. And anytime we want, maybe through a black hole or by bending space, we'll be able to instantly go Home. Perhaps for supper, sports, or just to answer a knock on the door from friends dropping by to visit.

"It's gonna be *so cool*—and even better than we can imagine . . ."

After a while Taylor said, "Know what, Dad? I'm really gettin' hungry." His attending grin held a hint, impossible to miss.

"You are, huh? So whaddya feel like? Nachos, maybe?"

"Yeah!" he growled with glee, knowing he'd won without a fight.

"Well . . . I guess we could go to Chili's. Mom's not gonna want to make supper. And she'll prob'ly be on the phone all night anyway . . ."

"All *right!* Let's go!"

And so we did, just the two of us. It was a meal for guys. We

wolfed down nachos dripping with melted cheese along with a deep-fried onion "blossom." For dessert we shared a hot-fudge brownie ice-cream sundae. Taylor gulped his favorite drink, Dr. Pepper, while I sipped mine, a solitary tall dark beer served in a frosted glass.

Taylor teased, "Now, Dad, give *me* the keys! After all, friends don't let friends drink and drive." His preachy tone was nyah-nyah-nyah. "*I* will drive us home!"

"You wish, bucko!"

During dinner we laughed, conferred, and made two key decisions. We talked about this weekend's telecast of the Children's Miracle Network.

"Taylor, you know you don't have to do this if you don't want to. Everyone will understand."

With a contemplative frown furrowed in his brow he took his time and then replied, "Yeah, I know. But I really think I should, don't you? . . . Yeah, I *want* to."

We also talked about the fun of going out to eat whenever Taylor got bad news. We had thought the custom was over. Until today.

2 CLOSE ENCOUNTER

OUR FAMILY WAS A HOMEMADE VERSION OF *IT'S A Wonderful Life*—before George Bailey jumped off the bridge. We were Mom Debbie, Dad Brian, and three sons: Christopher, Taylor, and Jonathan. While Debbie stayed home with the boys, I worked in the world of finance. My job was helping clients find their way to the mythical land of Economic Oz. At the same time I stood guard against the Wicked Witch of the West, Economic Loss, and her evil flying monkeys, stealing wealth away. I believed God himself gifted and ordained me to this work. Thanks to him I was smart and tough and good. Every day I turned to him and read his Word. My foremost prayer was from the Psalms: "Unless God builds the house, they labor in vain who build it." For me, the "house" was my business. I was convinced that God himself was building it with blessing.

If this vocation was my cake, the icing was opportunities to write and speak. Sometimes there were seminars, sometimes articles to write. But my favorite was radio. I was an intermittent guest on talk shows. And for several years across the land I reported and prognosticated on economic news. About three days each week the phone rang early in the morning. Stepping from the shower, dripping on the floor, sometimes with shaving cream smeared onto the earpiece, I'd make something up, a bite that sounded good. Then throughout the day, my comments were broadcast around the country. They sounded like the thoughtful and concise analyses of an economic prophet.

In truth, they were no better than my initials. But then, neither was anyone else's. The outside of my life was bright and fresh and radiant. As far as the eye could see, the future glowed with never-ending growth, the prosperity and blessing of status and respect.

Life in our suburban Dallas home was even better.

A skillful household manager, Debbie also has impeccable taste. Our house was homey, comfortable, well appointed. Bills were paid on time. Beautiful pictures in beautiful frames hung on the walls, perfectly arranged.

The boys had birthday parties I only dreamed of as a kid. And early on Debbie got each one involved in music, sports, and swimming lessons, along with activities at school and our local congregation.

Our homemade version of *It's a Wonderful Life* almost ended in the middle of production, about a year before our youngest son, Jonathan, was born. On a rainy Saturday in May of '92, Debbie, Christopher, Taylor, and I buckled the boys into our old Volvo. We were aiming for the Science Place museum near downtown Dallas, twenty minutes from our home. Instead we became the small and crumpled target of a jackknifed eighteen-wheeler hauling eighty-thousand pounds of dry cement. We should have died, but didn't. Although at first, for just a small eternity, I thought Christopher was gone, he was only unconscious. But until he came to I tasted the bile of an unspeakable horror.

In the end our injuries were minor. Still, it was a close, close call. That evening I told Debbie, "You know, in a way we died today. What we felt was just the same as untold millions who encounter, without

warning, an instant shock of terror then, like a light switch, their lives are just turned off. The only difference for us is that we're still alive. We must have been protected. God must have a plan, a purpose for our lives. And after this, we should never be afraid again."

How right, how wrong, I was.

3   THE DEATH-DEFYING TAYLORMAN

ESCAPING THE HORRIFIC CAR CRASH WASN'T TAYLOR'S first brush with death. In fact, it seemed like death was out to get him from the moment he was born, emerging bluish purple, umbilical wound around his neck. Unwrapping the python cord was harder than expected. Still, the doctor did it, saving his life at birth so that he soon glowed pink, squalling out his newborn cry of thanks. But later, as Debbie held her infant son, she had a premonition. It shook her up, made her sick inside. Not like morning sickness. It was worse than that. Much worse.

When she told me what happened, what she felt and why, for a moment I too was rattled by a sense of numbing fear. But racing at Mach four (or more), my mind tagged it as irrational and meaningless. I brushed it all aside.

"It doesn't mean anything, Debbie. You're just feeling backwash from the cord around his neck. And maybe some postpartum stuff."

To myself I thought, *Probably hormonal.*

"It wasn't a voice," she explained. "But it was a message. The message was, 'Love him well. He won't be here for long.'"

This message came, she said, with the feeling of a Presence. "The message made me sick. But the Presence felt like God."

When she told me this, I felt relief. It was hormonal after all. I knew God didn't speak like that to people. Part of me wished he did. I knew he used to. But not anymore.

People who think he still speaks are kooky, I thought to myself. *They're emotional, irrational, deceived. Not that they're bad; they're just untrained, unscientific, uneducated.*

I whispered an unspoken word, a prayer I'd one day rue. *Thank you, God, for saving Taylor from the cord. And thank you for my training. Thank you that I'm not like* them . . . *people who hear voices, thinking that it's you.*

Still, Debbie, at least, never quite forgot her premonition. One night when Taylor was three and Christopher six, it came roaring back. That night, like always, I went into the boys' room to share good nights and prayers. The first stop was with Christopher high up on the top bunk while Taylor waited underneath for his turn with Dad. Stone-blind to any danger, I goofed around with Christopher and then began to pray. As we did . . .

BOOM!

Bed and all, we fell. And underneath was Taylor! Heart pounding, shocked and terrified, I jumped over the collapsed bunk knowing I would find a badly wounded Taylor. Maybe worse. There was no sound. It happened so fast I thought he might be crushed, unconscious. Maybe even . . . dead.

No! No! No! I screamed out to God with soundless lips. Landing on my feet, I crouched with dread but had to look. When I did, I saw him. Unscratched. Untouched. But not entirely unfazed.

Eyes round and big, he looked at me in silence as if to say, *Wow! What was that?*

Instead of falling flat, as it seemed we should have, the top bunk landed at an angle, one long edge all the way down, pressing on the lower mattress. But the other angled upward, suspended just above my precious little boy. I pulled him out, hugged him tight. And prayed out loud our thank-yous.

Four years later on a Sunday afternoon, the falling bunk was long forgotten. It was a blistering hot day. Summer, Texas-style. After some cajoling Taylor grudgingly agreed to join me on a short excursion to Joe Pool Lake. To the dam road there.

Just a ten-minute drive from our house near Dallas, the earthen dam is at least ten stories high and two miles wide. It's topped by a stretch of an old state highway that extends another two miles along the edge of the lake. Isolated and remote, the dam road offers a fantastic view of giant sky and lake and prairie. Closed to motor traffic, the long and almost all-flat road was a perfect place for me to walk and learn to in-line skate. It was a place to exercise and look for God in a place of wild beauty. For two years, regardless of the weather, I went there almost every day. Alternating back and forth, I power-walked one day then Rollerbladed on the other. Usually I went alone, but sometimes Christopher and Taylor came along and rode their bikes beside me. This was our plan in August '95 when Taylor and I headed for the dam road.

On the way we reached a place where we could see the whole horizon toward the north. Taylor saw it first. "Look, Dad!" All across the northern sky, about twenty miles away, there was a thin black wall. Not tall, but very black and very wide. It snaked across the eastern boundary of the earth and sky. But to the west, not far it seemed, we saw a harmless, fading tail. It tapered off, disappearing into bright blue skies filled with fluffy clouds, tame, white.

Taylor saw it first, I think. Both of us said, "Wow!"

"Will it hit us?" Taylor worried.

"Nah, I doubt it," I assured him. "Up here and on the dam I've seen a *lot* of storms. They always move from west to east. And look! The western sky is clear. I'm sure we'll be okay."

"All right," he answered. But his tone implied, *If you say so, Dad.*

While pulling out his bike in the parking lot, I said, "Look, buddy. See where I'm hiding the keys? I really don't want you in the parking lot alone. But if you hafta come back ahead of me, use the keys, get inside the van, and lock it. Okay?"

"Okay, Dad."

Off we went, Taylor on his little bike and I on Rollerblades. Still new at in-line skating, my biggest worry was hitting a pebble or a crack and falling down, especially at the start of a short but disconcerting hill.

Once out on the dam, however, the road was long and flat. It also was high. The northern sky, opposite the lake, was an uninterrupted panorama. The wall of black looked mean. After a mile and a half, I said, "Taylor, buddy, why don't you stop here and wait for me to go to the end of the road and come back? Then you can join me. But . . . if the sky gets too scary for you, don't wait. Pedal as fast as you can and go back to the van, okay?"

He nodded. And I left him there.

Skating west I was relieved, encouraged. The skies were clearing up. But I didn't look behind me, back toward the east . . . until four miles out, four miles from the van, two and a half miles from Taylor's waiting place. That's where I turned around . . . straight into the open throat of a black and deadly fury.

In an instant the hot air dropped by twenty degrees. Just as fast the wind began to blow, starting out at twenty-five to thirty miles an hour, moving up to sixty, seventy, more, high up on the dam road.

"Oh, no! . . . Oh, God! . . . Taylor!"

Straw and dust blow furiously across the road. On my skates with all my strength I begin to climb back toward the east, toward the topside of the dam, toward the long and deadly open stretch to this storm from hell. The place where Taylor is.

I am angry, terrified. This storm broke the rules! It violated odds! It is irrational! And strong beyond belief!

And I, I, brought Taylor here, put him in the middle, exposed and unprotected. I brought him to the high place, now like an altar on the dam. I left him (My son! My son! My Son!) *like a sacrifice, easy to devour by death's horrifying howl.*

No one would even hear him, if Taylor yelled for help. Knowing that he knew this, I knew he wouldn't even try. But both of us, I also knew, would cry out to God.

Over and over I plead, "Oh, God! My son, my son, my son! Please protect my son! Let him live! Help him make it to the van! Spare him! Keep him safe! He is helpless, helpless, without you. Protect him too from paralyzing fear. In this screaming storm from hell let . . . him hear your voice! Let him know your peace. Make him stubborn and unstoppable with power straight from you. Help him make it safely to the other side."

But as I pray, the storm grows worse. Much worse. Small pebbles mixed with water shoot like BB pellets. Grass and straw are hurled like a million tiny needles, striking the left side of my face. Straight-line winds increase to sixty miles an hour—maybe eighty, maybe more. Thunder roars as count- less deadly lightning bolts hurl all around. This storm is alive. Enraged. Murderous.

My eyes are blind, squinted almost shut as I push my head down toward the ground and slightly to the right, turning away from the wind. Time slows down. I slow down, can barely move. Crouching low, I try a lower profile but still can hardly move against the wind.

In the raging storm skating, keeping balance, makes a strange demand. There is no symmetry in thrusting with both legs, first left then right. Instead, leaning to the left with almost all my weight, I thrust and thrust and thrust with every ounce of strength. But only with one leg—my right. And still I hardly move.

I think, If it's this bad for me, almost two hundred pounds, oh, God, how can Taylor stay upright and in control on his little bike?

Maybe he didn't try to go! Maybe he hid on the rocks under the bridge abutment where I left him! Maybe, maybe, maybe . . . If he did, I'll join him there. Even if he didn't, maybe that's what I should do.

This is nuts! I'm skating to my death. What good will that do him if he's made it to safe shelter?

Slowly, slowly, inch by inch, I count my thrusts up into the hundreds. Then, at last, I reach the bridge abutment. I stop. I look. Taylor isn't there.

Then I know. At some point, just before it hit, Taylor saw it coming. He saw the storm was bad. And when he saw he rode, pedaling with all his might to the shelter of the van.

Strength is gone. Should I go on? It would be insanity.

I do not stop. I go. And go and go and go and go and go. Angry, angry, angry with the storm I yell, I cry, I scream, "You're nothing! You're a wimp! You can't crush a flower *unless you have permission. God controls you with no effort! You are on a leash. You might take my life. Maybe you've already taken Taylor's. But not without permission. Cuz God, my God, knows and loves us even here and now. And even here and now, you can blind and blow and roar, but God, my God, is sovereign over you right now!"*

Then in my soul I hear a wordless whisper, "I Am, indeed I Am. And Taylor is okay."

Time crawls, but I do not stop. At last I reach the van.

Empty.

Oh, God, where is he?

"Taylor!? Taylor! TAYLOR!"

Then I see him! He's coming out from a cinder-block bathroom building with a young and scruffy man. The only other car in the parking lot is old, beat up.

Relieved and born again to fear, I think, Mister, if you have touched a hair on my precious son's head, you're dead.

Picking Taylor up, I hold him in my arms, kiss him, stroke his head, rub his back.

"I was so scared, Dad. I thought you might die."

"I thought you might too, sweet boy. But why were you in the bathroom?"

"Well, at first I got in the van. But the wind was blowing so hard the van began to rock. I thought it was gonna blow away. Then this man came over and said it might be safer to wait for you inside the bathroom building."

Still suspicious, I thank the man, an unlikely angel. Then together, safe, Taylor and I go home.

That night I asked, "Hey, buddy, what was it like for you riding in that storm?"

"I dunno."

"Well, did you pray?"

"Uh, sure." Intonation adding, "Duh!"

"So, what did ya pray?"

Always challenged in his speech by the letter *r*, Taylor was still clear. "Ovah and ovah in my head, just one thing: 'I can do all things through him who stwengthens me.'" Stunned, awareness hit me. God *does* still speak.

"Taylor, do you know what that was? It was more than just a prayer. That was God! God speaking to you in the middle of the storm. Cool!"

According to the next day's news, what hit us was a macroburst, a gigantic wind shear exploding across the ground like shock waves from a bomb.

Once again, Taylor survived and even prospered. Something inside this kid was stronger than the Grim Reaper. It was as if, whenever death itself came charging, Taylor simply set his jaw and fought and grinned. And never quit a battle. His sunny inner landscape undiminished, he never surrendered. Even to the greatest darkness of them all. The darkness yet to come.

4   CHANGES IN THE WIND

"HEY, DAD? WOULD YOU PULL ON MY LEG? IT'S HURTIN' again."

"Sure, buddy. Let's do it on your bed."

Lying on his back, Taylor reached above and back, grabbing on to the headboard.

"Which leg is it?"

"This one," he said, pointing to my right, "it aches."

Grabbing his left foot, I gently pulled, increasing force, sustaining it, until he said, "Okay, that's enough."

"Feel better?"

"Yeah, thanks, Dad. Ya know," he added with a smile, "growing up's a real pain . . ." Reading his mind, I finished the thought, as he often did with me. He twinkled and grinned, then ran off to play.

The aches began when Taylor was eight, in the second grade. He felt periodic soreness in his bones, especially in his legs. It was nothing more, we thought, than normal growing pains. Preoccupied with raging business battles, I didn't notice, didn't see, the obvious anomaly in our diagnosis. Every time he had these bone-aches, they were below the torso. And just a single limb. When he asked, the only leg I ever pulled was his liberal one—his left, not right. Always the Democrat, never the Republican. Always the ass, never the elephant.

But true to form, Taylor never let the nuisance of growing pains, or any other kind of pain, slow him down. At least not for long. Bruises, scrapes, cuts, smashed fingers in the door were to him like growing pains: inconvenient and annoying interruptions of discovery.

It was, for him, a magic time. Life was an adventurous delight, a kaleidoscope experience of fascinating beauty, endless fascination.

So much to do! So little time!

Ride the bike! Play with friends! Practice being Daddy to his little brother! Make big brother mad! Learn the violin! Go to school! Hit the ball! Compete with classmates! Tease the teacher! Conquer computer games! Climb trees! Explore the neighborhood! Discover secret places!

Spy on yucky girls! Fly a kite! Ride a go-cart! Go to summer camp! Jump on the trampoline! Swim like a fish! Dive like a dolphin! Splash like a cannonball! Make up jokes! Practice puns! Crash and watch TV—shows like *I Wuv Wucy!*

Not even Dad's disconcerting inattention or wounded grumpiness seemed to slow him down. The days were just too short and bedtime always came too soon.

Taylor's life was perfect. Fantastic!

Mine was just the opposite. Outside the home I fought on several fronts and died a thousand deaths. Tumultuous assaults were destroying my career. Companies I researched, in which I had placed faith and lots of client money, began to fail, fall, and slowly die from mortal business wounds. Like buildings wired with explosives at strategic points, these businesses, these vaults of client funds, collapsed. In slow motion each became a dusty pile of worthless broken concrete, landfill hauled off to the dump, thrown away, covered up forever.

My clients, my friends, were, to say the least, unhappy. My financial superpowers were exposed, no more real than those of gaudy superheroes inside comic books. At the same time, what felt like superforces were wrecking my career. Like rabid sadists roaring in orgasmic ecstasy, they raped and ripped my psyche . . . over and over and over again. There were days, many days, when death seduced my mind, my fantasies, mostly like romantic whimsy, sometimes just like lust. Even on the dam road there were times the only peace I saw was the enticing invitation of permanent relief beneath the blue and gentle waves on the lake below . . .

By Taylor's ninth birthday, our house in greater Dallas was on the market. We were moving east to Nashville, Tennessee, where, with a trusted partner and best friend, the foundation was being laid for an exciting new career, a venture with potential for expansion all throughout the South.

We moved to Tennessee with hope. But six weeks after our arrival my business partnership died, killed by accidental discovery of my friend's deceptive negligence. Our family struggled through long months, torn by heartache and despair—and from far more than the business. Just before we moved, Debbie's sister, Cynthia, died from cancer. Six months later her mother too was buried, also killed by cancer. Our boys mourned the friends and life they left behind in Dallas. Debbie mourned her sister and her mother. And I mourned the almost-certain death of my new career.

Taylor coped by goofing off at school and playing down the block with his new friend, Trey. He and Trey shared several common passions. Outside they played tag football: Trey the quarterback and Taylor the speedy, agile runner, fastest on the block. Indoors they indulged in their generation's mania: Nintendo and PlayStation games.

Trey—contemplative, passionate, and friendly but something of a loner—when combined with Taylor—sunny and competitive, something of a loner too—formed a perfect match. As only seems to happen in magic preteen years, they were best friends for life.

Trey's friendship was an anchor, his house and family a pleasant nearby shelter from the storm of stress and sorrow inside our rented townhouse at the dead end of the street. The place that Taylor now called home.

Then came news of yet another pending loss. Trey's dad took a job in faraway Las Vegas. Soon their house was leased, and they were gone. One night during evening prayer, I gently probed, asking Taylor about Trey. When I did, he sobbed and sobbed. Face buried in his pillow, he stayed awake long into the night muffling the sounds of a broken heart.

Then, all at once it seemed, Taylor's chronic growing pains turned into a limp.

Debbie and I thought it was related to the trauma of Trey's move. It wasn't. Months before Trey moved the nuisance ache, by itself, sometimes persuaded even Taylor to sit out from games, turn down a racing challenge, park his bike, or only watch a bowling match at a birthday party.

When Taylor's teacher expressed concern, tendrils of concern finally poked and slithered to the surface of my conscious mind. Debbie drove Taylor to the orthopedic clinic on May 5th, 1998.

"Something's wrong," the doctor said after examining x-rays. "Maybe some kind of juvenile rheumatoid arthritis causing inflammation in the hip." He suggested ibuprofen and the use of crutches for a week. At a follow-up appointment six days later, the doctor said blood tests ruled out arthritis. "Just so I can sleep tonight, let's do an MRI," he said, "a magnetic resonance image."

Taylor lay flat on his back atop a cold, hard slab. "Don't move until it's over," he was told. "If you do, the image will be blurry."

But almost instantly the cold hard table became an instrument of torture. Taylor cried out from exploding pain, "I can't keep still! It hurrrrts!" Involuntary tears erupted.

Using makeshift padding from pillows and blankets, technicians tried to cushion Taylor's painful backside. The table was aimed toward a huge thick plastic wall with a tiny portal sphere. It circled round the hard and chilly bed on which Taylor squirmed with muffled screams of pain. Hammering to life, the machine drowned out the boy. Slowly, almost imperceptibly, the table began its crawl through the claustrophobic portal. Beginning at the waist, it crept in and through the sphere, crawling down, down, down. All the way down his legs.

Taylor tried not to move. But crying out in agony and anger, he couldn't help wiggling a little. In spite of pain worse than he had ever known—and pain's companion, fear—Taylor's iron will (more than makeshift cushions) kept his body mostly still for the 3-D pictures.

Looking at the slightly fuzzy images, the orthopedic doctor tried to hide his shock.

When I heard the news it hit me like a vicious sucker punch. I couldn't breathe. Knees buckled. Like a broken thing, I couldn't sit up straight, couldn't even try. Bending forward like a sitting fetus, my torso collapsed to lap.

Time, already slow, so very, very slow, now stopped and disappeared. Croaks emerged, almost soundless gags. Heart pounded to the beat of jackhammer blows, breaking through the granite of my soul to the core within. I whisper-gasped the first and central syllable of a three-word horror requiem.

"Oooooooh, God, NOOOOO!"

Falling from the chair, I knelt on the floor and howled. Agony, despair erupted from unknown, unmeasured depths, from the broken core of me.

With tears and breaking heart herself, Debbie tried to comfort, reach me. But I was in another place, buried alive far, far below. It was a zone-dimension that gripped, suspended, held me out of human reach.

Taylor had a tumor almost filling up the left side of his inner pelvis. Even though there wasn't any bulge on the outside of his tummy, it was huge, "the size of a small melon," the doctor said. It was the biggest tumor the orthopedic specialist had ever seen.

This thing inside my son was cancer. But what I saw was death. And a terrible awareness: I could not rescue him; he could not rescue me.

Rescue, if such a thing existed, would have to come from Someone Else.

5 THE ODDS

"THE BIOPSY WENT VERY WELL. NO PROBLEMS." DR. Herbert S. Schwartz, Taylor's surgeon at Vanderbilt Hospital's Orthopedic Oncology Clinic, was briefing us. He'd just cut out and sent away a small piece of the hidden monster inside Taylor's pelvis. Confident the tumor was a Ewing's sarcoma, he conceded, "It *could* be an Osteo. Pathology will let us know early next week."

I spent hours on the Internet, searching, printing, reading with a pencil in my hand. I underlined and tried to translate, looking up countless words from the world of medicine, a whole language that hardly seemed like English. My obsessive efforts boiled down to just two things: treatment protocols and odds. Odds of survival. Or not.

In the end, protocols took second place. Everything proposed by Vanderbilt's pediatric oncology team was in lockstep with treatment plans by other topnotch cancer-fighting centers in the country.

Odds for survival, the likelihood of life, not death, depended on circumstances. The only good thing about Taylor's diagnosis was the cancer's apparent confinement to just one tumor. All the tests said it hadn't spread.

But only this was good. Almost everything else made long-term prospects grim. There were two bad things about Taylor's alien invader, and they were very, very bad. Size. And location. By any medical standard, the tumor was huge. And it was in a dangerous place.

Odds of long-term survival (generally defined as five years after diagnosis) were directly related to how much of the tumor's tissue could be killed by controlled infusion of poison drugs *prior* to surgery.

If 90 percent of the tumor was killed, the odds of long-term survival were pretty good—about 85 percent. But if less than 90 percent was put to death before surgical eviction, the odds that Taylor would grow up, get married, have children, pursue a career, and happily retire—the odds that he would *live*—were one out of seven.

One out of seven.

Then, buried deep in hundreds of pages printed off the Web, I stumbled onto a surgical procedure no doctor had yet mentioned. It was an operation called a *hemipelvectomy*. Bright red lights flashing inside my brain brought me screeching to a halt. What I saw and read looked like a dreadful prophecy, a secret peek at Taylor's not-too-distant future.

Simply put, a hemipelvectomy is surgical removal of up to one-half of the pelvis. It's done because some tumors, especially malignancies, leave no other choice. Depending on the tumor's size, it's possible a portion of the pelvic hemisphere might remain.

But if the sucker's really big, all the pelvic bones on one side must be cut away, including the acetabulum—the large and cup-shaped bone that forms the socket for the leg.

Without this socket, a leg is mechanically useless because pediatric prosthetic hips are still impossible. And if the acetabulum is removed, *there's no good reason to keep the leg attached.* If the leg's left dangling, a useless limb for life, it is, by any measure, medically or aesthetically, much more a liability than an asset.

The end result is an amputation unlike any other. There is no stump. The patient's moon is never full again. It is, instead, reduced by half. All that's left is fodder for dark humor in order to somehow anesthetize a lifelong extracruel dismemberment.

One scholastic summary I discovered reported results of people who'd gone under the knife and come out with no remnant of a hip. Among all these only one in three remained alive five years after surgery.

One out of three.

I never talked stats with Taylor. But I did pursue the matter with his doctors, senior members of the cancer treatment team.

"Are these studies accurate? Are they current? Are they right? Do I correctly understand them? Is it true that unless the chemo kills at least 90 percent of Taylor's tumor, his odds of long-term survival are only 10, maybe 15 percent?"

Most physicians cleared their throats, kept their focus on a chart—or someplace other than my eyes. One took the role of teacher to a child, "Now, Misss-ter Schrauger . . ."

No one meant to be unkind or rude. Quite the opposite, I think. Experts in their field, treating children with cancer, they knew the odds, the likely course of things to come. And they knew it from experience, not just from reports. I think they didn't want to "disturb the patient's family."

They shouldn't have worried. I was plenty disturbed already. Various responses to my pestering questions often went like this . . .

"Now, Misss-ter Schrauger, I do not know about the exact study to which you are referring. And you must be very careful about what you get and read from the *Internet*. But I do know you must keep in mind that Taylor is not a statistic. We are going to do everything possible to fight his cancer and defeat it. Meanwhile it's important you and your wife are 'there' for him. You must think positive and help him fight for life.

"As far as surgery is concerned, that's not our department. We treat the cancer. Dr. Schwartz operates."

At first I only heard condescending platitudes, a recipe of sorts: non-answers mixed with passing of the buck, a counterfeit cupcake frosted with professional compassion, but with all the nourishment and texture of a rock-hard hockey puck. It really ticked me off.

Then, upon reflection, I heard and understood.

Nonanswers from oncologists were truth in thin disguise. Under flimsy masks of axioms was the reality's repulsive face. It was full of open sores oozing sickly yellow pus, no less toxic than Ebola. My understanding of the risks, the odds—the truth—was all too accurate.

Dead on, so to speak.

Once again my son, the unexpected love of my life, was high atop the dam road caught in early angry winds of a terrifying storm. There was no place to hide. He could only move ahead, down the one-way road. And once again behind it all was that old Malevolence, a wild beast with razor teeth, a gloating dragon breathing fire, hungry to devour.

But this time, *this time,* Taylor would not be alone. No matter what the dragon did, no matter how he roared and shook the earth, I swore that with God's help I'd stay by Taylor's side all the way across, safely through and to the other side.

6   THE MOST IMPORTANT THING

THE INVADER INSIDE TAYLOR'S HIP WAS NOT EWING'S after all. It was an *Osteo*-sarcoma, an evil sibling of Ewing's. But darker, worse. Ewing's tumors come from soft tissue and create soft-tissue tumors—a deadly, pliable threat. Osteo-sarcomas come from bone. The tumors they create grow into stabbing, bony masses. At first, like bullies, they shove internal organs out of their way. Then, unless they're killed, they cut and tear with psychopathic glee, ripping, stabbing from the inside out.

Most of the time Osteos, like Ewing's, are first attacked with potent chemo drugs. But unlike warfare against Ewing's there are fewer weapons in the arsenal of medicine with which to fight the foe of Osteos. Radiation treatment, for example, is a course of last resort. This nasty kind of cancer is so viciously resilient, the only attempt to shoot it with a ray gun is when all else has failed.

The news wasn't good. But it really didn't change the near-term strategy of intensive chemotherapy followed by an attempt to surgically cut out the huge malignant growth. Five days after the biopsy Taylor returned to Vanderbilt for full initiation into cancer warfare. First, a Hickman catheter was surgically installed inside his chest. Just below his nipple on the left it tunneled through a mainline vein straight into the heart. Outside his chest the master hose erupted, a long and off-white dangly Y held in place with stitches, patches, tape. Both ends of the outer Y, the ports, were capped: one white, the other red. The gizmo allowed the medical team to draw blood and give drugs without needle sticks. That was good. On the other hand, the Hickman itself was a royal pain. Every day both ports had to be flushed to prevent blockage and infection. And every three days the sticky master patch had to be replaced. The biggest hazard was something getting in the ports like bacteria from swimming pools or air accidentally pumped into the heart through an IV hookup. Attending risks ranged from infection to cardiac arrest.

With the Hickman in place, Taylor was ready to battle the beast. Vanderbilt's superb medical army was going to war. They were, and are, the best: fully qualified and ready to fight.

Which begged the question, what was *I* to do?

Realization finally struck. My commissioned duties, my assigned roles, were communications and recruitment.

Taylor, only nine, almost ten, needed a liaison between doctors, nurses, and himself. Unusually bright and self-aware, he was, like any kid, somewhat overwhelmed by grownups—especially when they were doctors and nurses.

But he did confide in me. He told me how he really felt, what he really thought. And since he was my only patient, I became a student of my son. Watching. Learning. Listening to his words, his moods. Reading the expressions on his face. Hearing intonation. And so coming very close to knowing unsaid thoughts and fears.

I could encourage him. I could teach him to speak up for himself. But when he couldn't-wouldn't, I'd be there to help.

And I could recruit.

Taylor didn't need medical reinforcements. The troops at Vanderbilt were fully competent and staffed. But he desperately needed spiritual allies to help him fight. Debbie enlisted help by telephone, her tool of choice. Perhaps I could do the same, except by a different means. By writing. By e-mail reports.

Not good at prayer myself, I could still ask others to intercede with God for Taylor.

I ran my ideas by Taylor. He listened, shrugged, agreed, "No prob, bob," and then resumed his play or TV show. With no effort he simply let go of all the stuff he couldn't control.

Why can't I do that?

With recruitment on my mind (and a desperate need to think out loud) I sat down and composed what would become the first of many reports sent through cyberspace. Regardless of their skill or visibility, I wanted to recruit an army who would pray for Taylor—and also for his family.

Friday, May 22nd, 1998

Taylor's first round of chemotherapy begins this afternoon and lasts for three full days. Hopefully he'll come home next Monday or Tuesday.

Complete hair loss is expected in about ten days.

Vanderbilt's team of pediatric oncologists told us Taylor faces about twelve months of treatment.

There are two immediate objectives for chemotherapy. One is to kill any microscopic cancer cells that might be elsewhere in his body but are undetectable by testing. The other goal is to shrink the tumor to a point where surgical removal is feasible.

After surgery, there will be many months of additional chemotherapy in an attempt to prevent future recurrence.

The surgeon who will remove the tumor thinks the operation will result in a virtually useless leg. With all our hearts we pray that Taylor will recover full use of both legs *and* have no recurrence of the cancer in any form.

But the most important thing is this . . .

Please pray God will protect Taylor's *spirit,* even causing it to grow and prosper—no matter what happens to his body.

Taylor knows what's going on. Even so, the reality of what he's in for will come in stages—just like it will for the rest of us. This dynamic is, I think, a gift from God. And I am (mostly) grateful for it.

Thank you for praying for Taylor. And for his family too. All our emotional and spiritual resources are gone. And yet, somehow, we go on. It must be God, giving us his strength. This is the only explanation that makes sense. And I think he's making his strength, even himself, available to us through you. Through your faith, your love, your prayers.

Please feel free to pass along to others this current news—and our love and thanks as well. I'll do my best to keep you posted . . .

Brian

7 MIBs

TWO DAYS AFTER TURNING TEN TAYLOR YELLED, "HEY, Dad! C'mere!" When I came into his room he said, "Watch this!" Plucking out a pinch of thick blond hair from the middle of his head, he said, "This is so cool!"

"Taylor!" I protested. "Stop! You've made a bald spot bigger than a quarter!"

"Really? Oh man, I've gotta look in the mirror! . . . You're right! Cool!"

"Tell you what, buddy. Let's stick to the plan and give you a buzz. Otherwise you're gonna look like a polka-dotted head case. Let me get the electric clippers. I'll meet ya in the garage."

And so, while Mom took pictures, that is what we did. Without the clippers' plastic guide, I cut his hair to the shortest stubble. Along the way, however, we made a Mohawk, looked in the mirror, took pictures, and laughed. Then we cut the Mohawk, leaving just one tuft standing near what used to be his cowlick swirl. Debbie tied a ribbon to it; Taylor batted his eyes for another photo.

All his yellow hair went into a Ziploc bag. All mine, thin and gray, soon went in the trash.

One week later Taylor was a cue ball, stubble rubbed away, his head a shiny sphere. Thinking to myself, *Why not?* I snuck into the bathroom late one afternoon, lathered my entire head, and shaved it all away (hair, that is, not head). Upon presentation at the supper table, the unexpected sight of another skinhead in the house was to the sound of protest. From everyone but Taylor. He looked at me and grinned. "Feels kinda weird, doesn't it?"

"Yup, sure does. But we *look* cool!"

And so we both became, and stayed, MIBs, Men In Baldness, along with secret names, Agents T and B—our takeoff from the movie *Men in Black*. Out in public everybody was nice. They said how great we looked, how nicely shaped our heads. We MIBs agreed and proudly stayed that way.

During that summer of 1998, Taylor made five visits, spent seventeen long days, in a hospital we dubbed the Children's Vanderbilton. Newly remodeled, the wing where Taylor and other children stayed was almost luxurious. The halls were wide; the lights were bright and cheery; the color was light blue. Gentle whales swam in tiles on the floor while fishes drawn by pediatric patients swam in picture frames hung up on the walls.

But looks can be deceiving. This was no resort. It was, in fact, a battleground, a place where patients, parents, and pros engaged the enemies of illness and of death. The architecture was attractive, the arsenal impressive and all the people nice. But far too often battles became ugly and warriors got weary to the marrow. Especially the children.

During each stay poisonous chemo drugs dripped into Taylor's body. He was nauseated, threw up, lost his precious privacy. Urine was measured and tested. People looked at his stool before he flushed. He was poked and squeezed and subjected to a host of tests, most of which he hated.

Even so, he was always polite, charming in his misery.

Not I.

If the poisons dripping into Taylor's heart were chemo drugs, the poisons dripping into mine were sickening fear and helplessness, a slowly bubbling brew of unacknowledged rage.

Groveling with God, I pled, "Please spare my son—please, please, please, please, please—infinity times please. Take me. Take me instead!" I wept at least a million tears but never heard an answer.

Arguing with the doctors, no one confused me with Dale Carnegie. "Why does the hell of Taylor's nausea remain? Why not try Marinol [a drug derived from marijuana]?" They resisted, concerned he might be scared by the drug's effects. "They're not gonna bother Taylor; trust me. Why not *try* it, here in the hospital where you can supervise him? How could *anything* be worse than what he's feeling from the deadly chemo drugs?" At last they conceded, and the Marinol helped. Taylor's appetite was stimulated. And when he got a little high, we laughed at the irony . . . just say yes to drugs.

Through it all I also nagged for information: Is the chemo helping? Has the tumor shrunk? What are Taylor's long-term odds? When will he have surgery? What will it entail?

Finally, on August 11th, 1998, a round of tests was done: x-ray, bone and CT scans, and another MRI.

Eight days later, while Taylor rode the bus to school for the first day of fourth grade, I went alone to meet with Dr. Herbert Schwartz, Taylor's world-class orthopedic surgeon.

8 FIFTY-FIFTY

"THE TUMOR HAS NOT SHRUNK. IT'S GROWN."

Dr. Schwartz was blunt but plain. No matter what I asked, he answered with precision. His eyes were kind. His tone, matter-of-fact.

I tried to maintain a detached demeanor, to approach the horror from my head, not heart. The effort was surprisingly successful. Still, my eyes were leaky, painful. My tone was wobbly.

Much to my surprise, Dr. Schwartz never dodged a question, nor was he condescending. His unvarnished clarity was a breath of fresh air. But what I learned about the tumor was much worse than bad. On June 2nd the obscene mass had measured twelve centimeters in its largest diameter. Ten short weeks later, and while under harsh attack, the evil thing had *grown*. Almost faster than a weed. The hip would have to go, Schwartz said. But the leg, he thought, could be spared.

One week later Debbie, Taylor, and I met with him together. But since my private meeting seven days before, he was much more pessimistic. While Taylor listened, Dr. Schwartz made three things very clear:

1. Successful removal of the entire tumor would be a major challenge—meaning it might not be possible.

2. If possible, removing all the tumor would minimize the risk of the cancer coming back. But . . .

3. Successful removal of the entire tumor also meant there was a fifty-fifty chance Taylor's left leg would have to be amputated.

As the possibility of amputation sank in, Taylor pulled the bill of his baseball cap down low. Hiding his eyes, he leafed through an old issue of *National Geographic,* pretending to read, to see the pictures. He told Dr. Schwartz he understood.

When left alone in our small examination room, I held Taylor in my arms while Debbie rubbed his back. Burying his face in my chest, he sobbed. As we joined him in his tears we also prayed, thanking God he too was with us in the little room and that he too was weeping. We also thanked him for his strength, strength to keep on going. One day, one minute, at a time. Strength we did not have inside ourselves.

We acknowledged that he alone is the Great Physician. As such, we asked that he himself would operate on Taylor through the hands and mind and heart of Dr. Herbert Schwartz.

Monday, August 31st, 1998

It's two minutes past noon. Taylor's been in surgery since about eight o'clock this morning. Dr. Schwartz, Taylor's surgeon, called from the OR about forty-five minutes ago. "The entire tumor can be extracted," he said. "But the leg cannot be saved."

Before proceeding, however, we wait. Schwartz has sent pathology several lymph nodes close to Taylor's tumor. They *look* healthy, I'm told. But Schwartz wants microscopic evidence the cancer has not spread. If it has, he will leave the tumor and close Taylor back up . . .

Now, at last, results are in. They are negative.

And so, even as I write, Schwartz is extracting the tumor and amputating Taylor's leg.

This is a good day.

Taylor is safe. He remains complete. But not only this. He faces a future of profound grace, immense love, irresistible humor, enhanced productivity. And growth far beyond today's undiminished wholeness.

And so God instructs parents through a son, tutors teachers through a student, instructs grown men through a boy just ten years old.

Long day.

Lots of support.

Tumor extracted.

Leg lost.

Taylor spared.

Peace remains.

God is good.

More later.

With gratitude and love . . .

Brian and Debbie

At Taylor's side in the recovery room, his eyes are shut, his breathing calm and painless. I gently stroke his smooth and downy head then whisper in his ear, "Hey, buddy, it's Dad. Mom and I are here. You are doing great. I'm proud of you, sweet boy."

But does he know his leg is gone?

Moments later he tries to speak, raspy words I cannot interpret at a distance.

I whisper in his ear, "Sorry, buddy. I couldn't understand you. If you want to try again, I'll put my ear next to your mouth." And so I do.

Eyes still shut, he speaks again. In a teasing wheezing tone he says, "Now you'll have to carry me!" There's a gotcha in his voice. He's often nagged me with the mocking plea, "Da-ad, will you carry meeeee?" Until today I've (almost) always said, "No way!"

This time, with a breaking heart, I squeeze his hand and say, "I suppose I will. But not for long! . . . Only for a little while." Trying to control myself, I add, "Get your rest, buddy. You don't have to talk."

Perhaps a minute passes. I hear more mutters.

"Sorry, honey, but it's hard for me to hear, especially with that mask blowing oxygen. What did you say?" Again I place my ear close beside his mouth.

"Now—I—should—be—able—to—get—a—really—good—deal—on—shoes," he repeats. "At—least—50—percent—off!"

I laugh out loud then tell him unabashed, "You're the bravest man I have ever known."

A nurse filled us in. The first thing Taylor did when he woke up was reach down with his left hand, finding, as expected, only empty air. He knew his leg was gone long before I walked in through the door.

In his heart he'd said, *Thought so. Thank you, Lord. The tumor's* gone. *Now help me, please.* Then eyes still shut as if asleep he got excited, sharing with his God, *Now I get to use my lines on Dad! Please help me help him too.* And so he did—with courage unlike I had ever seen or heard. And thought I'd never see again. With determination, even glee, and with perfect timing, he flawlessly delivered lines prepared days before in secret, priceless gifts to give to Dad when he woke up without a leg.

Taylor's body was diminished. Radically. For life. But his spirit was unscathed. Intact. Complete. It was, in fact, enhanced. Strong beyond belief. It was as if he'd had two operations: radical amputation from his body and radical enhancement to his spirit. In the end he gained far more than he lost.

9 OUT ON A LIMB

FRIDAY, SEPTEMBER 25TH, 1998

Taylor goes back to Vanderbilt Hospital this coming Monday, September 28th. This will be his first chemotherapy treatment since surgery on August 31st.

The potent drugs he'll get over four long days will cause a lot of nausea—plus something new this time. We're told that chemo is likely to magnify his phantom pain. Looks like, once again, it might kick hard, and just as the ghostly jolts are starting to calm down. If you are someone who prays, please pray about this.

This past week has been much different than the one to come. Taylor's gone to school two times and to my office once. He's gone shopping with Mom and spent a day away, playing in the home of a friend.

When he was at school he played four square during recess, sometimes without his crutches. I can't imagine how he does it. But he does.

These days he's racing on his crutches, often going faster than I walk—even when I power-walk. Other times, inside the house, he puts his crutches down and hops from room to room! "Hey, Dad!" he said the other day. "Look! I'm a human jumping bean!"

Phantom pains still erupt from time to time. But Taylor's medication recipe combined with distraction therapy is pretty effective. And for the most part, his surgical incision is healing well.

Thank you for your prayers and many messages. We're getting e-mail from around the world: Zimbabwe and Brazil, Ethiopia and Singapore, Pakistan and Ukraine, Texas and Alaska, Michigan and New Jersey. And, of course, lots from here in Tennessee.

Keep writing! No matter how brief, we love hearing from you.

Gratefully yours . . .

Brian

※

Wednesday afternoon, November 4th, 1998

Dear Everybody,

This is Taylor. Sorry it's been so long. Instead of writing, I've spent most of my time in the playroom [here at Vanderbilt].

Since I wrote last time I've come to the hospital for three yucky, boor-*ing!* chemo treatments, including this one.

This time nausea and ralfing—or upchucking—haven't been bad at all. Phantom pains . . . okay, I guess.

For Halloween I dressed up as a one-legged pirate. And I was able to go to my school's Halloween party last Friday afternoon.

Guess what???

There's a guy from my congregation who works for News Channel 5 [here in Nashville]. He's filming me for the next coupla weeks. He's doing a story for our congregation's anniversary. And maybe for his TV station too!

He filmed me at my class's party last Friday. And he's supposed to come by the hospital sometime today or tomorrow.

Last weekend my family went with my friends to Rock Island State Park. There's a river there with lots of huge boulders to climb on. Mom thought I couldn't do it. Boy, was she surprised! I blew her away! I climbed all over the boulders and ended up taking the hardest path to a waterfall! Dad could hardly keep up. He said I was like a little rock crab—which I was!

I really hate long stories. And this one is long enough. Thank you for all your e-mails, letters, cards, and stuff.

Love,

Taylor

❧

Monday, November 16th, 1998

Hey, Everybody! Guess what I did last week?

On Monday [November 9] I walked around our whole, entire sub-division—by myself! Then on Tuesday I called Dad to tell him I just climbed a tree! Boy, was he ever shocked! I was *really* out on a limb! And

I was able to get just as high as I did with two legs! It was a BLAST!!!

Just before my friends came home from school I climbed a pine tree by the bus stop. When the kids got off the bus I yelled at them. They couldn't believe it!

There was a *fifth* grader who tried to climb up with me. But he could only get to the first branch of the pine tree! And here I am, a fourth grader with one leg, and I could get to the very top of the tree two stories tall! I couldn't believe it!!!

The next day I climbed a *huge* tree in front of my friend's old house [where Trey used to live] and got to the very, very, very, very, very, very, very top!

I climb by grabbing a branch. Then, with my leg, I kind of hop up the tree. After that, climbing is a snap. Not the branch, just the climbing!

On Friday I rode the bus to school! I'm all caught up with the rest of my class. Then, at recess, I played four square *without* my crutches—and made it all the way to the fourth square!!!

Ummmmm . . . Ummmmm . . . Ummmmm . . . BURP! (Ekskúze me!)

Then I got back on the bus. When it reached my stop, I just hopped off!

If you wanna see what the guy from News Channel 5 has filmed, come to our congregation on November 22nd at nine in the morning.

If your e-mail will take it, I'm sending a picture of me in my pirate costume from Halloween.

Good-bye until next time!

Love,
Taylor

10 BULLIES OF HARD TRUTH

As Taylor started a bright new year in January '99, I darkly started mine. Thrilled with Taylor's spirit and guardedly optimistic about his future health, my emotional energy was sapped by the stark realization that my business could not be, would not be revived.

During Taylor's illness I rebuilt the company's operational shell with shards from the badly smashed embryo—a Humpty-Dumpty uncooked egg my former friend and partner had splattered on the rocks. There were just two problems with my 3-D reconstruction. First, all ten thousand patched-up cracks were visible. Second, inside this cracked-up structure there was almost no liquidity. And the little puddle that was there smelled an awful lot like rotten egg.

When with a business plan in hand I asked new investors to put their money in, I was like a wannabe comedian telling a bad *yolk*. (And this to people who believe that, whether good or bad, money is *never* a yolking matter.)

In short, business losses were too much. Regardless of my efforts, the company could not be saved. But perhaps something could be salvaged for its investor-creditors. With this new focus fixed in mind, I waged litigious warfare against every deadbeat customer who owed money to the company—and almost always won. On paper. Almost all the vanquished fled to bankruptcy or simply disappeared, so that most judicial orders in our favor could never be collected.

In time I knew our original investors would do well to someday get back pennies on their dollar. And understandably upset, any one at any time might decide to pur*sue* me.

As my New Year 1999 began, bullies of hard truth were in my face, filling up my vision. The business was a cracked-up shell. I could not bring it back to life. Taylor faced more chemo. His cancer could come back. Our family could go bankrupt. And I had to find a job.

Even so, as time marched on in 1999, we celebrated Taylor's health. Chemo ended in February. In March all scans were clear! There was a celebration trip in April. Just Taylor and his dad in Gatlinburg. We lived it up and did it all without a handicap. Every day through May we prayed, asking God to glorify himself by keeping Taylor healthy, cancer-free. In light of all the evidence to date, the strength of Taylor's spirit, and the vigor of his body, we were (almost) certain God would grant us this request.

Then, in June, on our wedding anniversary, came news.

Like a twisted line from the movie *Poltergeist* we were told, *It's ba-ack*. But "it" was much worse than a ghost. This time the cancer was in Taylor's lungs.

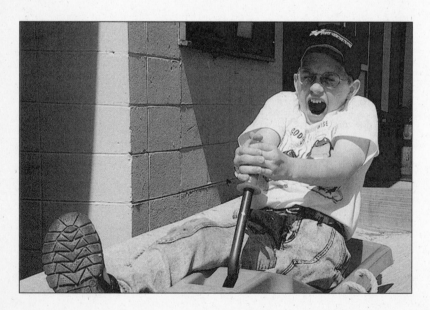

PART II
FULL SPEED AHEAD

11 SEVEN DAYS IN JUNE

MOVING AHEAD: A TAYLOR REPORT

Friday, June 11th, 1999

In the week or so since discovery of the cancer's recurrence, Taylor's days have been chock-full.

Last Friday, June 4th

Taylor had a birthday. He's now eleven, exactly one-fourth my age. Debbie spent the day getting ready for the party while I processed more than a hundred e-mail messages from friends. Over the next few days Debbie and I read them several times. We were strengthened, encouraged, and filled with gratitude for these expressions of your love. For your commitments to pray.

Late in the afternoon Debbie received a call from one of Taylor's doctors. Vanderbilt's Tumor Board has settled on a battle plan. They intend to counterattack the stubborn enemy in Taylor's body with a massive six-day infusion of chemotherapy, but from a drug he hasn't had before.

It's called ifosfamide (eye-FOS-fa-mide). We're told it shouldn't make him too nauseous. But it will knock the snot out of his immune system.

And for the third time he'll lose his beautiful blond hair.

Two or three weeks after this infusion, Taylor will undergo new scans. *If* the nodules in his lungs show any signs of surrender to the ifosfamide assault, he'll get another six-day round of the same stuff. Then more scans. After that, *probably*, he'll go under the knife again—to slice the suckers out.

So much for camps and vacations this summer. But Taylor remained thrilled about the new laptop I promised to get him. And he was excited about his birthday bash, only hours away.

That night at six o'clock about eight boys arrived. They were ready to party hearty. And so they did, complete with water fights and lots of wonderfully grotesque bathroom humor.

Later in the evening, after cake and presents, the gang grew strangely quiet. Climbing partway up the stairs, I heard talking inside Taylor's room.

"You have *five* tumors?" asked one incredulous friend.

"Well, five right now," Taylor explained. "Including the last big one, I've had *six*." The kid was bragging! Must be a preadolescent testosterone thing.

While spying I gave a name to that first monster: The Mutha. It wasn't a term of endearment. But it was accurate. Somehow this *thing* had hatched and spread her microscopic young before it was ejected into formaldehyde. In my mind I pictured the horrific parasitic monsters in Sigourney Weaver's *Alien* movie series.

"The biggest tumor in me now is only one centimeter," Taylor continued. "The rest are even smaller."

With authority in his voice, Taylor's best friend, Trey (who had moved back from Las Vegas), announced, "The good thing is, they found it real early. So there should be no problem getting it all out."

Standing on the stairs, I thanked God for Trey and prayed that he was right.

Finishing my climb, sneaking past the room, I took a secret peek. All the boys were sitting on Taylor's bed, clustered round a PlayStation video game. Just like that, *Snap!* The conversation was over, and everyone was teleported back to fantasy.

Saturday night, June 5th

Taylor and I arrived at Nashville's CBS affiliate, News Channel Five, about two hours before Taylor's scheduled interview. This was his big night. As one of two ambassadors for VCH (Vanderbilt Children's Hospital), Taylor was about to be a star on the opening broadcast of a telethon for the Children's Miracle Network.

People were wonderful; the food was good; the studios were *cool*. And Taylor was totally pumped. Behind the cameras, he raced around, sometimes hopping without crutches in order to initiate a sneak attack on Dad, tickling my ancient ribs—four *times* older than his!

Taylor's coambassador for the VCH is a girl, Lou Allyn. She and Taylor were interviewed *(live!)* at 10:40 P.M. Taylor grinned so hard his smile muscles hurt.

On camera he was asked, "So, Taylor, what's the best part about being this year's ambassador?"

Eyes looked up, mental wheels turned. Then straight into the lens he answered, "Popularity?" and grinned from ear to ear.

That night I chuckled all the way home.

Sunday afternoon, June 6th . . .

Taylor and I returned to the television station. This time Debbie too was with us. All three of us were scheduled for an interview that afternoon.

Soon as he walked in, swinging up his leg, kicking open doors, Taylor got the royal treatment. In less than a day everyone had come to know and love him, perhaps in part because they also knew about the cancer's recent reappearance—and that Taylor himself had learned of it only three days ago.

I watched, amazed, at the unconscious wonder in other people's eyes. What did they see? Then it hit me. They saw the same as I: an irrepressible spirit in the face of horror. An energetic, enthusiastic, witty boy. He wasn't perfect, but he was irresistibly magnetic.

Throughout the day and into the evening hours, Taylor was frequently invited back before the camera. In the lights! On the air! He helped accept gifts from corporate donors.

Driving home that night inside our darkened van, Taylor said, "Know what, Dad? It really feels good to know you're good at something and then to do it well!"

"You're right!" I agreed, once again surprised by his insightful self-awareness. While I drove we prayed. We thanked God for his gifts through people, people who give Taylor opportunities to do things. And to do them well.

On Tuesday evening, June 8th

The chemo fight began again at 6 P.M. Debbie took Taylor to the VCH and set him up for the night. I stayed home with Christopher and Jonathan.

That night I called Taylor on the phone. "So, what's it like?" I asked.

"Just like the bad ol' days," he dryly answered. Still, he remained thrilled with the promise of a laptop. Earlier that day I ordered it, a fully loaded Dell Inspiron 7000. It's a beauty, and with a price to match. I was grateful several helped by making contributions but also a little embarrassed that we needed help to get it.

On the other hand, whenever I ask, "Is Taylor's happiness worth personal embarrassment?" the answer was, and is, an emphatic *yes.*

On Wednesday, June 9th

Debbie was with Taylor most of the day. "He is exhausted," she told me on the phone. He went from the State of Boundless Energy all the way to Wasted in twenty-four short hours.

Suitcase packed, including my pillow and a Clancy novel, I showed up at four-thirty that afternoon. Taylor *was* exhausted, but true to form I found him in the playroom glued to a Nintendo game.

"Oh, hi, Dad," he said, barely looking up, not wanting to get killed inside Mario's world.

"Hey, buddy. I love you," I replied, sitting down to read my Clancy book while Taylor played, both of us trying to escape into lands of make-believe.

And today, Friday, June 11th

This evening, once again, I'll sleep in the room with Taylor. Several minutes ago he called me on the phone. With a begging tease he asked for microwave popcorn and nachos to eat as snacks tonight. I will, of course, comply. That's our kind of food!

His appetite makes it clear Taylor's tolerating well this round of chemotherapy. But is it working???

Before we go to bed tonight we'll watch movies, play games, eat junk food, and laugh—a lot. Then, as always, before the lights go out, I'll join him on his bed. I'll put my arm around him, and with his back against my chest we'll say our nightly prayers.

After we've repeated our treasured litany—"Good night! I love you! See you in the morning!"—I'll retire to my fancy cot set up by the window. When I get there I'll thank God for the grace and strength he's giving each of us through your love and prayers.

Love,
Brian

Husband to Debbie; Dad to Taylor, 11.02; also Dad to Christopher, 13.56, and Jonathan, 5.82. And reluctant guardian of Dempsey the farting boxer.

12 THE REST OF THE STORY . . . HOW MUCH DOES IT HURT?

WHEN TAYLOR'S ELEVENTH BIRTHDAY PARTY BEGAN on Friday night, June 4th, all nine boys engaged themselves in a rowdy water-pistol fight outdoors. Taylor played along at first but soon discovered it was too hard to handle crutches and a water gun. He asked his friends to come inside and play an indoor game in which he could take part.

But his guests, his friends, were so caught up in play, they hardly heard him, if at all. Giving up, Taylor came inside. He was devastated.

Distressed, he fought to hold back tears. When at last he told me why, I went outside and with my grown-up baritone brought all the boys back in. After that, everyone was happy and had fun.

Late that night, after cake and presents, after games and then good-byes, I sat alone with Taylor in his room. "Buddy, I'm sorry your party started out so bad. But it seemed to end okay, don't you think?"

Instantly his eyes filled up with unshed tears. "Yeah, I guess," he answered with a quiver then a pause. "But, Dad! When my friends were outside, they completely left me out! And when I asked them to come in, they wouldn't!" Painful tears began to flow.

"Ahhh . . . Taylorman, believe me, I know how much it hurts to feel abandoned by your friends. It's even worse when it happens in your own house—and at your own party!

"Your friends weren't cruel on purpose. But what they did was rude. If you *weren't* hurt by it, something would be wrong with you. Hey!

I'm proud of you for telling me how you feel instead of pretending. It takes courage to be honest about feelings. Now all you have to do is forgive your friends. But remember the lesson! Never forget how it feels to be rejected and ignored. It happens to kids all the time, especially when they're somehow different from others. If you remember how it feels, maybe you'll reach out to them when everyone else is making fun or leaving them alone."

Awareness hit his heart and bounced back through his eyes.

"Now, buddy, I have a question for you. I'm familiar with the kind of pain you felt tonight. I know it all too well. But what I don't know is how this kind of pain compares with what the body feels. You know, like all the stuff you've been through. You've had a major amputation, phantom pains, and nauseating chemo. You have firsthand knowledge of pain I can't even imagine. In fact, you already know more about suffering than most people ever will, or would, if they lived a hundred years!

"So here's my question: How does rejection compare with all the physical pain you've been through?"

Taylor's eyes turned thoughtful. Synapses in his brain fired off at least a million rounds. In his mind and heart he weighed the two in balance.

"Well," he finally said, his tone solemn and judicious, "I'd say they're both . . . pretty much the same."

His answer was stunning. A single instance of rejection hurt *just as much* as radical amputation, guerrilla-striking phantom pains, and twelve months of nausea from chemotherapy.

"Thank you, buddy," I whispered. "I've always hidden pain I feel from rejection and told myself, 'You wimp!' You've helped me understand this kind of pain is very real, very bad. It's no less hurtful than the worst kind of physical pain. And just think . . . the pain we feel when we're rejected must be a little like how God feels when we reject or ignore him. Taylor, I promise: This is a lesson I never will forget."

In fact, I never have. And I never will.

13 CAMP CRAZINESS

CALENDAR DAZE: A TAYLOR REPORT

Wednesday, July 14th, 1999

Hi. Once again, this is Brian, Taylor's dad. Here's a brief summary of what's happened since June 11th and a near-term calendar of things to come.

On Monday, June 11th

Taylor was almost done with his first round of chemo since discovery of the cancer's recurrence in his lungs. He did very well. From his room in VCH he called me at the office at least every fifteen minutes. "Is it here yet? Is it? Is it?!"

We knew the laptop would arrive that day. When it did, Taylor was ready to burst. "*Don't* open it, Dad! I want to be there!"

Over the next ten days, or so, from
Tuesday, June 15th until Saturday, June 26th

Taylor was thrilled with his new, incredible computer. His favorite game is Microsoft Motocross Madness, a dirt-bike simulation. The experience is awesome. The controller, graphics, and sound make it seem like the real thing.

The first and only DVD movie Taylor bought was *Waterboy*, a laugh-out-loud slapstick comedy, somewhat like old Jerry Lewis films. It was *so cool* watching a movie on the high-resolution, fifteen-inch laptop screen!

Taylor's laptop was a gift from many generous friends, most of you anonymous. You made it possible for me to keep my promise to Taylor, the promise I made the day we learned the cancer had returned. I was, and always will be, grateful beyond words.

While Taylor was at home recovering from chemo and glued to his computer, Debbie gave him daily shots to boost his white cell counts. They worked! Taylor's system never got as depleted as we thought it would.

He was tired and a little weak. But he never stopped living. He had friends over, visited their homes, played video games, and traded Pokémon cards.

Taylor did great. But during these days and in spite of help from friendly pharmaceuticals, I rarely slept well . . .

Then, for a whole week, from
Sunday, June 27th, until Saturday, July 3rd

Taylor went to camp, something we thought he wouldn't get to do this summer. It was his second year at Camp Horizon run by the American Cancer Society. It is a special week just for kids who are fighting or have fought Big C. Unofficially we call it Cancer Camp.

Does that sound gloomy, dark? Cancer Camp is anything but. It is, instead, a place where a kid can be a kid even if he or she is bald or weak, walking with a limp, or built a little different—like having just one leg. Everybody's *normal* (whatever *normal* is).

The week was full of stuff to do, just like any camp. The only difference is, this one's under the constant supervision of specially trained nurses and an on-site pediatric oncologist.

All week long Taylor ran full throttle—until each day he just pooped out. He was in the pool almost every hour it was open. That meant he always had to stop by Club Med on the way.

Club Med was headquarters for Head Honcho Nurse. She covered Taylor's Hickman line with a huge transparent patch before he went into the water. Her name's Elizabeth—Lizzy to her friends. She hails from St. Jude's, not Vanderbilt.

Taylor was always hopping with impatience to go swimming. While she taped up his chest, Lizzy wisely drugged him up with junk food: potato chips washed down with strong grape soda. They ate and drank together then competed for the loudest, longest belch. That's how she made her way straight into his heart. And when she did, he snuck in hers as well.

At every opportunity, many of which he created, Taylor pulled pranks (almost always on adults 'cause he didn't want to hurt the feelings of his fellow campers).

One day, with help, he even kidnapped Miss Piggy, the snooty stuffed companion of camp director Stephen, leaving him to sleep alone, without Miss Piggy's comforts, for at least one night.

For the talent show Taylor went as Elvis. He let the girls (especially nurse Elizabeth) put makeup on his face. He sported a specially tailored large white shirt, including huge lapels trimmed with ribbon gold. And on his now-bald head he wore a wig of Afro hair colored midnight black.

When it came time to perform, the king of rock-'n'-roll was ready; his imitation was perfect. Balanced on his leg, performing without crutches, he wiggled and he sang, "Un-un un-un . . . Ah'm awwwl shook up!" Then to laughter and applause he bowed and said repeatedly, "Un, thu-ank yew, thu-ankyewverymuch."

On Disco Night he had a date, dancing up a storm with nurse

Elizabeth. They whirled and they twirled. Taylor swung his date around the dance floor until, at last, she later said, "I fell flat on my bottom. Of course, Taylor laughed his way off the dance floor, hopping on one leg!" While taking a break, they inhaled grape sodas then belched so loud it even pierced the disco music.

Early in the week his scalp developed that now-familiar tingly feeling. For the third time in a year his hair began to fall in little clumps (most of which he pulled out on purpose with a laugh). Under slight duress he grudgingly let two counselors (only guys, not girls!) shave his head—which he promptly burned swimming without sunscreen in the afternoon.

After that, with cajoling charm, he persuaded nurse Elizabeth to give him her yellow-and-white umbrella hat. Not only did he wear it unashamed, he also brought it home and treasured it with pride.

In every camp activity, just like the pool, he dove right in. Always competing to win, he laughed it off when he usually didn't, congratulating other kids like him. He Hula-Hooped, played basketball and kickball, and even did the limbo.

He freely gave advice to those in charge, especially director Stephen and nurse Elizabeth. "Next year, you really oughta . . ."

His last night there was movie night. The shows were *Star Wars* flicks. Although he'd seen them many times, he joined the others watching on an outdoor screen. Sitting to one side near a case full of grape soda, he and nurse Elizabeth scarfed down all the bubbles that they could then had a belching contest.

Bored with the movie most had seen before, several other campers, even counselors, joined the competition. Some did well, but no one could come close to the volume and the resonance of Taylor's awesome barks. For two years in a row he was Camp Horizon's undisputed champion of burps! That's my son!

The only interruption in Taylor's week was Tuesday. Late that morning a nurse from camp (not Elizabeth) drove him to VCH for scheduled scans.

I drove there too, arriving early. With nothing else to do, I wandered into Vanderbilt's small and empty chapel near the main front lobby.

Walking in halfhearted, I feel awkward, helpless, angry, scared. I end up kneeling at the front, no one else around, baptizing myself with big drops of scalding tears.

These days I rarely pray—at least not in any conventional sense. There are no words. Only pain. I am keenly aware that God's name is not Aladdin. He's able to heal. But he doesn't have to . . .

I leave the chapel and several minutes later meet Taylor in the radiology department. He splits a grin, gives a hug, and fills me in on camp so far.

Once he's on the table the scan does not take long. Technicians get a kick from pictures of Taylor's stomach. It is stuffed with food recently ingested at a Taco Bell, something Taylor persuaded his chauffeur nurse to buy him while driving in from camp.

When his lungs are pictured on the screen the attending radiologist lets me take a look. She points out a node, just a tiny shadow, hiding in the dark, proof the evil Mutha has left a wicked litter.

Soon as it's over, Taylor hops off the table, pauses for another hug, and giddily returns to camp.

Next day Debbie got a call. She was told the nodules had "not grown." I guess this was good news. Our preference was to hear the nodules had shrunk or disappeared. Still, we were relieved that, with this news, Taylor's next round of chemo would not include a drug costing him additional hearing loss.

(He's already lost enough from last year's chemotherapy, from the drug cisplatin. It seems that ever since his hearing is like slightly fuzzy vision, just a little out of focus. He hears but often pauses as if translating a strange language—like, perhaps, Old English. And very often, too, we repeat things to him, slowing down and turning up the volume. We are grateful though that, for the most part, the pain from his tinnitus has almost gone away.)

On Saturday morning, I drove to Camp Horizon to join Taylor for breakfast and then bring him home. His hair was gone, his scalp recovering from sunburn. In short, he looked terrific. Once again we both were MIBs—Men In Baldness.

Before breakfast began, all the children gathered round camp director Stephen (now happily reunited with Miss Piggy) outside in the muggy morning air near a burned-out campfire. Just the night before the site had been alive with enchanted light. Now, beneath the rising sun filtered through a fleeting mist, the site of nightly magic was a pile of gray and lifeless ashes.

But with a gift Stephen stoked each heart, each soul, inside his special campers. They stood around him, unaware they were an entire congregation of pediatric heroes. Or that standing there together, their mingled spirits blazed far brighter than ten suns.

Stephen's gift was a song called "Friends," written and made famous by

Michael W. Smith and his wife, Debbie. Stephen, tall and thin, a single man with kind, sad eyes but always with a pleasant smile, unwrapped his hidden talent. With a voice of aching beauty he slowly sang . . .

> Packing up the dreams God planted
> In the fertile soil of you
> Can't believe the hopes He's granted
> Means a chapter in your life is through
>
> But we'll keep you close as always
> It won't even seem you've gone
> 'Cause our hearts in big and small ways
> Will keep the love that keeps us strong
>
> And friends are friends forever
> If the Lord's the Lord of them
> And a friend will not say "never"
> 'Cause the welcome will not end
> Though it's hard to let you go
> In the Father's hands we know
> That a lifetime's not too long to live as friends . . .

When the last note disappeared into the morning air, all the staff and counselors formed a long straight line leading to the front door of the dining hall. Then in slow assembly each camper received and gave away no less than thirty gentle, lingering hugs. And with each hug there always came a promise: "See you next summer!"

Standing outside the circle and far back from the line I swallowed hard and hid my face. I knew that many of these heroes would *not* be seen next summer, at least not at this camp.

After the holiday weekend, from

Tuesday, July 6th until today, July 14th

Taylor returned to Six South, his Vanderbilt home away from home. Once again, tethered to a pole on wheels, he stayed true to form. Almost every minute the playroom was open, Taylor was there. And when it wasn't open, he was lost in cyberspace sitting in his room, playing games or talking with unknown friends, like in Yahoo!'s cancer chat room. "I'm always the youngest one," he tells me.

During Taylor's stay Debbie and I were told his next CaT scan will be on Monday, July 26th. Subject to results, Taylor is scheduled for surgery on Monday, August 2nd.

The objective of this operation, as I understand it, is removal of the nodules on Taylor's left lung—and probably some eyes-on, hands-on investigation of his innards while his body's opened up.

All indicators are that Taylor's spirit remains remarkably robust. Mine, on the other hand, is dying. Not pretty. Not good. Especially for my family. But it's true.

Thank you for your love and prayers, for your encouragement.

Love,

Brian

Husband to Debbie; Dad to Taylor, 11.11; also Dad to Christopher, 13.65, and Jonathan, 5.91. Also reluctant guardian of Dempsey the farting boxer.

The next thing Taylor did was attend a *second* camp, this time with a slew of kids his age, all from our congregation. We're told he was a "wild man," blowing everyone away.

Unlike Camp Horizon, full of kids like him, Taylor was, at first, a shocking sight to his healthy friends, including the adults. *How will he do?* they wondered. *Will he be okay? How will he get around? What if he gets hurt? After all, "poor Taylor" has cancer and just one leg.*

When he arrived (one day later than the rest), the first thing Taylor did was patch up his Hickman and head off for the pool. Thrilled to see a diving board, he dropped his crutches, hopped up, hopped out, dove in. Then did it all again. Laughing when he belly-flopped, he just got out, got up, and did some more.

"How 'bout a game of killer ball?" he asked the awe-struck kids. Mostly speechless, they hesitated and slowly backed away. "C'mon!" Taylor said. "Let's play!"

A Native-American Mohican dad replete with long black hair watched and empathized. All his life he's known rude stares, blatant mockery. And worse. Taking off his shirt, he jumped into the pool. Taylor beaned him with a ball. The fight was on. Birdsong (a.k.a. Bill Miller) grabbed the ball and threw it back. Hard. Taylor dove, escaped, resurfaced, capturing the bobbing ball. Laughing at his deft escape, he took aim and threw again. Hard. A hit! Bill threw back. But diving for cover Taylor was impossible to get. And when the ball escaped the watery battleground, landing on the grass, Taylor never hesitated. Out he hopped, scooting to recover it, then hopped back in. *Splash!*

Bill, who is my age (pretty darned *old*), later told me, "I could not believe your son. His spirit was so powerful, so strong . . . As we played, everything he did was teaching me. I never will forget that day, for still my spirit needs to learn his lessons."

Later in the week Taylor joined the boys and men in canoes paddling down a river engaged in water fights and other stunts as if they were immortal. Although he rode with a very wary grownup, Taylor's canoe tipped over when the current swept it up against a horizontal tree trunk. Taylor popped up, laughing. But his custom crutches drowned, swept away forever. Someone found an old-fashioned replacement made of wood and crowned with half-moons for each underarm. Taylor was merely inconvenienced. The loss didn't slow him down.

At camp, Taylor was a wild man with an unfettered mighty spirit. Soon he would be back at Vanderbilt, enduring more surgery. But also attended by troops of nurses who adore him.

What a life. What an incredible, wonderful, fully lived life.

14   THE RIBBER AND THE RIBBED

EARLY MONDAY MORNING ON AUGUST 2ND, 1999, OUR family was at Vanderbilt's OR for kids. The time had come to cut away part of Taylor's lung. Taylor was excited.

When his surgeon Dr. John Pietsch (pronounced "peach") came in and asked, "How are you this morning, Taylor?" Taylor never missed a beat.

"Just peachy," he replied, laughter in his eyes. Pietsch's eyes laughed back.

Dr. Pietsch had just reviewed pictures from a CAT scan one week earlier. Four nodules were visible on the bottom of the left lung, and one small bump showed on the lower right lung. Because the latter was small and might not be cancerous, Pietsch said he'd probably leave it alone that day and take it out in a couple of weeks.

"Today," Pietsch said, "I want to focus on removal of the cluster on the left."

At least one of the nodes, however, was *inside* the lung, huddled near its sibling squatters in and on the bottom lobe. It would probably be necessary, he told us, to remove that part of the lung in order to evict all of these unwelcome tenants.

Because each lung has three lobes, this meant Taylor could lose one-third of one lung. We worried. Afterward would he have trouble breathing?

"Not at all," Pietsch told us. "The human body is designed with about twice the lung capacity it actually needs. Taylor will do fine."

When Pietsch left us to get ready, Taylor was given a preanesthetic: the goofy stuff. Within seconds it took effect. After kissing him good-bye, as he was rolled away he sang, "So long! Farewell! I mighta say I do-oo. I do, I do to you and you and you-ooo." Obviously *auf Wiedersehen* and *adieu* were not yet part of his vocabulary.

While Taylor was under the knife, we sat beneath a poky clock. Christopher and I drank free coffee from the nurse's station. We talked. I fiddled on Taylor's laptop. Then our friend, a leader from our congregation, came to visit. His presence, laughter, kindness, strength were God's gentle anesthetic for us. With him I always feel safe to be real—a rarity in life.

During the procedure, Pietsch's nurse briefed us. She said he was, in fact, removing about two-thirds of the bottom lobe, about one-quarter of the lung.

Around noon Pietsch himself showed up. Dressed in green scrubs, thin paper hair net on his head, a loosened mask around his neck, he gave us his report. It was encouraging.

One of the small nodules on the surface of the lung was crumbly calcium, apparently dead! Others would be tested by pathology.

While looking around, he said he found a fifth small node not previously detected. But after close examination he could not find any others. Apparently all the squatters on the left lung were evicted!

"And it's possible the nodule on the right might *not* be cancerous," Pietsch said. "It could, perhaps, be caused by an infection."

Between two ribs, Taylor's incision began about halfway down his trunk underneath his arm then angled toward his back, about six inches long.

"How did you get the lung out between his ribs?" Debbie asked. Pietsch's eyes and almost-hidden grin were mischievous, reminding me of Taylor. *This is what Taylor might look like when he's grown with kids,* I thought.

"It's a secret," Pietsch answered. "I could tell you . . . but then I'd have to kill you!" No doubt, this is a man who knows his ribs.

We laughed with Pietsch, thanked him, and soon were ushered into the recovery room, a large and open space that looked more like a high-tech warehouse than a "room." Taylor was awake, looking good but sore. "It hurts to breath," he grimaced. Pain meds soon removed the edge.

"I love you, buddy," I whispered in his ear, bending down. "And I'm proud of you. But, hey! Where are the wisecracks I expected?"

His answer was *the look,* a pause, and then a very dry retort. "It's hard to make a joke when you've got new nostrils in your lung."

I stroked the soft skin of his hairless head, chuckled at his imagery, and readily concurred.

Throughout the week Taylor made excellent progress. He was sore and a little breathless. But as soon as the drainage tube came out (oh, how he *hated* that thing), he was a brand-new man, rarin' to go—especially to the playroom.

On Thursday someone told us that, according to pathology, every tumor from that piece of Taylor's lung was dead!

A single nodule remained on the right lung. In spite of the wonderful report we heard, the plan was still to get the sucker ASAP, perhaps in just two weeks.

Saturday, August 7th, 1999

Today, while Mom was someplace else, all three boys and I went to the mall. The place was bursting with shoppers, just like us, eager to escape the heat. What they didn't know is that they would be hit with a shocking sight—a one-legged boy racing around on forearm crutches (we got a new pair) while his dad trailed behind, pushing a healthy five-year-old in his brother's wheelchair.

Shoppers were stunned. I was awed. Only four days before this one-legged kid had had his side cut open and a fourth of his lung removed. Now, here he was, on crutches, using muscles that should have hurt like, well . . .

For several hours, rich with joy, we joined the benign melee and finally came home pooped.

We're all exhausted. But we're also grateful for the wealth of God's love. Through you his love is tangible. Through you it nurtures and sustains us. May God do one thousandfold for you what you have done for us. For all our family, and with love . . .

Brian

Husband to Debbie; Dad to Taylor, 11.17; also Dad to Christopher, 13.72, and Jonathan, 5.98. And still reluctant guardian of Dempsey the farting boxer.

"I feel like I'm diagonally parked in a parallel universe."
(Source unknown)

🌿 15 ENCORE: T-2

FRIDAY, AUGUST 13ᵀᴴ, 1999

Last night, feeling a little shocked by the prospect of another operation in three short days, I asked Taylor how he felt about it.

"I just want it over with," he answered. "Besides, the last operation really wasn't that bad . . ." His sentence trailed off as the television recaptured his attention.

I shook my head. He still amazes me. Less than two weeks ago he had his ribs stretched open and one-quarter of his lung cut out. Now he shrugs and nonchalantly says, "It really wasn't all that bad"?!

Meanwhile, our youngest, Jonathan, turns six on Sunday. Tomorrow afternoon Debbie's throwing a huge pirate birthday party for him. Jonathan is thrilled. And I am grateful. He's getting a day, a special event, entirely for him. So much attention has been focused just on Taylor . . .

Until next week, with love and thanks . . .

Brian

Jonathan's birthday party was a huge success. *Fourteen* five- and six-year-olds were at our home. Thanks to Debbie's administrative skills, everything stayed under control. Christopher and Taylor, both dressed up as pirates with penciled mustaches, welcomed each kindergarten guest. After cake and ice cream they crouched behind the paneless window inside a faded plastic fort. While boys and girls sat on the other side, big brothers (with the help of Taylor's best friend, Trey) did an improv puppet show, just like they used to do for Mom and Dad when they were much younger.

I hid behind a camera with a big zoom lens, taking lots of pictures, recording for posterity this miracle of joy.

Jonathan and friends, too young to comprehend, laughed and played in blissful ignorance of suffering and death. Christopher, a somber sweet thirteen, smiled self-consciously. Tightening his shirtless abs, he was in that awkward place between the man unfolding and the present but departing boy.

I love each son with all my heart. Still, in these fleeting moments, Taylor was the greatest marvel. There he was, completely bald, dressed up as a pirate, well aware of surgery to come. But living fully in the *now*, not *then*. And living to the hilt. He laughed with unpolluted pleasure, especially in the puppet show, when, barely hidden behind a toy wall, he performed with zest, sharing his performance skills with the "little kids."

Not wanting to spoil the fun, I tried to reinflate the tattered life raft of my spirit. *I. Am. Not. Alone!* I told myself while lost in unseen stormy seas, whole oceans locked in combat. Up and down I rose and fell on mountain waves of love and grief and poignant joy.

I always told Taylor everything about his battle as I understood it. But I never talked about the odds. I never said to Taylor, "There is, at least, a 95 percent chance that *metastatic* Osteo-sarcoma will take your life."

In fact, as much as possible, I hid this threat even from myself. Instead, I told him, "Just like you, I'm thrilled with the pathology report. So now we need to decide . . . continue with chemo or wait? Because, in spite of this good news, there's still a *chance* the cancer *could* come back . . ."

As for Christopher . . .

It's tough enough just to be an adolescent. It's even harder, though, to be one with a brother fighting cancer. Throughout these long and almost endless days, Christopher loved Taylor but felt invisible next to him. Almost every time he was out with Taylor, or even just with me, people (understandably) focused eyes or words or love on Taylor, often blind, oblivious, to Christopher standing right beside us. My terrific oldest son: kind but hurting on the inside, almost flawlessly polite but feeling so alone, trying to do right but often ready to explode. He is, more than my other sons, a lot like me.

⚘ 16 FULL SPEED AHEAD

A TAYLOR AND FAMILY REPORT

Friday, September 17th, 1999

About a month ago Taylor had his second thoracotomy. Since then, in thirty-two days, he's not only recovered, the kid has gotten *busy*. A new student at the same school where his brothers go, he is a full-time fifth grader.

His favorite job at school takes place twice a week early in the morning. Standing at the curb where parents drop off children, Taylor helps a child get out of the car then scurries on his crutches and opens up the building door so that the younger girl or boy can easily walk in. And all the while he grins from ear to ear.

I think he likes the greetings—"Hi, Taylor!"—and gets a kick from dumbstruck looks. But most of all he loves to prove, both to himself and others, that he can do anything, just like a normal kid. This is what he longs to be. But, of course, is not. And never will be.

Even in phys ed he takes full part, including bangs and bruises I wince to think about. I think this is where he shows his greatest courage. For here his intense sense of privacy does battle with a fierce determination to do it all, to prove himself and thereby win the casual, not awe-struck, acceptance of his classmates.

The irony, of course, is when he does it all, his fifth-grade peers are usually more awe-struck, not less.

"So, buddy, how do you change shirts in private?"

"Actually, I don't. Other boys are with me."

Inwardly I chuckle at the mental picture of ten- and eleven-year-old boys making sideways looks, aghast at what they see. On both sides of Taylor's chest are two long scars from surgeries in August, one thin and healing nicely, the other broad and red, healing too but stretched, not thin, a scar that may not ever disappear. And from the center of his chest erupts that long white tube, the Hickman to his heart. The tube, with its dangling branches, is taped to Taylor's chest. Always hidden by

a shirt, the Hickman is something people on the "outside" just do not remember.

"Does anyone ever ask about your scars?"

"Nah, not usually. Once or twice, I guess, a kid has asked me what happened."

"I'll bet!"

"But, Dad, the other day in gym we were playing tag ball. One kid on the other side threw it at me *hard*." Unfallen tears brimmed up in his eyes.

I cringed but said, "Well hey, buddy, that's the game. I'm sorry you got hurt. I know how much that rubber ball can sting."

"Yeah, Dad, I know! But this kid acted mean, like he really wanted to get me. I hardly know him!"

"Ah-ha . . . and do you know the reason why?"

"No!"

"Well, I do. I know it makes you uncomfortable, but you are loved and famous at your school. That makes some people jealous, even angry. I know it's nuts, but it's kinda funny too. Here you are, a cancer fighter with an amputated leg, and this kid is *jealous!* He wishes he could be like you! You've almost gotta laugh."

Taylor didn't laugh, but understanding dawned inside his mind, a light that dried up watery eyes.

"Listen, buddy. *Everyone's* a cripple. Everyone. Everybody's wounded on the inside, crippled in their heart. But because it's on the inside out of sight, most people lie to themselves. They pretend they are okay. They don't admit how much they really hurt. Instead they try to ignore their crippling pain, forget it.

"But when they look at you, they see themselves in the mirror of your loss. They are reminded of the truth. They see they too are wounded cripples. They too are mortal. Someday they will die.

"That's why most grownups glance at you and quickly look away. It's not about you. It's about them. Okay? Do you understand?"

"Yeah, Dad. But I still don't like it," he protested with a smile.

I haven't written for a month because I've been upset, almost apoplectic. This turmoil, a hidden uproar in my mind and heart, began with the pathology report that followed Taylor's second thoracotomy.

Turns out my understanding of the report from Taylor's first thoracotomy was wrong.

I thought all the nodules were dead. They weren't. Nodules extracted from both lungs had live cancer cells.

The good news is that in both surgeries the margins were clear. That means there was no indication of cancer on the outer edges of extracted lung tissue.

But . . . the same thing was true when Taylor's left pelvis and leg were amputated one year ago—on August 31st, 1998. Even with clean margins and additional rounds of intense chemotherapy, the cancer came back. In spite of this history, and because margins from lung surgeries were clean, the Vanderbilt Tumor Board recommended Taylor *not* continue with chemotherapy.

It was a difficult call.

Do we hit him hard with chemo now in order to attack and kill microscopic cancer squatters that may or may not be there? Or do we take lots of pictures, praying for no more recurrences but retaining chemo as a treatment option if they do come back?

While Debbie and I agreed with the decision to stop chemotherapy, I battled a hurricane of emotions. It was provoked by the Tumor Board's decision to also limit future CT scans just to Taylor's lungs. What if it returns in his brain? Or pelvis? Or maybe his right leg?

Granted, lungs are the place where the cancer is most likely to recur. But I know people who've had it come back elsewhere. One, a son, had the monster pop up in his brain, unseen because unscanned. Once discovered, after symptoms could not be ignored, it was too late. The tumor was too large. The boy died.

Believe it or not our insurance company came to the rescue. Apparently, getting paid was the real issue. Lots of times hospitals don't get reimbursed for taking tests deemed unnecessary by bureaucratic drones who Just Say No.

Thankfully, our insurance company's caseworker assigned to Taylor did not hesitate to say the company would gladly pay for periodic CT scans of Taylor's brain and lower abdomen—as well as of his lungs.

Hallelujah.

So, here we are. A family full of school and homework, cross-country and soccer (by Christopher and Jonathan), music lessons, and work. Also lots of driving (mostly by Mom). And lots and lots of stress.

All of us are grateful for your love, your encouragement and humor, your patience, and your help. Your prayers. We are *not* strong people. It is only because of God's help, usually through you, that we persevere.

Love,
Brian

Husband to Debbie; Dad to Taylor, 11.29; also Dad to Christopher, 13.83, and Jonathan, 6.09. And plugged-nose guardian of Dempsey the farting boxer.

17 THE LONGEST DAY

SCANS TODAY

Monday, September 20th, 1999

This afternoon at 5 P.M., Debbie's taking Taylor to get his CT pictures taken.

Don't even feel like making a "cat" pun.

I *think* shots will include brains, lungs, lower abdomen—plus a full-body x-ray.

Calling all prayers . . .

Brian

The next morning, at the start of my Longest Day, Taylor went to school and after school, with Mom, straight to his piano lesson. Debbie said CT results would not come in till sometime after lunch, after 1 P.M.

All morning long the only place I lived was in the State of Nauseating Fear, making just one plea: *O, God! Please, please*, please, *let the scans be clear.*

After lunch I waited, looking at my silent phone until, at last, I called. Then I wrote . . .

TERRIFIED
Tuesday, September 21st, 1999, 2:20 P.M.

Just called Pediatric Oncology, Taylor's medical team. Asked if they had results from yesterday's CT.

A nurse came on the line. Her voice was piercing, nasal. Even though she knows it well, she mispronounced my name. Why?

"Mr. Skrangrr? Uhh, I will have our doctor who's on call get back to you."

"How long?"

"Oh, probably within an hour."

"Can you tell me anything about the results?" My voice was weak, a faint and hoarsey whisper.

"Well, uhhh . . . I haven't seen them. I'm sure they're in the pile here. I'llhavethedoctorcallyoubackjustassoonaspossibleokay?"

"Okay."

Brian

After that each minute was its own millennium inside my office tomb. I died at least ten thousand deaths and yet could not escape. Time and utter solitude mocked my midnight soul.

She knew but wouldn't tell ya, they scoffed. Wanting to throw up, I couldn't even make dry heaves.

"How will I survive this wait? How will I survive? Where are you, God? *Where are you?*" I prayed and prayed. And prayed. Screaming. Angry. Scared.

But the skies were wordless. From them there came no answers. The cosmos, just a wild, brainless sponge, sucked away my pleas into its black holes. Creation didn't even grant an echo to my questions.

Doodle words, I finally thought. *Doodle words.* With horrible penmanship I began to write on paper, something I later gave a title called . . .

a musing
in my quiet office
i am alone
unknown
terrified
weeping with fear
weeping in prayer
begging God to intercede

then
in my quiet office
my heart hears
Something indefinable

still
i am terrified
weeping with fear
weeping in prayer
begging God to intercede
but not alone
and not unknown

What creation couldn't do, in some strange faint way the Creator did.

Seconds after penning the last word, "unknown," my phone began to ring, bringing me the news. Before rushing to the house, I followed up with our unseen team of readers . . .

SCAN RESULTS

Tuesday, September 21st, 1999, 4:05 P.M.

Finally got a call from a different nurse in Pediatric Oncology. She did not seem happy with all the calls many of you made during the last ninety minutes. But they worked. She gave me a report.

Taylor's left lung is clear.

Taylor's right lung indicates a "density." This might be nothing more than scarring from surgery on August 16th.

But . . . there is also a new, separate mass on that lung, an anomaly radiology does *not* think can be attributed to scarring. Worst of all, there is a five-centimeter mass in Taylor's boneless pelvic sphere, on the left, right next to his rectum.

The primary oncologists with whom we've worked are out of town.

Dr. Pietsch, who did the thoracotomies, is in surgery.

I asked he call with his opinion as soon as possible.

The nurse promised to pass along my request.

Weeping from a bottomless well of tears . . .

Brian

I locked my office door and in a daze drove home. Only Christopher and Jonathan were there. I had forgotten about Taylor's piano lesson. There was another hour to wait.

I was such a wreck, Christopher insisted that I tell him what was wrong. When at last I relented, he put his homework down, went inside the bathroom, and locked the door behind him. Bible in his hand, he went to read, to grieve, to pray. It was his necessary business.

Later that same hour Dr. Pietsch called. While I sat at the kitchen table, Pietsch said he was looking at the CT scan even as we spoke. I told him, "It's the pelvic mass that really scares me."

Pietsch responded with a provisional analysis. The mass, he said, does not *appear* to be all tissue (that is, cancer). Instead it seems to have three parts: part calcium, part fluid, part tissue.

Is it surgically accessible, I asked? It is, *but* . . . because of its size and position Pietsch expressed concern about getting clean margins. Said he'd like to see some shrinkage before attempting an extraction.

I was grateful for his kind, clear answers. Still, to me, the news was devastating. The problem is, *none* of Taylor's chemotherapies to date had shrunk *any* of his Osteo-sarcomas. Granted, 60 percent of the original pelvic tumor (the evil Mutha, as we call it) died from chemo poisons. But even as it died, it *grew*. Its size increased by *20 percent* during those three months of nauseating treatment prior to extraction.

Pietsch reassured me that the Pediatric Oncology team would consult with other specialists around the country before proposing a new treatment plan. Or plans. But with half the group out of town, we had to wait. Thanking Pietsch, I said good-bye. And waited.

Finally. The garage door rattled opened. That familiar auto-engine song moved in with a crescendo and then abruptly quit. Car doors opened, paused, then shut.

Thump-plop, thump-plop, thump-plop.

Taylor was the first to climb up wooden stairs and come inside the house. "Hi, Dad!" he greeted with grin, looking up the inside flight of stairs to the landing where I stood.

"Hey, buddy," I tried to smile but failed. "Listen, I need to talk with you and Mom. Would both of you come to our room once she gets inside?"

"Okay."

In our bedroom with an odd if only momentary calm, I told them the bad news. Then with Taylor and with Debbie we cried. Together Mom and Dad touched their son with hands on head and shoulders, and prayed.

Suddenly we understood why Taylor had been uncomfortable since the start of school. We thought his aching backside was simply due to sitting down on chairs designed for people with two legs and a full-boned hip (as well as a doubly cushioned tush). The theory made sense. It just wasn't right. The real problem was a new and very nasty tumor growing in his rear.

Twenty minutes later Mom left to work the phones while Taylor and I lingered in the master bedroom.

"Hey, buddy, wanna know the *good* news? The good news is, for the next two days at school, you'll be able to get away with *anything!*"

I won a grin as his mind ignited possibilities.

"Know what else? There's a tradition we've gotta keep, remember? Every time we get bad news, we go out to eat. I get a beer; you get nachos. And this time Christopher can go with us."

Taylor's neurons blazed. There was a momentary silence, a contemplative frown, and then a twinkle. "Okay, but *only* if we can *add* to the tradition by getting me some new Pokémon cards!" He split a mischievous smile.

Who could say no? At lightning speed the white flag of my heart flew up.

So off we went to eat, stuffing ourselves on heavenly fatty foods. Christopher worried that my solitary lager might have too much effect.

If only. I worried there would be too little. Gorged with high choles-
terol (*this* was my bad example), we three hunter-gatherers then went
to the superstore. Our task: to capture and bring home new packs of
Pokémon. But the store was sold out. I was relieved but not off the
hook. Taylor wasn't about to let me forget my promise.

And so on this, my longest day so far in life, Taylor bounced right
back.

Debbie and I did not. We hadn't hit the bottom. Nor was it in sight.

For myself, in the dark and falling, I couldn't see a thing. But all
around I heard the endless cackle of maniacal glee. Death was laughing as I tumbled blind.

PART III

UNCOMMON SCENTS

18 WAITING

Sunday, September 27ᵀᴴ, 1999, was a landmark day. At the end of morning worship, just before the sermon, Taylor with his mom and I stood center-left before the congregation, a human potpourri of about two thousand people with backgrounds from nearly every kind of faith and denomination.

Pastor Charles explained this important event was being specially done for Taylor because of Taylor's schedule in days and months to come. Soon it would again be filled with battle, engagements by a preteen veteran in his new Third War against an enemy invader, cancer in his triply wounded body from Wars One and Two (which, in turn, had claimed one full leg and two partial lungs).

While Charles spoke I stood with Debbie on my right, arm around her waist. Taylor stood on the left, my other hand resting on his shoulder. Then all at once Taylor was brought forward several steps. Still in sight but out of reach.

Outside my empty hand, held on to just by God's, Taylor stood alone, a man. He fearlessly confessed his faith in Y'shua as God's Son, in Y'shua's sacrificial death in Taylor's place, in Y'shua's resurrection from the dead. To every question posed by Pastor Charles, kind but sober to the bone, Taylor answered clear and calm, "Yes sir."

Then all two thousand people stood on pairs of feet, joining Taylor as he stood with crutches on one-half a pair. When they did, Taylor was baptized "in the name of the Father and of the Son and of the Holy Spirit." With water dripping from blond hair onto smiling cheeks, Pastor Charles made an introduction.

"I now present to you, this body of believers, a full and fellow member of this, our congregation, with all its privileges and responsibilities. Do you, this body, pledge your full support, to pray for Taylor, to help him when he needs it?"

"We do!" Soft thunder answered in response.

Tuesday, September 28th,1999

I received an e-mail from a friend who works in the cafeteria at Taylor's school. The subject line was titled "Lunch Lady to a Star." She wrote: "Taylor made me laugh today. I asked him if he liked watermelon. 'Not really,' he replied. 'Just the seeds for spitting on people!'"

Last night I asked, "So, how're ya feeling about stuff? Especially the new tumors?"

"I really don't think about it," Taylor answered right away. Then paused, twinkled, gleamed, "Except when I get presents!" Like Old Faithful, he once again erupted with an uncontainable, awesome grin.

Wish I could say the same. In fact, it's just the opposite. It's been eight days since new tumors were discovered, but still no treatment plan. I think of nothing else. And in spite of Taylor's honest answer early in the evening, he thinks about it too, though mainly late at night.

In just eight days discomfort in his backside has increased. Now and then he also feels an ache below his knee. Has the cancer come back there as well?

We wait. And wait. And wait. When will a treatment plan be proposed??? Maybe this afternoon.

Thankfully, we do not wait alone . . .

Brian

Husband to Debbie; Dad to Taylor, 11.32; also Dad to Christopher, 13.86, and Jonathan, 6.12. And air-afflicted guardian of Dempsey the farting boxer.

I feel like death will be a breeze compared with this.

Thursday, September 30th, 1999
From: Brian Schrauger
To: Dr. Robert Janco, pediatric oncologist

Look forward to seeing you this A.M. at 11:30. Thought our time might be more productive by sharing these thoughts and concerns . . .

In light of his diagnosis of metastatic Osteo-sarcoma, an extremely dangerous mass in a very bad location, and failure of past chemo treatments to shrink the primary tumor . . . Taylor's intermediate to long-term prognosis is grim. His odds for survival are less, probably much less, than 20 percent.

I don't think this in any way means that we don't fight. We *do* fight. But at some point there is an issue of balance between a vigorous fight for his life and protecting his quality of life.

It is for these reasons Debbie and I are currently inclined to skip the carboplatin infusions in the proposed ICE protocol [ifosfamide, carboplatin, and etoposide]. Your thoughts?

Thank you . . .
Brian

19 COUNTEROFFENSE

THE MEDICAL COUNTEROFFENSE BEGAN OCTOBER 4TH. Taylor was admitted to Vanderbilt Children's Hospital where he would be treated the remainder of the week. After several days of intensive research, meetings, and e-mails, Taylor's doctors and our family settled on the ICE treatment plan—three chemo drugs with which Taylor's body would be blasted for five days. Taylor was included in the decision-making process.

The carboplatin troubled me. A related drug, cisplatin, had already caused permanent hearing loss (my guess was about 30 percent). And with the loss, at first, Taylor also suffered hearing pain, an affliction called tinnitus. Now the terrible reality was finding a balance between the fight for Taylor's life while protecting his quality of life.

Four days before, immediately after seeing Dr. Janco, one of Taylor's primary-care physicians, I went home and reported to Debbie. Then, alone, to Taylor. Told them the conversation was very helpful. "So, buddy, after meeting with your doctors I tend to agree with 'em. We've got to launch a counterattack. Now, not later. After looking over several options, I think that ASAP you should start two rounds of the ICE."

"Why not operate right now and take the pelvic tumor out?" Taylor asked.

"Believe me, buddy, I nagged the heck out of those guys asking that same question. Bottom line is everyone, including Dr. Pietsch, is convinced it's just too dangerous. Your bowel, rectum, or bladder could easily be nicked, causing an infection that could kill you. Keep in mind, just like Dr. Schwartz needed clean margins when he took out the Mutha, Pietsch needs clean margins too. If he accidentally cut into live cancer cells, it's almost guaranteed the cancer would spread all throughout your body."

"Yeah . . . I know." He understood the predicament but didn't like it. He knew as well as anyone that past chemotherapies hadn't shrunk his tumors. Sometimes they seemed to stop the growth. But even then they never shrank.

I continued. "The good news, if you can call it that, is that the tumor in your pelvis isn't life-threatening. Even though they're small, the spots on your lungs, if in fact they're tumors, are more dangerous.

"There's no guarantee this new mix of chemo will be able to shrink the tumor in your pelvis or kill the buggers in your lungs, but we've gotta try. But *trying* means you'll also hafta take the *C* in I-C-E, a drug called carboplatin. Remember cisplatin?"

His eyes responded, "How could I forget?"

Well, carboplatin is like cisplatin. It's just not quite as strong. But taking it means there's a chance you'll have more hearing loss."

"Whadja say?" he asked, perplexed.

"There is a chance you'll have more hearing loss," I said again, notching up the volume, slowing down the words.

"Huh? *Whadja* say?" he asked a second time.

Conned again.

"You turkey!" I snorted in surprise, tickling with revenge. "You are *such* a turkey. How do you ever expect to survive Thanksgiving?"

He just laughed and laughed, thoroughly pleased with himself. Then he tickled back, delighted that he scored a point against me in our daily game of pranks 'n puns.

"Y'know, I think you actually like the idea of putting everyone on mute anytime you wanna!"

"Huh?" he asked.

Finally, out of breath, we took a break. "So what do you think?" I panted.

"'Bout what?" he panted back.

"'Bout takin' all three drugs in ICE, including the carboplatin."

"Whatever." Taylor shrugged, resigned. "Why not?"

Over the weekend he remained active, visiting friends, driving a four-wheeler, trading Pokémon cards, and vigorously engaging in several video games. But each day he also grew more tired. And the nature of his symptoms hinted the new tumor in his pelvis was growing.

Taylor's medical condition was dangerous. And he knew it. So did everyone else. But in spite of ubiquitous red-eyed grownups with barely muffled sniffles, Taylor's spirit remained undaunted. Gleefully defiant. Bashful. Honest. *Fun.*

Why focus on fear when you can lean on God, Mom, and Dad— and *focus* on *fun* stuff?!

When with Taylor it was easy to laugh in the face of death. But when I wasn't with him . . .

So with this life on the one side and that life on the Other, Debbie and I hung on by our fingernails to a swinging pendulum, dangling back and forth, back and forth, over the snarling pit of black despair . . . thankful for the net even though we could not see it . . .

Writing to our e-mail friends all around the world, I once again signed off with conviction,

I feel like death will be a breeze compared with this.
And I'd gladly die, if I even thought that it would help.

20   FAME AND INFAMY

DURING THE FIRST WEEK OF OCTOBER, WHILE TAYLOR was enduring the chemo, a nondenominational prayer meeting was held for Taylor's benefit. Organized and promoted by a go-getter friend, the event was supervised by a leader in our congregation. When, at first, he asked how I felt about the idea, my stomach twisted in a knot and in my soul I growled.

"Okay, I guess," is what I said out loud. "But with one nonnegotiable provision," I whisper-snarled, feeling menace. "At *no* time in the meeting must there even be a *hint* that God's name is Aladdin or that he is like him, granting any wish we want if we'll just rub him the right way or say or yell some formulaic words, grunting till we're red in the face, believing hard that God will 'put-out' so that, in fact, he will." I grew angry at the thought. It showed.

"I promise. None of that," the supervising leader said. "Now then, Brian, will you speak?"

Shoot. "I'm supposed to stay with Taylor during the prayer meeting. I'm thrilled for anyone to attend and pray—anyone but me. Not only do I not want to speak, I don't even want to go."

"Okay." Calm intonation. Reassuring. Challenging. "Just think about it and do what God tells you, all right?"

"Yeah, okay."

"I don't want to go. Why do you insist?" I argued with my Maker for several days on end, trying hard to wiggle out. Then, "Okay, I'll go.

But I will not prepare a speech. That is up to you." I grumpily surrendered. But I was not a happy camper.

So I went. Squirming with discomfort, I sat on the second row with Debbie on my right and Cliff, my brother, on the left.

For at least half an hour highly skilled musicians led the group behind us in songs of "praise and worship." I didn't sing along.

To me it felt like eating cotton candy while cruising through the carnage of a Nazi prison camp. *There is a place for cotton candy. But not here. Not now,* I stewed inside my woundedness.

There was a Bible on the backside of the bench in front of me. I opened up the Torah to the book of The Beginnings (or First Things) then scanned until I found the story of Jacob, a father of God's people. Jacob was a guy who messed up in his life at least as much as I had messed up mine. Still, Jacob became Israel, the namesake for the nation of all ages. But only *after* he wrestled, hand-to-hand, in the dirt and all night long with an Opponent known as Elohim—God himself, who picked the fight. God, who started it.

When, at last, the singing stopped, I was introduced. Wound up with irritation, blinded by the platform lights, I stood up at the podium. With undilated eyes I tried to see people in the dark, "out there," but failed. Standing still I gathered thoughts, wanting to be clear, not rude.

Silence stretched the human psyche of the room, making people start to squirm. I knew but didn't care. Then, at last, I spoke. My words were halting. Slow. Off the cuff. Improvised as I went along . . .

"Thank you all for coming. Thank you for your prayers. Without them our family could not have come this far. Without them I would not be standing up, let alone here in front of you. And thank you for your love, especially for Taylor. As I speak, he's at Vanderbilt. With toxic chemo dripping into his body, he is playing games, waiting for me to show up with microwave popcorn.

"Tonight while singing, there's been a lot of talk about God. God, our protector. God, our refuge. God, our helper. God, who rescues us from trouble, loves without condition, who strengthens when we're weak.

"While all these things are true of God, none of them are front-and-center truths with God and me right now. Right now God is not my helper, my deliverer, my friend—at least not primarily."

At this point you could have heard a pin drop on the carpet.

"Primarily, instead, he is, by his own command and invitation, my divine Opponent. He insists I wrestle with him. And I do. This is a summons I believe everyone receives at some point in their life. But it is a posture, a kind of engagement with God no one ever talks about. Let's talk about it.

"Remember Jacob?" Opening the dog-eared Bible stolen from the pew, I read the story to the invisible congregation. "Jacob wrestled with God himself, the Creator of all things, who with a puff of breath could have blown away this stubborn, flawed, and little man. But he didn't. After all, God's the one who started it. God's the one who summoned Jacob to wrestle in the dirt. And so he did. Tired, filthy, smelly, bruised, Jacob fought and fought and fought. Then, when all his strength was gone, Jacob refused to let go. Bloody and defeated but still somehow alive, he clung to his Opponent, unwilling to quit.

"Jacob wanted something. Facing certain death at the hand of his brother, Esau, from whom, by deceit, he stole what wasn't his, Jacob clung to God. With unbelievable audacity, he demanded that God bless him. And God *did*.

"Somehow Jacob's insistence on a blessing was an act of faith—even in a God who beat the stuffing out of him. Jacob's request pleased God so much, he blessed him by changing his name to Israel, the name of

God's own people, a nation yet to come. But the other part of blessing that God gave was the *opposite* of healing. Instead God touched Jacob's hip, making him a cripple for the rest of life.

"*This* is where I am with God. Wrestling. Angry. Confused. Undone. Perhaps it's where you are too. Or perhaps you too can hear his summons, 'C'mon, *fight* with me!' I urge you to accept. Fight with all your heart, with all your might, refusing to let go until he blesses you. But, fair warning . . ."

Pointing to myself, including Taylor and his cancer by the gesture, I said with shaking voice, "The blessing you receive might just look like this."

I sat down in silence, weeping, pleased, thanking my Opponent for his help. The moderator of the event stood and said some words, I don't remember what he said, but he sounded disconcerted. Even so, he invited all who wanted to step forward and pray with us to do so. They did. Afterward came many hugs and tears.

All in all the service seemed to turn out okay. Still I was uneasy. While friends stood in line to hug us, part of me wanted to yell out, "Hello! This isn't a funeral yet!" Another part screamed, "People! People! This isn't about *us*."

My chronic emotional nausea stemmed, in part, from a deep suspicion that some might be tempted to idolize Taylor, Debbie, or me. God *forbid!* I was also disturbed by the probability that there were many who had surrendered to an abracadabra God-is-Aladdin kind of "faith."

But while I wrestled, Taylor played . . .

From: Mary Sue
To: Brian Schrauger

While you and Debbie went to the Tuesday evening prayer service, I stayed with Taylor in the hospital. Vanderbilt's Life Flight helicopter pad was outside Taylor's window—just over the edge of a flat rooftop, one floor below. We could see and hear the choppers as they came and went.

After it got dark we heard one approaching. Taylor said, "Turn off all the lights!" Then he got the remote control for his bed lights and turned them on and off, on and off, pretending to signal the approaching helicopter as if he were bringing it in to land!

I can't imagine what the pilot must have thought as he saw a patient's window blinking at him while he landed! It was so typical for an uninhibited eleven-year old boy . . . I loved it! And I thought you would like to know.

Mary Sue

Later I wrote our friends to let them know that on Saturday, October 9th . . .

Debbie brought Taylor home. The first thing we did, of course, was shop. As usual Taylor flew from store to store down the causeway of the mall, using his wheelchair as a scooter.

I tagged along behind, chest puffed out proud, holding Taylor's crutches, grinning at the now-expected looks on shoppers' faces, morphing from disgust to shock.

"I sure wish you could see 'em, buddy."

"Me too! I've *gotta* get rearview mirrors on this chair!"

In the seven days he's been set free from the prison called VC, he has, nonetheless, spent a lot of time in Funkville. Daily shots to boost his blood's white cell count cause bone pain, especially in his shoulders and lower back. So, lots of backrubs from Dad.

The new tumor in his pelvis we call the Little Mutha also bites, on average twice a day, usually at bedtime or in the morning hours—today at 5 A.M. Pain meds work but sometimes make him itchy or upset his stomach. And for some reason he's had a number of irregular bouts with killer headaches.

But in between, he still swings in high gear. Still provokes tickle fights and pillow battles. Still is eager to get out and *go*. Still is thrilled with junk food and with Pokémon. Still is the only person I know who cannot contain a grin of pure delight when he sees *me*.

If Taylor's blood cells bounce back to acceptable levels, he'll return to VC captivity, tethered to a rudely beeping pole, on October 23—a Saturday, I think. After a second five-day-long assault by chemo drugs he'll get another CT scan of his pelvis. Then we hope, we pray, surgical excision of the Little Mutha will be feasible—and successful.

If not, Plan B is an even more toxic chemo protocol and, perhaps, a "stem cell rescue" (a virtual bone marrow transplant, if I understand correctly).

For now, we live. We laugh. We cry. We play. One day at a time. Thanks, of course, to a strength that isn't inside us, but is, instead, a gift . . . given, paradoxically, by our one and same Opponent, who also really cares, a gift delivered by your love and endless prayers on our behalf.

Living in the eerie, sunny eye of a homicidal storm—at least for now . . .

Brian

Husband to Debbie; Dad to Taylor, 11.36; also Dad to Christopher, 13.91, and Jonathan, 6.17—all growing far too fast, even under Dempsey's breathless air.

Give me ambiguity or give me something else. (Source unknown)

21 THE CaT COMES BACK

THE CaT COMES BACK—AND OTHER NEWS

Friday, October 22nd, 1999

The CaT report came back "unchanged."

I should be glad the tumors haven't grown. Instead I am dismayed. They haven't shrunk.

If anything the Little Mutha in ar*rears* has grown a little bit. After all, *shrinkage* is the primary objective in order to evict her and her parasitic siblings inside Taylor's lungs.

Yesterday Debbie took Taylor to the Vanderbilt Children's Hospital Hematology/Oncology Clinic. (In short, the clinic.)

Taylor's platelets were low, too low. He needed an infusion. Platelets are the protoplasmic drones that keep us from bleeding to death from a cut or scrape. Taylor's platelets dropped to unacceptable levels as a direct result of his last round of chemotherapy.

According to the schedule, Taylor, once again, was supposed to surrender to the VC tomorrow morning. But because his white and red cell counts have not rebounded, round two of this extratoxic chemotherapy has been postponed until November 1st.

Meanwhile Taylor remains determined to grab all the gusto he can get. Today he and Christopher are imploring me to spend the night inside our aging van, something they used to do a lot before we moved to Nashville.

"Pleeeeeeeeease, sweet-wonderful-Dad-best-Dad-in-the-whole-entire-universe!" Taylor begs with batting eyes, head tilted, mouth turned down, then blowing me a kiss.

Neither one will get the rest he needs, but both will have fun. And in spite of Taylor's overt flattery, I hear the sounds of wistful memories, nostalgia, underneath his plea. So I'll prob'ly fold and let him do it—probably already have! Taylor and Christopher will be "camping out" tonight.

Meanwhile I dialogue almost every day with Taylor's doctors, pushing hard for other treatment options—Plans C and D, if in due course Plans A and B don't work.

Separately, it seems most other dads like me, dads with suffering children, find some refuge in their work. I'm glad for them but jealous too. This prob'ly is self-pity, but here goes . . . When I drive to my office (almost) every day, it is to a dying business I arrive. In spite of all my efforts, it is on life support. I could just "pull the plug" but feel that would be wrong.

So I live in constant fear: Will "family members" of this living corpse blame me for malpractice committed by my former partner? Will they sue me and destroy me? Litigation scares me because in a separate matter I have been named, along with thirty others or so, in a malicious class-action suit filed in another state by attorneys living in yet another, far, far away from Tennessee. Mostly dormant for two years, the enemy has now begun a full assault, an attack against which, though meritless, I simply have no resources with which to make defense.

It feels like being mugged by a ruthless thug. But I am not alone. My wounded family's with me. A psychopathic lawyer points a cocked and loaded .44 at the center of my forehead. His finger twitches on the trigger as he screams, demanding money. When I say, "There isn't any," he yells, "You lie! I know you've got some on you. I'll find it when you die." His finger starts to pull.

And according to our laws, he has the right to shoot.

Plugging ahead, looking for laughter—grateful when it finds me. And grateful, very grateful, for your prayers . . .

Brian

Husband to Debbie; Dad to Taylor, 11.38, also Dad to Christopher, 13.93, and Jonathan, 6.18. Time flies while Dempsey's aromatic skills never blow away.

❧ 22 MIBs and MIPs

A Taylor and Family Report

Wednesday, October 27th, 1999

"Dad, you've gotta shave my head tonight!"

Taylor was on the phone, calling my office. This was his fourth falling out with hair. By now we knew the symptoms. Just before shedding, his follicles feel like ten thousand tiny needles. This now familiar prickly feeling began the day before. Twenty-four hours later he was easily plucking out fingerfuls of thick blond hair.

When I walked into the house about an hour later, Taylor bounced around me like a happy hoppy kangaroo.

"C'mon, Dad! Let's *do* it!"

"Gimme a coupla minutes to change my clothes," I grumbled. "Then I'll buzz ya.'"

"Okay! *Okay!*" he cheered, undaunted by my antonymous mood.

Standing in front of our bathroom mirror while I changed, he strategically pulled out large clumps of hair.

"Look, Dad! Hey, Mom," he yelled, "c'mere! You gotta see this! I've
gotta bald spot! Of course, it's not as big as *yours*, Dad—that is, when
you have hair. But I've got one! . . . Hey, Dad! Maybe when you buzz
me you could make a really big bald spot on my head. Then I'll look
like an *old* man—just like you!"

Turkey.

"Oooo-kay, *spot*," I growled. "Instead of using the electric clippers,
how 'bout I *pull* out all your hair?"

Laughing, he turned around and resumed his task with vigor. On
purpose he dropped globs of hair all over the sink, sprinkling some
inside my drinking cup!

He won, of course. I laughed, tickled my revenge, then buzzed him
bald. As always, I saved his hair inside a sealed plastic bag. By supper-
time his head was crowned by a thick, short bristle of blond whiskers.

Shaving with a razor blade was postponed till the next night. Then,
fully lathered for the task with menthol shaving cream, he looked in the
mirror and erupted.

"Looks like I have a lady's swim cap on!" He grinned and made con-
torted faces at himself, fully entertained.

"You better hold still," I warned. "I'd *hate* to draw blood." Several
minutes later he was again a chrome dome—and without a single nick!
And once again we both were MIBs: Men In Baldness.

"Remember, Dad! Just like in the movie, you are Agent B, and I am
Agent T!"

In spite of everything, the boy is full of wit. Several days ago he
responded to my brother Cliff. Taylor wrote . . .

"Dear Uncle Cliff . . . You said if you eat a frog every morning, nothing worse will happen to you the rest of the day. Well, something worse will happen . . . YOU'LL CROAK!"

Humor is our family's medicine of choice. And we are desperate for it. The reason we are desperate is because our whole family's PITA level's peaking. [PITA is our acronym for Pain In The A . . . And the PITA *rating* is measured on a scale of one to ten.]

Taylor's PITA really *is* a PITA. And when the Little Mutha bites, there's nothing funny about it. While these attacks of pelvic pain remain irregular, they are increasing in intensity.

On Monday night, two days ago, Christopher and Taylor finally spent the night sleeping in our van. With doors locked tight, shades pulled down, equipped with flashlights and walkie-talkies, they nested in their sleeping bags atop the folded-down backseat. They had a blast, slept well, and apparently Taylor had no pain. Perhaps he was medicated by the sheer nostalgic fun, reliving something he did with his big brother when they were six and eight years old—almost halfway in the past of Taylor's life.

Regardless of the reason, if there even was one, last night was a different story.

Less than an hour after lights went out, Taylor was knocking on our bedroom door . . .

Knock-knock. Knock-knock. Knock-knock!

Debbie and I leap out of bed, instantly aware of who and why.

"What number is it, buddy?"

"It's a five," he cries, annoyed and hurting.

"Okay. What kind of pain is it?" By which I mean, is it regular pain, stabbing-achy? Or is it the more elusive evil, phantom pain?

"It's tumor pain!" he weeps, impatient. By which he means it's some of both. A horrific combination.

Debbie gives more medicine while I go to get my pillow. Thirty minutes later, lying down beside him, the additional dosage Debbie gave still has no effect.

Taylor is miserable. Unable to find a comfortable position, he finally just stands up. Moments later, frustrated past tears, he curls up on the floor beside his bed, covering his head and ears with a feather pillow.

I reach down and rub his muscular shoulders. It's like giving Popeye a backrub. My personal PITA peaks as I marvel in dismay . . . How can such a strong, dynamic, super kid be in such mortal danger?

How can I, his dad, be so completely helpless? Only capable, it seems, to watch him fight this cursed cruel beast?

Yes, I pray. I beg. I cry and laugh, encourage him, and coach. I try to teach and play. All as best I'm able.

The two of us are soul mates, hearts knit in love as one. Together we are MIBs, Men In Baldness. And MIPs as well. We are Men In Pain.

But still these facts remain: I cannot fight in his place. I can only watch.

Eventually Taylor climbs back in bed as the pain subsides. Lying on our backs, I rest my right arm on his left; my hand envelops his. In the descending haze of sleep, our limbs are fused, made one. Like recalcitrant lightning bolts lingering behind a fading evil storm, I feel residual jolts of pain stab upward through his arm, my arm, even as at last, together, we surrender to exhaustion.

Brian

Husband to Debbie; Dad to Taylor, 11.39; also Dad to Christopher, 13.94, and Jonathan, 6.20. And still the reluctant guardian of Dempsey the cacophonous canine.

The darkness is my closest friend. (Psalm 88:18 NIV)

23   NUMBER 22

ON FRIDAY, OCTOBER 29TH, 1999, TAYLOR WALKED front-and-center before the entire student body at his school. He was escorted, and dwarfed, by two football players who looked like Goliath's brothers.

As the undefeated team welcomed its new honorary captain, every student, every teacher, every person there stood up on their feet. Then, as one, they erupted with thunderous applause. Standing to the side against a concrete wall, Jonathan was perched up on my shoulders. We also clapped and cheered. While that thunder rumbled on and on, there also came from many eyes, including those of macho football giants, a gentle rain of tears.

High-school senior Adam Tipps, leader of the team, gave Taylor his own royal purple jersey, his own white number outlined with a ribbon of pressed gold.

Number 22.

This season Adam carried the ball 1,860 yards in just ten games, scoring twenty-four touchdowns along with an even pair of two-point conversions. Among all athletes in the state of Tennessee, he was at the top. Now Taylor shared his number.

Like Taylor, the jersey was radiant, clean . . . yet strikingly scarred. No mistake about it: This jersey had seen battle. It had known great pain. It had endured uncommon wear and tear. It was intimate with blood and sweat, breathtaking grunts and fear. But it also was no stranger to exhilaration, fun, and victory.

It was a perfect symbol, one that Taylor wore eight days in a row.

And during which he quickly added his full share, and more, of blood and pain, tears and fear, anger, fun, and hope.

After the ceremony our family left on a weekend trip high up on a mountain. It was the very peak of fall. With leaves ablaze in dazzling yellow-orange-red, backlit by piercing rays of sunset, the time and place seemed like a glimpse of heaven. It was visible for just a moment, just long enough to whet the appetite. It was a whiff, a smell, stirring up a famished hunger. But a kind of hunger no food, nothing in *this* world, could begin to satisfy.

Then all at once the vision and the smell were whisked away, ramrodded to the past, leaving only hunger from a poignant memory fading into night, a longing unfulfilled for never-ending beauty, never-ending peace.

The beauty of the brilliant leaves about to fall was enhanced by Taylor's joy. But diminished too by recurring pain and bouts with silent fear. "I just need to be alone!" he said several times, scurrying

away with deft hops and skips inside his purple jersey. Perhaps, in part,
he dreaded his pending week of chemo, while at the same time he felt
the Little Mutha stabbing, undeterred.

I understood the need to be alone. And so I tried, but found it hard,
to let him freely go.

Back home early Monday morning Debbie loaded up the boys,
drove Christopher and Jonathan to school, then delivered Taylor to
Vanderbilt. There, again, he was admitted for five long days of poisonous infusions. When I arrived that afternoon Taylor was in full-
bore, prechemo, rock-'em, sock-'em form. Crutches left behind, he
mobilized himself by scooting with his single foot, then jumping on
the base of his six-wheel IV pole.

As he sped around the hallway race-pole track, his purple jersey,
Number 22, rippled like a flag. As he drove and dodged he also flung,
without discrimination, verbal puns at everyone along the way—fellow
patients, nurses, staff, and doctors—even if he didn't know them.

He was grabbing the chemo tiger by the tail and yanking hard. His
fun was infectious. But it also had an edge: vague, but troubling . . .

At 7 P.M. Tuesday, Taylor asked for and received another dose of his
regular antinausea meds. Minutes later, jersey on, Number 22 was off
to the playroom, where he plopped down on an empty chair and
joined a game of Sorry!

I sat down to watch.

"Know what?" he loudly asked. "I'm feelin' kinda drunk!"

Seconds later the blue box on his IV pole beeped a shrill staccato.
The little screen flashed the warning in luminescent green: "line
occluded." Taylor quickly checked his lines, saw they weren't occluded,

reprogrammed the dumb box, then turned back to play Sorry! with the kids in the playroom.

Almost right away the dumb box beeped again. This time a quick check revealed blood and IV fluids squirting from one of the two ports in his Hickman line. After eighteen months and lots of wear, his line had sprung a leak.

Refusing his crutch, or any help, he hopped down the hall to his room, bombing the whale suspended in the tile floor with large raindrops of red blood. Sometimes he missed and hit his foot. "Looks like sweet-and-sour sauce!" he cracked.

The leak was no big deal. It was quickly fixed. But Taylor was in crisis. When his nurse walked out, he turned to me in tears. "Dad, it's like I'm really, really angry. Not at *you*. I *promise*. I'm mad but don't know why. *Unnnn!* I just wanna *hit* something! If only I had a punching bag!"

"I know what you mean, buddy. And I'm proud of you for telling me instead of hiding or pretending. Fact is, I'm surprised you haven't gotten mad like this a long, long time ago."

"Actually, Dad, there have been times I've hit stuff—like my pillow with that little baseball bat."

I laughed and said, "Well, shoot. Why not do that now? The heck with dim lights and deep breathing! Let *me* be your punching bag. Tell you what. Let's take a second to pray, then I'll hold a couple of pillows and you can punch away: hard as you want, long as it takes."

"Can I kick ya too?" His question was dead serious.

"Uh, you bet . . . Let's pray."

After thanking God that he's in control even when we're not, it was time to hit.

"Give it all you got, buddy. It's *okay*. God can handle your anger, and so can I. I just have one request—puh-lease make sure you don't hit my nose above or private parts below the pillows. Remember where you came from!"

Number 22 smiled, scowled, and swung, hitting *hard.*

Bam! Bam! Bam!

He hit with one fist then the other then paused for a breath before he went again.

Bam! Bam! Bam!

Then leaning back against his bed, propping up with both strong arms, his leg and foot exploded like a piston. I tottered, worried just a little, then braced for more.

Pow-Pow-Pow!

We kept it up for more than an hour. He hit and kicked. I prayed and wished I'd worn a cup. Winded, he finally announced he'd had enough.

"You sure?"

"Yeah. Sure wish we had a punching bag at home . . . Let's watch a movie now."

Lying on his elevated bed, propped up at an angle, we watched *The Flintstones* movie. Yabba-dabba-doo.

Afterward we prayed and said good night. As he took his glasses off, handing them to me, he said, "Y'know, Dad, this has been a *really* strange day."

I kissed him and agreed, went to my cot but didn't go to sleep. Taylor had confessed his rage, agreed to hit me, then slugged away with all his might. When he did, *because* he did, I never loved him more. I'd never been more proud. It took courage, but he'd felt safe to share, not hide, his rage—even to express it, to take it out on me. Because I asked him to.

Is this what God wants too? I wondered. *Is this how he feels when I punch it out with him?* Instantly my spirit heard the answers, felt the love. I wept and finally went to sleep, knowing that my turn would come to punch with all my might. And that when it came, God would hold the pillows, thrilled and proud.

How strange. How very strange, indeed.

Unfortunately the next morning was harder than the night before. Even with his jersey on, Number 22 was bored.

"Wanna talk?" I asked.

"Sure, why not?" He shrugged.

I took a deep breath, said a silent prayer, adopted a matter-of-fact tone, then brought him up to date about the cancer in his body. I filled him in on what I'd learned.

"Yes, we hope to shrink the Mutha with this chemo regimen then have it taken out. But only if it shrinks. If Dr. Pietsch tried to take it out

without clean margins, there's a chance the cancer would spread fast."

It wasn't the first time we'd had this kind of talk. But for Taylor it was the first time the gravity of truth pulled from outer space the risk of his condition. Like a nasty meteor, it burned an awful trail through his conscious mind then hit the surface of awareness, radiating shock waves.

Alone together in his VC

room, he cried with brokenhearted tears. "But I don't *want* the cancer to spread!"

"Neither do I. Neither do I. But buddy, it already has. Twice. That's why we're fighting so hard. That's why we're praying so much. That's why people around the world are praying for you all the time."

When Debbie arrived, the three of us prayed. We claimed God's protection, power, peace—things that he has promised. We asked him to heal. We thanked him for his presence, his compassion, his control.

Unwilling to leave, unable to leave, I lingered with Taylor and Debbie until a schoolmate came to visit him at noon.

The next day Taylor's old familiar smile returned. But his eyes were older. Much older.

Finally Friday came. Taylor was released late that afternoon. Together we drove straight to the battlefield, a football play-off game in the stadium at school. Taylor's team is the Lions. How appropriate. If nothing else, Number 22, honorary captain, is a roaring lion.

Tonight he marches, shy but proud, to the fifty-yard line. There he'll flip a coin, call it heads or tails, and with that call determine who starts out with the ball. He'll walk with players three times his size. But in the stands and on the field everyone who sees will know: Taylor's bigger than them all.

He is, in fact, the biggest man I've ever known. He is my son, the lion, a hunter hunted, badly wounded but unscathed. Tonight, like every other player in the heat of bruising battle, Taylor won't be feeling pain. And I'm sure he'll want a hot dog.

Bursting with pride, I'll also remain . . . unshaven, unpolished, un-rested, undone . . .

24 DATE WITH A CAT

A TAYLOR AND FAMILY REPORT

Tuesday, November 16th, 1999

Tomorrow is Christopher's birthday. He turns fourteen. If you're so inclined, he'd love to hear from you.

All our boys love animated birthday cards through the Internet. The best thing is they're *free*.

Taylor is inundated with all kinds of supportive attention. But I'm afraid Christopher and Jonathan suffer from a deficit, especially from me.

Christopher is a terrific brother. He handles Taylor's fame quite well. Still, it would thrill me to see him get a flood of attention for several days. How 'bout filling up the in-box at his address?

If you don't know him, Christopher is self-motivated, a hard worker (too hard, I'm afraid), a topnotch student, and a long-distance runner. He also plays the piano and loves a good story. *Star Trek* shows are a mutual favorite.

Almost every day Jonathan, who's six, asks me to check his e-mail. I do, but there's rarely much inside his box. He is especially delighted with animated cards and links to Web sites designed for children.

Meanwhile, as I write, Taylor is receiving a much-needed infusion of platelets. His body is still recovering from the toxic effects of chemo drugs received two weeks ago.

In six days, on Monday, November 22nd . . .

. . . Taylor has another date with the dreaded CaT. Based on subsequent results, major decisions will be made. My hope and prayer is that surgical removal of the Little Mutha, the tumor in the rear, will be feasible.

From Tuesday through Sunday, November 23rd to the 28th . . .

Our family plans to visit relatives in Michigan during the Thanksgiving holiday.

CT scan results will be faxed to us while we're there.

Then, perhaps, the week when we return Taylor can have surgery??? This is one of my *pleasepleaseplease* prayers.

Thank you for loving our family. God bless . . .

Brian

Husband to Debbie; Dad to Taylor, 11.45; also Dad to Christopher, 13.996, and Jonathan, 6.25—flying on the wings of time held up, in part, by Dempsey's heavy air!

Honesty is the best policy, but insanity is a better defense.
(attributed to *Steve Landesberg*)

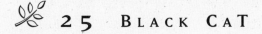

25 BLACK CAT

WEDNESDAY, NOVEMBER 24TH, 1999

My sister-in-law Su, married to my brother Larry, is Mom to triplets (two girls and one boy). They are about eight months younger than Taylor. This week Su and her family are hosting us during our stay in Lansing, Michigan. Yes, she's very brave.

I'm writing from the basement guest room at their home. Tomorrow all the Schraugers will celebrate Thanksgiving with a feast and rowdy play by twelve children—all sired by just three brothers: Cliff, Larry, and me (Cliff, with Vicky's help, wins the Sire Prize).

The food will be delicious. Kids will explode with play. But to Debbie and to me the feast will taste like straw. The sound of children playing will mock our dumbstruck souls.

Two days ago Taylor had a CT scan, testing for results from two long rounds of toxic chemotherapy.

Those results were faxed to us this morning . . .

The tumor in Taylor's boneless left-side hem*ass*phere, the Little Mutha, has not shrunk. In fact, it's grown a little bit.

In the lower lobe of his right lung, a new tumor has grown out of nowhere, rapid as a weed. And it's done so in spite of the last two rounds of heavy-duty chemo poisons.

According to the attending radiologist, this new tumor "is a spherical density that measures 1.8 centimeters in diameter [about one inch]. . . . I think [it] is a metastatic deposit."

Taylor's oncologists at Vanderbilt concur.

The bottom line (so to speak) is clear. The cancer inside Taylor's body has plowed over our most recent counteroffense. Instead of retreating, it has vigorously advanced.

There remain no conventional chemo protocols. Doctors are recommending a trial chemo drug called Topotecan.

But not surgery. Maybe later, but not now.

Taylor's reaction?

"I *thought* I felt something in my lung. Didn't say anything. I thought it was just gas."

He paused and sighed. His shoulders slumped.

"I'm so *tired* of all this."

"I don't blame ya, sweet boy," I agreed. "Me too."

Then, all at once, as if a switch was hit, he lit up and said, "Hey, Dad, know what? This means you've gotta take me out to Chili's again!"

I grinned and agreed. "Okay, but you know it'll have to be after we go home to Nashville."

"Yeah, Dad, I know. But don't you forget!"

"Don't worry. Besides, I'm sure you won't let me."

Hearts linked, we sat alone, but not alone, in silence. At last I spoke.

"Y'know, buddy, it'd be real easy for both of us to not have fun while we're here. But that's not what I think we should do. I'm your dad, so listen up!

"If you're hurtin', tell me and I'll get your meds. When you're tired, take a break and rest. But! Concentrate on having fun, as much as possible. Okay?"

"No prob, bob," he replied insouciantly.

And so, full throttle (the only speed he knows), that's exactly what he's doing. He's building forts and beating up on bad guys in Nintendo games.

Hopping without crutches, he goes to battle against his cousins in no-holds-barred pillow fights. When that gets old they all play hide-and-seek.

This afternoon he joined us at the theater, marveling at the movie *Toy Story 2*. And he laughs with pure delight, romping with his cousins' sixty-pound puppy, Oreo.

This Thanksgiving there is a lot for which we're grateful, not the least of which is *today*.

But time won't pause.

Tomorrow's chugging, "Bittersweet . . . bittersweet, bittersweet . . . bittersweet, bittersweet, bittersweet, bittersweetbittersweetbittersweet . . ."

Picking up speed, it roars down the track straight toward the present. And it will not be silenced, let alone stopped.

And it's hard. So unspeakably hard . . .

Brian

Husband to Debbie; Dad to Taylor, 11.46; also Dad to Christopher, 14.00, and Jonathan, 6.26—hurling down the tracks of time while Dempsey is at home!

"What is the difference between denial and faith?"
(Cynthia Carlson, Debbie's sister, a day or two
before her death on July 9, 1997)

While visiting his cousins, Taylor followed my advice. He lived life to the hilt, even jumping on his uncle Larry's trampoline. On a sunny afternoon he emerged from his bedroom after yet another secret bout with pain. Looking out the sliding window-door, he saw me jumping on the trampoline with his little brother, Jonathan. His eyes lit up with pleasure from the memory of fun times our family used to have on the trampoline when we lived in Dallas. Running outside, he cried, "My turn!" Taking off a well-worn shoe, he hopped off the deck, over the grass, then with a single fluid move, jumped up and swiveled round, landing on the trampoline.

While Jonathan and I stood on the side, Taylor started jumping. Higher. Higher. Higher! His balance was perfect, amazing.

"C'mon, Dad! Jump with me!" This is something we've not done for more than two years. So, I join him. Holding his beefy, muscular hands, we jump together. Just like the good ol' days.

Someone inside sees us and yells out to all the family, "C'mere and look at this—Taylor's jumping on the trampoline!" Soon cousins, uncles, aunts cluster round the clear deck door, watching with amazement. No one's ever seen a sight like this. For almost an hour we jump and play, just the two of us. Later Jonathan comes back outside to join his dad and brother. Three at once atop the trampoline is against the rules. But we receive a special dispensation.

After all, trampolines, like life, are full of risks. Rules help minimize the risks but, as I'm learning, never eliminate them.

Pay attention, heart.

There is no life without risk. And without risk there is no life, no real living. Careful though I am, every breath, every effort, every loving laugh and hug and kiss . . . all taunts and tempts that cursed foe, Death—who, in the end, always wins.

Should I, then, stop living? Should I abandon laughter, love, and play?

It's often tempting. Very tempting. Death cannot be avoided. No matter what I do, no matter where I hide, Death always finds his prey. Even when he's hunting for those I love the most. In Death's game of hide-and-seek he hides his face and counts. Sometimes to one hundred. Sometimes just eleven, maybe twelve. Then at a whim Death shouts with chilling glee, "Ready or not, here I come!"

And so he does. He always comes.

But just as I'm ready to surrender in despair, Someone reignites my failing heart with a painful jolt of joy. Uninhibited, unconditional love. Laughter. Delight. Even through my wounded son, the one whom Death now circles like a ruthless, hungry carnivore.

(Oh God! Spare him! Heal him! Give him a long life!)

I wonder . . .

Since Death always wins, how can love be real? In Death's cold shadow, isn't this thing called love nothing more than denial's drug of choice, socially correct, deluding us, deadening the pain of certain doom?

Get behind me, demons. Do you hear me, hell? The answer's No!

My fun-loving, full-of-life son is not delusional. He is, instead, amazingly aware, refreshingly sane. It's inexplicable but true: warts and all, he also flat-out loves me. And I him . . . like no other I have ever known, nor none I ever will.

And so, even in despair, I am compelled to admit that this thing called love is Real. Undiminished. Even stronger in the face of Death. And because love's real, Death isn't all there is. It can't be.

Because love's real, there must be something More, something Better, something Stronger. Someone Else.

Duly purchased at great cost, I surrender. Owned by Love, Death will come for Taylor and for me, but he will not win. He. Will. Not. Win.

Finally exhausted and with cousins begging for a turn, Taylor and I get off. We leave the trampoline behind us. But not forever. Rich with memories and forever bound by love, we will be back.

Yes, tomorrow always comes. But Death is not the last tomorrow.

26 NEW HOPE

ON DECEMBER 2ND WE STARTED A NEW OFFENSE against all the Little Muthas that had invaded Taylor's eleven-year-old body. Just before the new assault, we drove home from Michigan. I thought traffic would be bad on the last day of Thanksgiving weekend, but it wasn't. The drive was easy, even fun.

With his Popeye hands, Taylor kneaded my shoulders, massaged my chrome-dome head. He's an excellent masseuse. At one point he took a turn in his favorite seat, sitting shotgun up in front with me. When we hit a rain shower, I turned the wipers on. They were set to move without an intermittent pause. Concentrating on the road, I was suddenly distracted. From the corner of my eye I saw Taylor's head moving back and forth, back and forth, in rhythm with the wipers.

"Hey, Taylor! What the heck're you doin'?"

"Oh, nothin'." He grinned. "I just wondered what the world looks like from a windshield wiper's point of view."

Laughing so hard my seat shook, I finally said, "Buddy, I don't think anyone in history has ever thought of that. You've gotta be the first. But ya know, you're really kinda *strange!*"

"Like father, like son," he trumped. It was the ultimate compliment.

We made it home by sunset, unloaded the van. Taylor had an appointment at Vanderbilt the next day. Not knowing what he faced (so what else was new?), we boys went out to eat.

It was Taylor who reminded me again of our tradition: Every time we get bad news, we go out for beer and nachos. This time bad news came while we were out of town. Now that we were home, it was time to keep my promise. Debbie wasn't hungry. So it was the Guys' Night Out. All four of us, from six to forty-four, had a blast.

Monday morning Debbie and Taylor *thought* they were going to the clinic for tests: blood, liver, kidney—necessary analyses before starting an experimental chemo drug called Topotecan.

But by the time they arrived, Dr. Whitlock had a different idea. (Dr. James Whitlock is Head Honcho of Vanderbilt's department of Pediatric Hematology and Oncology—*the* HH of VPHO.)

While we drove home from Michigan, Whitlock hunted for experimental treatment plans appropriate for Taylor's battle. And one in which he could be accepted. (The vast majority of clinical trials exclude children.)

He found one. It was the study of a drug that's been around awhile but is rarely used. Something called Trimetrexate. The scientific trial was being done by the Sloan-Kettering Cancer Center in New York.

Taylor came home thrilled with the possibility of a trip and extended stay in the Big Apple. That afternoon he called my office and sang into the voice mail, "N-Y-C! Yeah!" His animated imitation was an interesting mix of Presley and Minnelli.

Just before supper, Dr. Whitlock called. The study was closed. But . . . Taylor could implement an identical protocol under Whitlock's supervision. Trimetrexate is commercially available. But the cost is breathtaking.

Tuesday morning Whitlock received a copy of the protocol from Sloan-Kettering and faxed it to my office. The next day Debbie, Taylor, and I met with Whitlock to discuss the procedure.

While we talked, making life-and-death decisions, Taylor ripped off wide sheets of thin paper used to cover the examination table. Wadding them into "snowballs" he bombarded Whitlock and peppered him with verbal pellet puns while we talked.

For two years in a row Taylor and Whitlock attended Camp Horizon, where they quickly became sparring buddies. Their friendship was . . . unique.

This time Taylor *drank* his chemo—at home, twice a day for three full weeks—usually as a cocktail mixed with flavored Gatorade. It was a heck of a lot more toxic than alcohol. And it had a different kind of kick. We prayed the kick would be strong enough to knock the Little Muthas out of Taylor's body into some black hole.

Once three weeks were up, perhaps on Christmas Eve, the CaT was coming back. And with that CaT scan we'd learn if God had authorized Trimetrexate to execute the Little Muthas.

We prayed—how we prayed!—he had.

If he didn't, what then? I shared my worries—and my hopes—with the e-mail list.

A TAYLOR AND FAMILY REPORT

Friday, December 3rd, 1999

Worry is a well-known wormy parasite living in my gut. I'm also stubborn, slow. But with baby steps and often falling down, I'm *learning* to expect manna from heaven in exact accordance with our needs.

Faith is such a difficult thing. But in the end the discomfort of trusting God is nothing compared with gut-wrenching spasms of worry.

If only I could remember this . . .

Meanwhile twice a day Taylor holds his glass up high, says, "Cheers!" and then gulps down his three-hundred-dollar drink. After full-body shudders from the taste, he practices a drunken Bing Cosby rendition of "White Christmas."

He also insists the only thing he really wants for Christmas is a gym-style punching bag. In lieu of Dad holding pillows while he kicks and hits (and with due consideration for the patriarchal jewels), I'm certain Santa will get him exactly what he wants.

Grateful for my baritone, void of any tenor-envy—and with a new ray of hope . . .

Brian

Husband to Debbie; Dad to Taylor, 11.50; also Dad to Christopher, 14.04, and Jonathan, 6.30. Burning in the flame of time, fueled by Dempsey's methane.

I know God will not give me anything I can't handle.
I just wish that he didn't trust me so much.
(attributed to *Mother Teresa*)

December 4th, 1999
From: Michael W. Smith
To: Taylor

taylor,

how are you? i hope you are doing well. i'm glad i got to come over and see you. i'm in greensboro, south carolina, doing a concert. i'll be back sunday night, so i'll call you and check in.

we'll stay in touch via e-mail if that's ok with you.

love you and praying for you. see ya!

michael

27 EAGLEMAN

THE BOYS AND I ARE IN A HUGE ATHLETIC WAREHOUSE kind of store, on the hunt. We are looking for a punching bag—Taylor's Christmas present. But as soon as they are sighted, the boys head off on their own pursuits, leaving me alone to contemplate the pros and cons of different bags. Standing there alone, I see a prowling salesman who has zeroed in on me. Resenting the unavoidable, I avert my eyes and squirm inside, waiting for his shot.

According to the tag on his shirt, the approaching invader is "Jim." He carries a slight paunch. His eyes are puffy, sad. His hair is wispy thin, disheveled. His skin is kind of grayish. Jim doesn't look like a healthy guy. A stinging sliver of sympathy stabs my heart's defense. Almost simultaneously I am assaulted by a terrifying thought . . . is this me ten years from now?

As if afraid others might hear and with a tremble in his voice, Jim asks, "How did the boy lose his leg? Was it an accident?"

As all defenses disappear, vanishing like magic, I reply, "No, cancer."

"I was afraid of that," he groans. "Had colon cancer myself not too long ago. Now I'm in remission."

"His name is Taylor," I respond. "Wish I could say the same for him."

Jim's already watery eyes fill up and almost overflow. "It's just too much," he says, then quickly escapes down the well-stocked aisle.

Deeply moved by the compassion of a stranger, I look up and find that all the punching bags and gloves are out of focus, blurry. A couple minutes pass. Jim comes back.

"Do you mind if I give this lapel pin to your son?" he asks. "My daughter makes them."

"Not at all . . . Hey, Taylor! C'mere a second. This is Jim. He has a present for you."

With shaking hands that threaten to fumble, Jim nonetheless succeeds. He attaches the pin to Taylor's shirt. It is a small but bright and golden eagle captured in full flight.

"Now, I want you to wear this all the time," Jim instructs. Taylor politely nods his head, giving his consent.

"This eagle," Jim continues, "is God's promise to you. You can find that promise in Isaiah, chapter forty." With warm, fresh water filling up his eyes, Jim nods then walks away without another word.

From the stock of barbells, maybe twenty feet away, Christopher witnesses the exchange. He approaches and asks, "What happened, Dad?"

I explain and for the first time see tears well up inside the eyes of my oldest son. No question, he is a brother who cares.

As soon as we are home I ask Christopher to bring my Bible and call Taylor aside. When Christopher returns I speak. "Jim said the eagle pin represents God's promise. Do you know what that promise is?"

"Uhhh, nope."

"Well then, guys, listen up! Here it is . . .

The everlasting God gives strength to the
   weary and power to the weak.
Even children get tired and worn out;
Even young men stumble and fall.
But those who hope in the Lord will renew their strength.
They will soar on wings like eagles;
They will run and not get tired;
They will walk and not wear out!"
(author's paraphrase)

I pause. Then, like in a cartoon on TV, a light bulb turns on above my head. When it does, I laugh. "Guess what, Taylor? God's promise is that if we put all our hope in him, we will either fly or run or walk straight through—or over—anything!

"Well, Christopher's a cross-country guy. So he's gotta be the runner. I do that stupid-looking power-walk almost every day, so you know what that makes me. . . . No, not stupid! A walker. But Taylorman, with one leg you can't run or walk. And God doesn't say anyone has to hop. That means you've gotta be the eagle.

"Every day you have pain attacks that make you screech. But no matter what, you've always had, and have, a spirit that flies high. And you always will. You are the Eagleman!"

Taylor grins and shrugs, pretending nonchalance. Wrapped around his right-hand wrist are no fewer than seven fabric bracelets. Neon green, bright red, blinding yellow, and bright blue, they are impossible to miss. He wears them all the time. The only time they are removed is when, just before some surgery, he's forced to take them off. Even then, he worries and commands, "Put 'em in a bag! Don't lose 'em! I want 'em back as soon as I wake up!" When he does, he asks, "Where are they?" then deftly rethreads each one through its plastic loop, his wrist again colored like a rainbow.

One's been sported for almost a year—and looks it.

"Why don't you throw that one out?"

"No way! That's the first one I ever wore. I'm never gonna take it off!" His loyalty is fierce.

"Okay, okay, whatever!" I comply, amused-bemused.

Each bracelet is emblazoned with four letters: FROG: Fully (or forever) relying on God, and WWJD: What would Jesus do? There is no question where his hope is fixed. He is, indeed, the Eagleman.

He's looking for another bracelet he's heard about but hasn't found. One with the letters PUSH—Pray until something happens.

Shoot, if he finds a source, I'll wear one of those.

With the help of high-tech crutches and powerful arms, Taylor hops away to play. At best, I plod with a limp, weary to the bone. But still alive and moving. Now, though, as I move I hope, I pray, that someday God will make me as good a man as Jim.

28 CHRISTMAS '99: BAM-BAM!

THROUGHOUT DECEMBER, WHILE TAYLOR DRANK flavored chemo hemlock twice a day (Trimetrexate, that is), his daily bouts with pain grew worse. We called them what they were, *attacks*. When they struck we shouted, "Taylor's having an attack!"

When he was in public, in the light of day or inside with his friends, Taylor sparkled with good cheer, radiating zeal. Perhaps he hid the mounting pain. Or, more likely, his enthusiasm for a life of fun and action was a potent anesthetic.

It was alone, inside his room, inside our home, when sadistic pain attacked as if inflicted by a drooling, gleeful demon, turning dials up and down, switches on and off, sending bolts of shocking pain from his bottom to and from his brain, making his whole body quiver with spasms from the torment.

Even in his room, even with his door shut, even muffled by a pillow, Taylor's moaning cries penetrated through the walls, stabbing to the very marrow of our souls.

We were living in hell's torture chamber that, like some operating rooms, was surrounded by an amphitheater. Every seat was taken. Half the unseen crowd, intoxicated by the anguish of a child, howled and cheered and stomped their cloven feet. The other half sat silent, sober, simply watching. One of these stood up. But even he didn't make a move to intervene or rescue.

Trapped inside ourselves, our cries for help unanswered (or worse yet, denied), we were powerless to prevent the torture of our son and brother. Granted, I was frightened by the thought of giving up my son to God even for his glory. But *saying*, "I surrender him," and *doing so* were very different things.

If he must die, I thought, *so be it. But why, God, why? Why does he suffer on and on and on while you are silent, doing nothing to alleviate his pain?*

Every day my anger grew, brewing into rage. This state of mind and heart was expressed but watered down in a report I shared with the e-mail list.

TOMORROW'S CAT
A TAYLOR AND FAMILY REPORT

Wednesday, December 29th, 1999

Thought it wasn't going to happen till next week. But just found out this morning. Taylor's CT is tomorrow afternoon.

Last Thursday, Christmas Eve, Taylor swallowed his last dose of Trimetrexate chemo. Now, once again, the CaT comes back—and he ain't the one from Dr. Seuss.

Our holidays have been a gladiatorial combat against cruel pain with brief, sporadic time-outs for incongruous fun.

Over the past two weeks Taylor's tumor pain has evolved from a one-headed monster of electrifying jolts to a two-headed beast of chronic aches punctuated by sporadic bolts of lightning. And assisting this beast, who's *way* beyond ugly, are soulless, clown-faced, psychopathic drones assaulting Taylor's leg, lower back, and head.

More tumors?

One thing Debbie and I will never forget from these last days of our millennium is an iterative midnight sound on our bedroom door.

Knock-knock!

Knock-knock!!

KNOCK-KNOCK!!!

Every time we hear, we instantly wake up, fly out of bed, fully aware of answers to the questions Who? and Why?

With an incredibly high tolerance for pain (and desperate not to be a bother), Taylor has, once again, waited too long to ask for help.

We open the door, find him standing there, leaning on his crutches.

Face scrunched up in tears, he softly weeps: angry, scared, alone. Then we follow, close behind and wordless, as he hastily retreats to his room-cocoon. When the door is shut behind him, he moans, he weaves, an oscillating crescendo-decrescendo cry of agony.

On a scale of one to ten, the level of his pain is often seven, eight, and all too often off the scale at twelve.

I give him meds, grab my pillow, join him in his bed, then stroke his arm. His back. His head. And with two fingers caress his soft, wet cheeks—praying all the while for the pain to go and stay away.

Countered by the drugs, pain does retreat somewhat. Though less and less each day. I pray and pray and pray. But always it comes back. Always it comes back.

Knock-knock!
Knock-knock!!
KNOCK-KNOCK!!!

When I hear the sound I leap up and run to my son. I kiss; I hold; I pray; I try to help. But poorly. I cannot take away the pain, the relentless, horrible, damnable pain. But I know Someone who can.

Knock-knock!
Knock-knock!!
KNOCK-KNOCK!!!

Just like Taylor knocking on our bedroom door in the middle of the night crying out in pain, I also stand at God's big door and knock. But unlike Taylor's parents, he doesn't answer. He doesn't run. He doesn't kiss. He doesn't hold. He doesn't help. He doesn't take away the pain.

Knock-knock!
Knock-knock!!
KNOCK-KNOCK!!!

Where—Are—You???????

Brian

Husband to Debbie; Dad to Taylor, 11.57; also Dad to Christopher, 14.11, and Jonathan, 6.37—all growing up too fast while Dempsey's gas gets worse . . .

Taylor got his punching bag for Christmas, a padded cylinder standing red, erect from a large black base filled to the top with water.

With brand-new boxing gloves, he punched away and sometimes kicked. But in spite of its size, in spite of its weight, the punching bag always moved away. It retreated from my son's attacks.

Just like pillows, it could not stand the blows unless I stood behind and held it.

One day after Christmas Taylor came to my bedroom door, a hollow thing, but still a door and shut. He was looking for me. This time, however, he had on boxing gloves.

BAM-BAM!

BAM-BAM!

Like a giant drum the hollow door amplified the sound as it rattled in its latch. An involuntary yell escaped my lips. My heart pounded in its cage.

"Who is it?" I responded with a flash of anger from the shock.

"Hi, Dad, it's me!" Taylor smiled as he and Christopher opened up the door. "Did we scare ya?"

"Yes, you did," I answered, growling just a little. "I love you, but please don't do that again. You scared me to death!"

"Okay," he answered sheepishly, then with a twinkle asked, "What-cha doooo-in'?"

"Tickling you! And you can't get me back, cuz you've got big fat gloves on!"

"Yeah, but I could hit you." Disabled by gasping laughter as I "played the piano" on his ribs, his threat was empty.

"Dad, watch out! My scars! My scars!" by which he meant the fully healed incisions from his thoracotomies.

"No fair!" I protested. "You've got scars everywhere. Bu-u-t-t-t . . . you haven't got one here. Or here. Or here!"

"My scars!" he cackled. "Da-ad, you gave me hiccups!"

"Poor baby," I commiserated as we caught our breath.

He wasn't hurting when he did it, but when he knocked, BAM-BAM! he really got my attention. Even though all he had to do was knock to bring me running.

For me it was this very thing, BAM-BAM, that brought me to the ring to fight it out with God. Just like he'd done with Jacob, this was his invitation to punch it out with him. To open up my anguished outraged heart. To hit and slug away while he held the pillows. While he absorbed the blows. While all the time he wept with empathy, loving me just as I loved my son. And just like he loved his.

There were no answers to my loud and angry questions. It's only when I paused to catch my breath I heard him softly whisper, *Welcome to my heart.*

29   ANOTHER READ CAT

A TAYLOR AND FAMILY REPORT

10:34 A.M., Monday, January 3rd, 2000

Results of Taylor's CT scan, taken last Thursday, just came in. The tumor in the bottom lobe of Taylor's right lung has "increased markedly in size."

On November 22nd, it was 1.8 centimeters in diameter. Now it is twice as big. A small density just below it "has also increased slightly."

And there are two new nodes in the bottom lobe of Taylor's left lung. (After last year's surgery, he was left with only two lobes out of three.)

As for the pelvic tumor, it "has not changed appreciably in size since the prior study" (on November 22nd). Radiology's report further describes this tumor as a "large, partially calcified, partially necrotic mass to the left of the rectum."

There is no evidence of a mass in the right leg.

Taylor doesn't know this yet. Soon as I send this e-mail, I'm heading home so that, together, Debbie and I can talk with him. And pray.

Early this afternoon all three of us are scheduled to meet with Dr. Whitlock. (Remember him? Head Honcho? *The* HH of the VPHO?)

He'll help us interpret the report. And discuss, What next?

Will keep you posted.

Brian

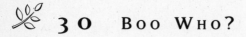 ## 3 O   B O O   W H O ?

A TAYLOR AND FAMILY REPORT

Friday, January 7th, 2000

In about forty-eight hours Taylor and I will be checking into the Children's Inn at the National Institutes of Health (the NIH) in Bethesda, Maryland.

Taylor is so excited about the trip, he's called me at the office several times a day this week. Last Wednesday, while deep in thought, my phone rang. Without preamble I heard the impish words . . .

"Knock-knock!"

Inwardly groaning, I consented with a grin, "Who's there?"

"Boo!" Taylor answered as if playing hide-and-seek.

Groaning again, I dutifully responded, certain of the punch line that would follow.

"Boo who?" I answered with a weary okay-so-I'll-do-it monotone.

All of us are excited about the trip to Maryland because it is a combo deal: another round of hope plus a free vacation. We get to fly, rent a car, try a brand-new treatment, and see some D.C. sites—Washington, D.C., that is.

Groundwork for the unexpected trip began with a very sober meeting. Last Monday afternoon, January 3, Taylor, Debbie, and I sat down with Dr. Whitlock. He confirmed that the most recent chemo trial, a three-week binge of Trimetrexate mixed with Gatorade, did not work.

In five and a half weeks all the tumors grew. One doubled in size. And two new deadly spots appeared.

Not good.

While Taylor's pelvic tumor is his source of chronic and horrific pain, it isn't life-threatening. Tumors spreading to and growing in the lungs are.

In more than eighteen months not one of many chemo poisons has shrunk a single tumor. None. In fact, just the opposite. In every case the tumors have grown. And if the cancer continues its current rate of growth in Taylor's lungs? . . .

In our meeting with Dr. Whitlock, top priority was addressing the desperate need to arrest Taylor's never-ending, monstrous agony. Phantom pain and tumor pain have formed an unholy, but successful, alliance.

On a scale of one to ten, level ten is the worst pain possible—like being skinned alive. At the other end, pain at level one is real but minimal—like a stinging paper cut or, perhaps, a needle shot. Over the past six weeks the torture has increased. It often skyrockets from a level one to seven in ten minutes, often less. And in spite of powerful narcotics, Taylor sometimes weeps, *"It's a twelve!!!"*

Dr. Whitlock referred us to another physician who specializes in pain control. The result was a mixture of new meds. Even so, pain levels have only diminished. They haven't gone away.

With his pain now reduced to an average level of three and a half, Taylor squirms, practicing positions, always looking but never finding one in which he is, even for five seconds, torture-free. While hunting for a comfortable posture he composes variations of his lyrics, "Ouch, ouch, ouch!"

He sings them to different tunes. Like the "Hallelujah Chorus:" "Ouch, ouch, ouch, ouch-ouch-ouch, ouch-ouch, ouch, ouch. Ow!-leluya! Ow!-leluya! Ow!-leh-eh-lu-ya . . ." Other tunes include *The Sound of Music*'s "Do-Re-Mi," Christmas carols, television jingles, and various compositions by Bach and Beethoven. I never sing along. All his moans, even put to music, are torture to my soul. But especially his tuneless cries in the night.

During Monday's meeting with Dr. Whitlock, running neck and neck with pain control was the objective to find another treatment plan. All that's left are *feel*-better therapies and experimental treatments.

Shots of intense radiation to the pelvic tumor might shrink it but would not address the deadly tumors inside Taylor's lungs. Radiation, then, would be an attempt to only treat the symptoms, to reduce the pain. This option meant surrender to the Little Muthas.

If we chose to fight, Dr. Whitlock told us about the availability of one or two experiments with new chemo drugs. But after eighteen months of total failure by all other chemotherapies (along with all their sickening side effects), these options felt futile.

The only other fighting opportunities were experimental, non-chemo drugs, biological agents by which medical scientists are trying to block the growth of tumors, shrink them, and maybe even stop their reproduction elsewhere in the body.

Taylor listened in on all of this. He fully understood the essence of the problem. But when I asked for input, he was noncommittal: "Whatever."

And he was just a little insolent.

When Dr. Whitlock asked him, "Remind me of your age," Taylor responded with the jousting familiarity he'd won with Whitlock after two summers at camp.

"How old're *you?*" he answered with a question, throwing a wadded paper "snowball" at Whitlock's head—and hitting it.

Whitlock gamely smiled but with his eyes seemed to catch the essence of Taylor's stinging prod . . . "You oughtta know. But what difference does it make? You're a whole lot older than I will ever be."

After we were done, Debbie and Taylor went home. I stayed behind, alone with Dr. Whitlock. Debbie knew the reason why because I told her. Taylor knew the reason because he knows me and I know him.

I stayed to ask The Question: How long?

Debbie made it clear she did not want to hear the answer. So I didn't tell her. Nor did I tell Taylor.

The next morning Dr. Whitlock called with news. Two studies were available. One at Sloan-Kettering in New York, the other at the National Cancer Institute (the NCI) in Bethesda. (In case, like I, you did not know this, the NCI is one of many divisions of the National Institutes of Health.)

The NCI study is for a drug called OncoLAR. Unlike any other study we've seen, this one is specifically for Osteo-sarcoma patients!

As I understand it—and my understanding is very limited—Onco-LAR's objective is to turn off, or block, the tumors' access to the body's growth hormone and thereby disable this kind of tumor's growth. Osteo-sarcomas are unique, I'm told, because they do not have their own internal growth mechanism. Instead, they depend on the body's normal growth hormones. Block those hormones; block the growth!

A few hours after Whitlock's call, I was speaking on the phone with a physician at the NCI, Dr. Mackal. She briefly explained the study. Then she invited Taylor to visit as soon as this coming Monday morning, January 10th.

Our visit to the NCI will be for five full days. If Taylor's eligible, and if we agree, he'll be accepted into the study and immediately receive his first dose of OncoLAR. If he's accepted, the NCI pays for travel, lodging, and treatment.

That night, Tuesday, we started to pack.

In spite of bad bad news, I must admit we are excited, especially Taylor. And that helps.

It was from this odd mix of bad news and excitement that Taylor called on Wednesday morning with his knock-knock joke.

"Knock-knock!"

"Who's there?" I said, sounding like Pooh's donkey friend, Eeyore.

"Boo!"

"Boo who?" Eeyore again, expecting the obvious.

But I was wrong.

Taylor's concise retort was amazing, replete with wisdom way beyond his years.

His words were words from God through a preteen boy—through a crippled, pain-wracked kid armed with nothing more than faith; faith summarized on fabric rainbow bracelets; faith animated by a zealous, twinkling wit; faith underscored by lopsided grins, mischievous and spirited. Words from God through an underaged and bloody knight, a solitary warrior engaged in battle up against an ancient evil dragon, an ungodly beast that has already ripped away and devoured a child's hip and leg and with its dragon claws twice sliced at Small Knight's ribs, leaving red harsh scars— scars that pulse, that throb, beating to the rhythm of the young boy's heart.

But the dragon doesn't quit. The blood that it has drawn, the boy-meat it has tasted, ignites inside its scaly-maggot heart a lust for nothing less than all the body parts, especially the unscarred and valiant heart, pumping strong, undeterred, inside Small Pilgrim's wounded body.

"Boo who?"

"Don't cry, Dad. It's only life."

Stunned, I paused then stuttered my applause. "Taylorman, those words are straight from God. And they're for the record. I'm writing them down as we speak so that I never will forget them."

Thanking him, I hung up, once again grateful, once again amazed . . . This wounded warrior-boy, this man, loves *me* with all his heart. And just think . . . this hero to all heaven is my son.

At the same time, in the same moment, an intensely profound and passionate Spirit echoed those same healing words from God's own heart to my own wounded soul.

"Don't cry. It's only life. It's only *Life*."

And if you will receive him, I know the Author of these words, and his attending promise, are for your soul as well.

So . . . off we go to Maryland, to the NIC on the outskirts of D.C.

I walk with a limp.

Taylor soars with a howl.

Together we cry and we knock.

Knock-knock. Knock-knock.

And thanks to you, all heaven resounds with sound,

Knock-knock . . .

Brian

Husband to Debbie; Dad to Taylor, 11.59; also Dad to Christopher, 14.14, and Jonathan, 6.39. Along with knocks on every fleeting day while Dempsey blows her horn.

❧

January 3rd, 2000
To: Charles
From: Brian Schrauger
Subject: Desperately needing feedback

Dear Charles . . .

Earlier this afternoon, Taylor, Debbie, and I met with Taylor's primary oncologist. After Taylor and Debbie left, I asked him The Question.

Here's his answer. Given the current momentum of the cancer in Taylor's body, he probably has four to six months to live.

Debbie explicitly asked me not to tell her what the doctor said. I understand and want to honor her request. So, for now, this must be kept strictly confidential.

I continue to believe Taylor will, in fact, die from this cancer.

But (except for doctors) everywhere I turn, *every* voice I hear explicitly condemns my horrible, unspoken belief. People without faith tell me I must . . . *Stay positive! Don't be negative! Keep fighting!!!* People of faith tell me, *God wants to heal Taylor. Believe harder.*

Does my horrible conviction mean I'm giving up or facing reality? Am I guilty of stubborn unbelief or "negative thinking"? Am I thereby blocking what is otherwise God's willingness to heal Taylor?

If not, is it now my job to prepare Taylor to die? To prepare Christopher, Jonathan, and Debbie for his death?

If so, how in heaven's name do I do this? Not only do I lack the knowledge, I lack the strength, the means. I am an emotional paraplegic.

Or am I just nuts, waaaay out in left field? (Given, of course, I was born nuts and have always lived so far in left field no one ever mows the grass . . .)

Thank you,

Brian

31   THE NCI AND DC2

A TAYLOR AND FAMILY REPORT

Thursday, January 20th, 2000

Ten days ago Taylor and I spent our first full day at the National Cancer Institute. On the second morning we were almost forced to leave.

We left Nashville on Sunday afternoon, January 9th. Our Southwest flight took us straight to Baltimore. First one on the plane, Taylor picked his window seat of choice. Full of people traveling to work on Monday At The Office, every seat was taken on the jet, sardining me in the middle on a row of three.

Not prone to talk with strangers, I opened my book. Before a single paragraph was read, the lady sitting next to me on the aisle side turned her head and said, "I think I know you and your boy." Turned out she is a member of the congregation we attend. As we flew I filled her in on Taylor's story and the purpose of our trip.

Minutes after our conversation was over, a man sitting in the sandwich seat in front of me stood up and turned around. He awkwardly leaned over the high back of his chair. He was a total stranger.

"Mister," he said, introducing himself, "sorry to interrupt. I couldn't help but overhear." His features said he was concerned I might be offended. But those same features also showed his heart, especially through his dark, wet eyes.

He didn't have to worry. Anyone who loves my wounded son loves me and is a friend forever.

"I live near the NCI," he continued. "Here's my card and home phone too. If there's anything you need while you're in town, please call."

I took his card and thanked him. When he turned around, I turned back to my book but found I could not read. The words had gone all blurry.

The Baltimore airport was an overcrowded zoo full of uncaged, single-minded predators. Scurrying on crutches, Taylor walked and dodged single-minded travelers for at least a mile until at last we found and nabbed our overweight luggage—and his wheelchair. When at last we sank into the seats inside our rental car, I think we both said, "Ahhhh."

In the dark, about an hour later, we somehow found our way to the Children's Inn. It's a large, luxurious facility, a home away from home for parents with sick children undergoing treatment at the NIH.

Both of us were pooped. But as usual, Taylor had a bout with agonizing pain, at least a level seven, keeping us awake late into the night.

Next morning, blurry eyed and grouchy, we took a shuttle to the entrance of the National Institutes of Health. After going through admissions, we found the overcrowded elevator bank we needed.

Going up, we stopped at almost every level until, at last, we stepped off on the thirteenth floor. To our left a door whooshed open and, like a vacuum, sucked us in. We were at the NCI.

Everyone on staff was wonderful. They were compassionate and professional, a rare combination among overworked people in an already stressful branch of medicine. Throughout the day Taylor was given a bed on which to rest and play his Nintendo Gameboy. It was his private parking place while nurses poked and prodded, drew blood through his Hickman line, a place from which he traveled to and from radiology for scans. But most of all a place where we waited, waited, waited. To win acceptance into the experimental study Taylor had to get passing grades on lab analyses.

Returning the next morning we were told he'd flunked a vital test. Admission to the study required a liver enzyme count no higher than an eighty-two. Taylor's was in the nineties, probably a residual effect from the daily chemo drinks he'd finished four weeks earlier.

Heart sinking down to toes, my stomach followed suit. It lurched then twisted into a knot. After nurses drew blood for a second test, I leaned over in my chair, cramped with sickening fear. With the bile taste of anger and despair, I prayed, I begged, "Please, God, let Taylor pass the test."

Thirty minutes later we were told his enzyme count was eighty-one! Taylor was accepted. With room for only twenty-four patients in the study, Taylor was number sixteen or seventeen. *Thank you, God!*

Taylor was in. People were kind. But the pain attacks were terrible, often clamping on with strangleholds at levels four or five or six. And for hours on end. Although I'd given full report of this, NCI professionals witnessed an attack on Tuesday afternoon.

Even pros, like Doubting Thomas, often need to see in order to believe. Once they saw his agony and heard his anguished cries, new and stronger meds were promptly prescribed. They helped. (As I write, however, the pain's gained ground again, attacking five, six times a day—and with excruciating regularity.)

On our fifth day at the NCI, last Friday the 14th, Taylor received his first dose of OncoLAR but not through his Hickman line. Instead it had to be injected into fatty tissue. And the only place he has any is in his lower right-side hem*ass*phere. Ouch.

According to the study's protocol, Taylor gets this shot once a month. In between, twice a day, he takes a pill, a drug called tamoxifen, a well-known weapon against breast cancer. Both drugs have demonstrated an ability to inhibit growth hormones manufactured by the pituitary gland, especially the specific hormone factor on which Osteo-sarcomas (those nasty Little Muthas) "eat" so they can grow. If the drugs work, Taylor might be short. But he'll be alive.

"What happens after Taylor's received his last shot of OncoLAR according to the protocol?" I asked the NCI physician in charge of the study.

He paused, looked at me with kindness, and never glanced away. Then he verbalized his answer.

"Mr. Schrauger, if your son lives until the last shot's given, we will rejoice and then decide what next to do."

Although distinctly out of focus, I too maintained the gaze, grateful for his empathetic clarity. I thanked him. Then both of us turned, looking away, blind and deaf for just a moment's time to the fading world around us.

"So, Taylor, what do your bracelets mean?"

After several eight-hour days with the same people, one brave nurse, Kimberly, mustered the chutzpa to ask.

One by one Taylor pointed at each.

"FROG means Fully relying on God. WWJD means What would Jesus do? And PUSH means Pray until something happens."

"So, do you ever take 'em off?"

"Never!" Taylor said. "Unless they *make* me cuz of surgery."

"Cool!" said the Jewish nurse. "I'm proud of you."

Later, out of Taylor's hearing range, Kimberly asked about my lone bracelet, PUSH.

"So what do you do after you've prayed and something has happened?" Her inquiry was keen, real.

"Good question." I was caught a bit off guard. "You know what I'm praying for. Guess once I get the answer, there'll be plenty of other things to pray about . . . if I'm able to . . . if I'm willing . . ."

"Well, let me know, would you?" Kimberly asked.

"Sure. And hey, thank you for your kindness to Taylor about the bracelets. I know you prob'ly don't believe Y'shua is Messiah. Your gracious response, especially to WWJD, is a credit to you. God bless."

"God bless you too," she said.

On the weekend we did D.C., Saturday was bitter cold. Taylor and I took trains deep underground all the way to the National Air and Space Museum, where we spent the day. I brought the wheelchair, but Taylor almost always used his crutches—or the chair as a scooter. I think we both said *Cool!* and *Awesome!* more than any other words that day.

Sunday was a little warmer. This time we drove to the world's hub of power. We toured the National Cathedral, the Capitol, the Jefferson Monument, and the Lincoln Memorial.

"Y'know, buddy, heaven honors heroes too," I told Taylor while we gawked at monuments to men. "Heaven's heroes are people who, no matter what, chose to trust in God, to take him at his word, to live and even die by faith. Some of them are listed in the Bible. But heroes *there* are rarely recognized *here*. In fact, they're often hated. I think you are one of heaven's heroes."

"Can we go now, Dad? I'm freezing."

We didn't see it all. But that was fine with us. We were grateful when we left. Without regrets for what we missed, we happily flew home.

One week from today, Taylor returns to the NCI for a day of tests. This time Debbie will go with him. But for now Taylor's daily battles are against physical pain and loneliness, even some depression. Each enemy is being fought. None are yet defeated.

And we are weary. Every member of our little family is weary to the edge of despair. Thanks to you and your prayers, I don't think we've yet fallen in. Or if we have, we're dangling in midair, not unlike Wile E. Coyote in *Roadrunner* cartoons.

Grateful for you and for God through you . . .

Brian

Husband to Debbie; Dad to Taylor, 11.63; also Dad to Christopher, 14.17, and Jonathan, 6.42. And mocked by the Roadrunner Time, unstoppable even by Dempsey's explosives.

32   THE UNSEEN TEAM

A TAYLOR AND FAMILY REPORT

Friday, February 4th, 2000

In spite of the meds, in spite of *doubling* his daily dose of morphine, Taylor's pain attacks have grown much worse. They often reach, and sustain, levels four or five or six (on a scale of one to ten).

And when attacked, his moans, his agonizing moans, cut to the bone, stab the heart, grab the gut, physically hurt the ears and stomachs of each brother and each parent. All of us who hear are deathly ill with horror, fear, despair.

Two nights ago Christopher called me to his room. He shut the door and wept. "I'm going crazy and I can't do anything about it! I can't stand it anymore. I don't even want to live here!"

I thanked him for his honesty and assured him that I understand. I understand too well.

"Christopher, buddy, it's *okay* to feel that way. I often feel the same. Something would be very wrong if we didn't wrestle with these feelings.

"What you've gotta do is get the rest you need and pray. You've gotta rest up so you can get up with new strength to fight one day at a time.

"And please, buddy, don't ever give up. Do your very best to love your suffering brother now. That way if he dies, especially if he dies, you will know all your life you loved your brother well and with all your heart."

Last night in Taylor's bedroom while the two of us watched the Discovery Channel, Taylor was moaning, then suddenly exclaimed, "Dad, it feels like I'm being poked on the inside. And right down here, where it should be soft, it feels like a bone!"

With his cautious guidance I touched the sore zone. It *was* as hard as a bone. It *is* bony. It is the pelvic tumor. It's what this horrific cancer, this Osteo-sarcoma, makes: bulbous bony growing killers, stabbing on the inside. And from the inside out.

This morning, after consultation with the NCI team in Bethesda, Debbie took Taylor to the clinic at Vanderbilt. Tests must be done. Decisions must be made.

This is such a lonely battle, such a lonely race.

Yes, there is a host along the way. We know you are among them.

Grateful for your shouts of encouragement and praise, your refreshing cups of water, this is still a race from which there's no escape. We cannot quit. There is no end in sight. And we are exhausted, sick with horror. But thanks to our unseen Captain, we are members, players, warriors for a mostly unseen team. Out of sight we fight for him, members of his team that in the end shall win.

And on this team no member is ever alone.

Brian

P.S. If you're not yet a member-warrior of the (mostly) unseen team, you're welcome to join!

Husband to Debbie; Dad to Taylor, 11.67; also Dad to Christopher, 14.21, and Jonathan, 6.47, each one a rare and priceless plant. With dubious defoliants by Dempsey.

*A despairing man should have the devotion of his
friends even if he forsakes the fear of the Almighty.
(Job)*

 33   THE CONVERSATION

A TAYLOR AND FAMILY REPORT

Wednesday, February 9th, 2000

It is *The Talk* no parents want to have with their precious, early-adolescent son or daughter, with their bright-eyed, witty child. A child still vibrant with the innocence of youth but also with the early blossom of adulthood beautifully unfolding in face, features, form.

Actually Taylor and I have talked about *It* several times the past two years. While I've tried to keep our discussions on topic, it has been difficult. It's been hard to zero in on how *It* relates to him, what he will do with the information.

I've dreaded it. But for months I've known a man-to-man talk was on the way. In my mind I've composed, rehearsed, and endlessly edited what to say, how to say it.

During this time I've gently prodded, poked, and nudged. I've lightly knocked on Taylor's conversational door, hoping he would open it—hoping he might wait a little longer. And all the while I've wondered, wondered how much of *It* he already knew.

Then, without warning, it was time. It had to happen. Of course nothing went according to plan.

After last Friday's visit to Vanderbilt, including a new CT scan, Taylor's coterie of doctors reached a turning-point consensus. He must begin radiation therapy of his horribly painful pelvic tumor.

It starts tomorrow.

As a general rule Osteo-sarcomas are highly resistant to radiation. That's why, up till now, it hasn't been tried. But we are out of options, low on time. Everyone is desperate to provide relief.

We agree. Still . . . the necessity of this new direction is a sucker punch to the emotional gut, knocking out all wind, suffocating hope.

Radiation therapy means Taylor cannot continue in the NCI's OncoLAR study, our last best chance for killing off the multiplying tumors.

It means the primary direction of treatment has changed course. The ship of medical care is no longer on a curative vector. Instead, its primary heading is for the nearest quiet harbor of Symptomatic Relief, also known as Palliative Care. And its speed is full ahead.

For Debbie, for me, this ice-cold, rock-hard reality is almost impossible to face. For Taylor it is a possibility he considered once or twice but then put out of mind, getting on with life. It was a *possibility* he had faced but not a *reality*. Until yesterday.

Debbie was driving Taylor home from a "dry run" at Vanderbilt's Radiation Oncology Clinic. Doctors and clinicians assessed coordinates and practiced taking shots with harmless laser beams. It will be two days before they aim and shoot the beam that makes its human targets swell and glow.

While Debbie drove she talked to Taylor. I don't know how it happened. I don't know words she used or her nuances of tone. But I do know she displayed remarkable courage, love, and grace.

Debbie told him his doctors believe that Taylor's body will lose its battle against cancer. And probably soon.

Taylor took it hard and sobbed. So, instead of going home, Debbie brought him to my office.

To me it was as if they appeared out of thin air. Preoccupied, I had run down the hall, irritated with my body's quick response to a single cup of coffee. Walking back, deep in thought, Debbie stopped my charging stride, marching down the hall.

"Oh, hi! What're you doing here?"

"Taylor's with me," she whispered.

"Great!" I started to move past her.

"No, wait," she said. And then she filled me in.

Together we went inside my office and shut the door behind us. Taylor sat in one of two chairs on the front side of my messy desk. I joined him, sitting in the other. Leaning over, I cupped his soft wet cheeks inside my just-washed hands.

"C'mere, buddy."

He tumbled off his seat into my embrace. Burying his downy head on my chest just above the heart, Taylor wept, soaking my shirt with tears. Debbie stood behind him, resting her hand on his muscular back.

No one said a word. I just shut my eyes, touched his heart with mine, and held him.

Time went by.

Taylor moved back to his chair. Debbie agreed to leave him with me. She went home to find friends with whom Jonathan and Christopher could spend the night. And while Taylor and I talked, she once again recruited a spiritual platoon to pray.

"I love you, Taylor. And I'm so sorry . . . Didn't you know how serious this is?"

Through muffled sobs trying to erupt again, he answered without words. Shell-shocked, he shook his head: left-right, left-right, left-right.

In the ensuing silence I could only imagine how frightened he must be. How do I comfort my son? How do I reassure him?

A brainstorm hit. Grabbing a CD program disk, I said, "Hey, buddy, know what this is?"

He nodded yes.

Taylor loves computers. It's a passion that we share. For a long time we've been learning from each other. I teach him, he teaches me—back and forth we go, thrilled with new discoveries, techniques, applications.

"Okay," I continued. "Now, if this program is on my computer and it crashes or blows up, what happens to the program? Do I lose it?"

Although he looked a bit perplexed ("Where are we going with this, Dad?"), my question succeeded. It piqued his curiosity.

"Well . . . noooo. Not as long as you have the disk."

"Yes! Exactly!"

"In fact, the disk itself is only a cheat sheet to remember the software! Every program is unique, a creation of *ideas,* thoughts translated into numbers, into codes written on the disk. So. How much do numbers weigh?"

"Nothing, I guess."

"Right! So, how tall are numbers?"

"Well, unless ya write 'em down, the question's dumb."

"Yes, but . . . how much space do numbers take up?"

"None, unless ya write 'em down."

"Exactly. And that's what software is. It's a complicated creation by smart people who write down what they've created so it can't be forgotten. But the software *itself* is just a bunch of codes with no height or weight or space.

"Now pretend for a minute that your body is a computer that's caught a really nasty virus, probably through e-mail, right?"

He nodded.

"So. Your computer's got a virus that's so bad, it's gonna crash. When it does, what happens to the software? When your body dies, what happens to the *real* you?"

I plowed ahead.

"Nothing! Because God always has the latest version, the essence of who you are, fully backed up in his infinite, flawless memory!

"What's more, when your computer crashes, when your body dies, you have nothing less than God's promise that, because of his Son, you're going to get an immediate upgrade to perfect hardware! . . . Complete with two strong legs—and forever free from pain and death! Cool, huh?"

No answer. Taylor looked away, staring through the walls, gazing down the road. His eyes filled up with grief, frustration that I didn't get it.

"But Dad!" he protested. "I'm not afraid of dying. I *know* I'm gonna go to heaven. What worries me [sobs] is how [. . . long pause . . .] *everyone* here will get along without me!"

With a soundless thunderclap, a lightning bolt of awareness strikes my soul. Large, ice-cold teardrops, like unexpected winter rain, fall down my cheeks, roll and splash, disappearing in the carpet at my feet.

Taylor isn't all that worried about himself. Instead, he's mostly worried about his mom. Christopher. Jonathan. And me. ("Everyone" is a polite euphemism for "you, Dad.") His concern is not without due cause. After all, we know each other's heart—and he is a most perceptive man.

"Oh, buddy, buddy. I had no idea. Now please, please listen! You simply cannot, must not, carry our load, my load. God doesn't want you to carry it, and neither do I. Your load is heavy enough without carrying mine—or anybody else's.

"Each of us is given his own stuff to carry. But only our own stuff, not other people's stuff. Not even the stuff of people we love.

"I love you more than life. If I could, I'd take your place in a heartbeat. But I can't. I just can't. I can walk with you all the way to the end. I can walk you Home. But I cannot take your place. And you can't take mine.

"I know this is hard, unbelievably hard, but here it is. I must put you in God's hands and trust him to help you. And you must put me in God's hands, trusting him to help me.

"Will you promise not to carry my load? Will you promise to trust God to help me, to help Mom and your brothers, just like we're gonna trust him to help you?"

He agrees.

Suddenly the whole room feels lighter, brighter. I shut down my computer, gather up my things. Taylor grabs his crutches as together we leave and walk out to the van.

Honoring tradition, we go out to eat. Just the two of us indulging in a little beer, a soda—Mr. Pibb (cuz they don't serve Dr. Pepper). We eat deli-cious fatty food. But do not taste it very much.

And eye to eye we smile. Mostly quiet, knowing looks, telepathing treas-ures of sadness, love, and hope.

It was easy to forget him. But now I know the Monster's real. The one inside my closet as a child. The same one who wrapped the cord of life, like a noose, round infant Taylor's neck in the dark and early hours of his birth. The one who tried to smash our family in the pavement of Highway 35. The one who, many years ago, high up on the dam road, tried to blow away a little boy and his soul-sick dad.

But now Death is exposed. With Suffering at his side, they are an ugly pair, more disgusting than my imagination ever pictured. They are, in fact, as ugly, as repulsive, and loud as Dante's hell.

But with God's help, we will not look away.

We will not change our course.

We will not separate.

Together we shall move ahead.

Because the bloody Monster's cursed.

And we are going Home.

Brian

Husband to Debbie; Dad to Taylor, 11.68; also Dad to Christopher, 14.23, and Jonathan, 6.49. Tonight, at least, Dempsey smells like roses.

I know that my Defender lives, that in the end he will stand upon the earth. I know that after this body has decayed, this body shall see God.

(Job)

34   LOVE AND METHANE

A TAYLOR AND FAMILY REPORT

Friday, February 25ᵗʰ, 2000

Our boxer, Dempsey, has always been an accomplished gasser. Lately, however, she has achieved all-time records, and ungrateful recognition, in several categories of flatulence: frequency, range, sustained impact, and density.

Debbie thinks Dempsey's notable advances in her singular skill are caused by stress. I don't really care about the cause. My chief concern is making sure she's not by my chair while I'm sitting in it.

Amazingly, however, both Jonathan and Taylor still want the old girl *sleeping* with them. Jonathan wants her in his room when he goes to bed. And Taylor, more often than not, wants her right up *on* the bed when he goes to sleep—strategically positioned, of course, but still right next to him.

And so, about half the time for the past few weeks, after Jonathan's asleep, the groggy dog (through deadly fog) is summoned into Taylor's room. She staggers in and barely jumps up on his bed. I manually shift her backside south, which Taylor delicately covers with his sheets, assuring me he won't go to sleep with his head beneath the covers.

It must be love.

This arrangement works because Taylor almost always goes to sleep long after everyone else in the family. That's because tumor phantom pains almost always strike at night.

Overall, the frequency and intensity of these attacks have diminished quite a bit during the past two and a half weeks. But they're still regular, still bad. And lately they've included a motley crew of peevish little fiends, malicious dwarfs like Briefly Blurry Vision, Leg Pain, Eyebrow Pain, Backaches, Headaches, Nausea, Respiratory Distress, and Hot Flashes. How many of these stumpy illegitimates are birthed by anxiety? I don't know. I'm pretty sure some are; some aren't. But it doesn't really matter.

What matters is, in spite of lesser pain, Taylor's doctor doesn't think the radiation's working.

Taylor's lower left hem*ass*phere has blown up like an overinflated balloon. The skin is taut, burnt red, tender to the slightest touch, exploding in pain with just a little bump.

Apart from these developments, Taylor tolerated well his first exposure to radiation—just as he has every other kind of treatment. Unfortunately both he and the aliens inside him tolerate them all too well. Or so it seems to me.

Taylor has one more week of radiation therapy. Then comes a two-week wait. After that the truth will be exposed in pictures from another CT scan.

Although Taylor's pain attacks have decreased, his bathroom problems have grown worse. Ever since the amputation, Taylor's had to "sit" on his hands while on the ivory throne, holding up all his body's weight—often for thirty to forty-five minutes. And now, more than ever, he doesn't dare to rest his aching wrists and shaking arms. Because if he did, just a little bit, it would cause unbearable pain even from the lightest touch on that bright red swollen buttock, on that evil pelvic tumor.

Still, all that downward pressure, in spite of herculean handstands, triggers tumor pain. The added unseen horror is that these efforts, along with their results, seem to indicate the pelvic invader is slowly squeezing shut his inner rectal wall.

Once the pain abates, usually around midnight, Taylor often sleeps twelve hours.

In appearance he remains remarkably robust. His arms and chest are muscular. His growing hair is blond and thick. His smile and his zeal are infectious. The only hint of some small malaise is his indoor pallor. When he doesn't hurt, you'd think the kid was on vacation. Or, perhaps, a professor in the graduate school of Warped Humor.

Several days ago when I came home from work, Taylor hopped up on the sofa and commanded, "Come here!" When I did, instead of an expected tickle attack, he jumped, grabbed me round the neck with Popeye arms, and wrapped my waist with his python leg. I carried my silly soul-mate son to a nearby mirror. Cheek-to-cheek we posed, like we often did when he was a little boy.

"Hey, Pale Face," I joke. "Look at this! Me, red-faced Tonto; you, white-faced Kimosabi. Or is it Casper?"

But as we look at our reflection, he's tickled by something else. Standing perpendicular to the mirror, Taylor's legless left side faces forward. His right leg is invisible.

"Hey, Dad!" he laughs. "Look! Looks like you're dancing with a double amputee!"

I see; I laugh; I marvel. Where does this kid get his ingenious sense of twisted humor???

It's usually from the dull drab states of loneliness and boredom that he phones me at the office. Although creative, his Taylorian chant follows a common theme . . .

"Hi. It's me . . . Guess what? . . . What-cha dooo-in? . . . When're ya comin' ho-ome?"

And almost every night, according to lifelong tradition, we pray at bedtime. Our efforts are often perfunctory, predictable. But sometimes they're poignant and enlightening. Like one night last week. In a matter-of-fact but weary voice he prayed . . .

"And please, God, get rid of the damned tumors—and *all* the cancer in my body."

He gets it!

The cancer and the tumors are not his. They are not part of his identity. They are, instead, illicit illegal invaders. Regardless of their painful success, he does not, will not, regard them as his own.

They are evil. And because they're evil, they are also damned, so sentenced by the judgment made, and paid, by God's own blood.

But by that same judgment, that damnation of all evil, Taylor knows that his identity, his essence, his unique life is forever separate. He, himself, Taylor, has been rescued from the attack of cancer—even from the assault of Death. (Fascinating . . . we are *rescued* by the vicious but vicarious judgment of God. Amazing.)

After prayers, Taylor summons Dempsey to his bed. Perhaps her noxious fumes *are* proof she is a dog who loves her wounded master. After all, if Taylor's moans carve scars inside my soul, is it really any surprise they cause Dempsey indigestion?

In uncontaminated innocence they sleep together. Because in spite of disconcerting sounds followed by unpleasant scents, it's better than being alone.

Taylor and Dempsey have an interspecies fellowship made holy by Love. Love that, for its part, "covers a multitude of sins"—including sounds and smells from the snoring mammal close beside.

As Debbie herself will readily attest . . .

Brian

Husband to Debbie; Dad to Taylor, 11.73; also Dad to Christopher, 14.27, and Jonathan, 6.53. And grudgingly grateful guardian of Dempsey the farting boxer.

Above all, love each other deeply. Because
love covers a multitude of sins.
(Rock)

35 NOT IN KANSAS ANYMORE

DURING THE SECOND WEEK IN MARCH THE INTENSITY of Taylor's pain attacks decreased. They were just as frequent but not as intense. Then a change occurred. One Tuesday night the invaders' penetration was so deep they provoked heart-wrenching cries. On the other hand, fierce as it was, the main force of the attack lasted only thirty to forty-five minutes. As usual, residual aftershocks coursed through Taylor's frame. They too retreated but only after Taylor fell asleep.

Predictably, the onset begins with a necessary trip to the WC (or, if you prefer, to our padded porcelain throne). Anticipation and execution of this private but universal practice should result in feelings of relief and well-being. Instead, in Taylor's case, it triggers immense anxiety. He knows the effort will expose him to a barrage of lightning-bolt javelins thrown with vicious accuracy by a legion of crazed sadists.

But something's changed since Tuesday. Last night was different. For the first time in many months, Taylor's trip to the WC was a trip to the

DMZ—or, if it wasn't demilitarized, the enemy didn't fire. Or, perhaps, an unseen Ally held the demons at bay so that they could not?

It seems the dramatic decline in pain attacks are due to a massive counteroffense that has three parts: Neurontin, touch, and a massive campaign of prayer.

As mentioned last week, Taylor's pain doctor tripled his daily dose of Neurontin. Nerve pain, or phantom pain, is a mysterious, ephemeral foe. It apparently haunts the brain from the body's hidden halls, its complex nervous system. Phantom pain frightens synapses with screaming sensations from a missing limb, resulting in intense distress—pain that's very real but like the limb that's gone, untouchable.

As any amputee attests, phantom pain is somewhat tamed by the mind and time. But it is never exorcised this side of the grave. Virtually impervious to regular narcotics (like morphine), phantom pain can be minimized by anticonvulsive drugs like Neurontin—primarily a drug for controlling epilepsy.

And so, an increase in Neurontin has helped.

But so has touch.

When Taylor's body involuntarily lurches, a hand on his upper body— front or back and with varying degrees of reassuring firmness—seems to act like a kind of shock absorber, softening convulsive impacts, imparting some degree of calm to his hyperactive nervous system.

It's as if touch reassures terrified synapses they are not alone in the stormy din of battle.

And then there's prayer.

This is something that I do, but poorly. I'm grateful many others do it well. An unknown host of people have made Taylor and his family the focus of their countless prayers to God. For these efforts I am forever grateful.

Over the next week, there was an unusual outpouring of prayer from friends on the e-mail list and from others too. A lot of it happened in our presence. But a lot of it was strange—at least to us. It was a kind of prayer *way* outside our experience. It was also a kind of prayer that took us deep inside very different places than we'd ever been before.

This disconcerting journey began when our Jewish friends, Marty and Jennifer Goetz, came by to pray for, and over, Taylor. Marty brought his velvet encased *tallith,* the beautiful prayer shawl he received at his bar mitzvah ceremony many (many!) years ago. The Goetzes also brought their priceless *chuppah,* a large embroidered swath of special cloth. The *chuppah* is a tentlike canopy, symbolizing the ancient bridal chamber, under which Marty and Jennifer were married.

Marty's a hoot. He did a great job making Taylor laugh and feel at ease—no small accomplishment by an adult Taylor didn't know. "The tassels, or *tzitzith,* on each corner of the prayer shawl," Marty explained, "are just like the ones God's Son wore on the lower edge of his everyday clothes. Remember the time when he was caught in the traffic jam of a dense crowd? The time when a sick woman pushed her way to him, reached out, touched his garment, and was healed?"

Taylor nodded yes.

"Well," Marty continued, "it was tassels just like those you're touching now on the corners of the prayer shawl! By touching his tassels the woman told God two things. She told him she believed Y'shua was *able* to heal. And she was *asking* him to do so. In her case, God did. But, the *tallith* and the *chuppah* are not magic. When you touch the tassels and pray, when you lie beneath the *chuppah* as your blanket, it's just a way to let God know that you want to be healed, that you are asking him to do so. So, let's ask him! Are you okay with that?"

"Sure!" Taylor answered without a moment's hesitation.

After placing a light dab of olive oil on Taylor's forehead, both Marty and Jennifer prayed brief prayers. In simple terms they asked God to demonstrate his mercy and compassion by healing Taylor's body.

But they also asked that God, by whatever means, would glorify his Son, Y'shua, his sacrificial Lamb, who died in Taylor's place. The One whose blood satisfies God's judgment so that he forever *Passes-over* Taylor. And blood that also makes my wounded son, Taylorman, a co-inheritor with the Father's wounded Son, Y'shua.

"Thank you, Yahweh, that along with many others, Taylor is an heir of all creation. He is an adopted member of your family—into which, like Taylor, his countless siblings have been born by faith alone. In Y'shua's name, so be it."

Loaning Taylor their *tallith* and their *chuppah* (such a gesture!), the Goetzes said, "Shalom!" and left.

"Well, buddy," I said, "that was interesting. And very, very kind."

Sitting in his sofa bed covered by the *chuppah* as a temporary blanket, Taylor fingered tassels on the prayer shawl and with a thoughtful look, distracted by my words, nodded his agreement.

Four days later a man named Mickey Robinson, with several friends in his wake, whooshed into our house to pray. Half of Mickey's face presents a handsome profile. But the other half, like the Phantom of the Opera unmasked, is at first a shock to see. Disfigured, discolored, massively scarred, this half bears the horror of third-degree burns and subsequent surgeries from an airplane crash more than twenty years ago. Married with children, Mickey tells the world that when his plane went down, he died and went to heaven—but was sent back.

(*Bummer,* I have often thought. *Please, God, don't do that to me. When I get there, I want to* stay.)

Mickey and his friends weren't screamers or religious manipulators. My highly sensitive antennae and delicate nose can almost always detect, to the edge of paranoia (and beyond!), shysters hiding under cloaks of piety. Anybody emitting so much as a whiff of this kind of offal con would get, from me, das boot on das butt out das door.

There was, however, none of that. All that was transmitted was compassion for Taylor and his family. When our new friends prayed, they asked God to heal Taylor's body. But they did not demand it.

Doubtful but hopeful, I too begged, but with wordless prayers.

But that same night, after they left, the phantom pain defiantly returned.

Frustrated, infuriated, I called Mickey from Taylor's room, interrupting a prayer meeting in his home. "Listen to this!" I almost yelled, then held the phone up over Taylor's bed from which he screamed and wept. Bringing the handset back to my ear and mouth I barked, "Pray harder!"

"O Lord in heaven, have mercy," he responded with an ancient prayer. "Brian, we will."

Grumbling a thank-you, I disconnected in despair.

But then, within minutes, the attack began to dissipate and Taylor, exhausted, went to sleep.

Probably just the medicine, my spirit griped to God.

Mickey and his friends did more than pray that night. They also made arrangements. The next morning we received a call from one of Mickey's praying friends. "Our private aircraft is at your disposal today," the friend said.

The "private aircraft" was, in fact, a Lear Jet.

Just before noon Taylor and I were welcomed by two pilots who flew us high and fast to Charlotte, North Carolina. On the way we ate gourmet lunches packed in boxes, fiddled with the folding seats, drank sodas, gawked out the windows. After a forty-five-minute flight we landed and hopped out (but then, Taylor *always* hops out). A young, clean-cut Brazilian man, André Schroder, met us at the airport. He drove us to meet Mahesh Chavda.

Raised in a devout Hindu home by Indian parents (native to India), Mahesh was raised in the port city of Mombasa, just south of the equator in Kenya. At age sixteen, contrary to his family's faith, he accepted Y'shua as God's Promised One, God in human flesh, the perfect sacrificial Lamb.

Now in his early fifties, Mahesh's life is devoted to a ministry of Christian evangelism (like Billy Graham)—and physical healing (*not* like Billy Graham).

Whoa.

Only weeks ago anything close to this kind of vocational claim would have sent me flying west, not east, toward Tarshish, not Charlotte.

There is one reason I took Taylor east, not west.

While I don't believe God *has* to heal anyone of any physical ailment, I know he's *able* to—but at his sole discretion. What persuaded me to fly east was Mahesh's frank admission, as a matter of public record, that he has prayed for many who have not been healed—or healed in part, not whole. To me, this was a refreshingly honest admission from someone who has focused on prayers for physical healing throughout his entire adult life.

Recovering from the flu(!), Mahesh presented his impressively rotund self, casually dressed in extra-*extra*-large sweats and with a slightly skewed toupee. Soft-spoken, kind, he was the polar opposite of flashy. He completely lacked the nauseating, charlatan quality my antennae have invariably detected over the years—schmaltzy schlocks in congregations and on TV in every flavor from the super-moussed, bejeweled, and blazing-eyed to religious belligerents. And clothed in everything from smelly rags to (more often) thousand-dollar suits. Impressed by Mahesh's humanity, especially his skewed toupee, I nonetheless was disappointed, desperate.

I felt just like a dad who lived two thousand years ago. A dad whose son was afflicted by raging self-destructive seizures. Pleading with a Rabbi named Y'shua, that dad begged, "If you can do anything, take pity on us and help us."

"If you can?" said Y'shua. "Everything is possible for him who believes."

Immediately the boy's desperate dad prayed my lifelong prayer, "I do believe! Help me overcome my unbelief!"

Amen to that, I thought to myself, sitting with Taylor on a small sofa in an untidy storeroom office.

Mahesh spoke so quietly he almost whispered. Dabbing Taylor's forehead with a fingertip of oil, he prayed for Taylor and for me. No lightning bolts, no thunderclaps. Just a touch on head and shoulder while he prayed.

Touch! my mind cried out, surprised. *That's one way Taylor's pain has been mitigated! Appropriate, loving touch is no less important in prayer . . . Perhaps, in fact, it is a* part *of prayer . . .*

Jetting back to Nashville at thirty-nine thousand feet, Taylor was a goof. He opened and closed hidden trays, played some solitaire. Fiddling with headphones, he switched a reading lamp on and off, on and off. He also did a show for one: covering his face with hands then moving them aside, he flashed a clownlike smile. Then covering his face again, he switched to an instant frown of bright-eyed fury—back and forth, back and forth. Not at all unlike the way he fights the cancerous Little Muthas, refusing to surrender, determined to have fun.

We left our house at eleven in the morning and were home by five that afternoon. As for the horrendous phantom pain attacks? Well,

there wasn't one on Wednesday. Nor, more significantly, on Thursday after Taylor's prolonged WC excursion which, for now, seems to be a DMZ that is well enforced.

How does Taylor feel about all this?

"I dunno," he shrugs.

"Me either, buddy. Me either."

We still can feel the pelvic tumor.

This coming Monday I have an appointment with Taylor's primary-care oncologist. It's time to make plans for Taylor's probable death. Stuff like use of oxygen, hospice or no hospice, signed documents to resuscitate or not to resuscitate if Taylor dies at home or anywhere outside the hospital. Stuff like that.

Then Tuesday morning, March 14th, Taylor gets another CT scan.

Meanwhile our family continues, best as we are able, to play and pray, looking for joy, creating memories, refusing to surrender to the agony in our hearts.

36 GROWN

IT WAS 10 P.M. ON FRIDAY, MARCH 17TH, 2000, WHEN Taylor and I celebrated our new nightly tradition: communion in his room. I read the words, we ate a little bread, drank a little juice, prayed a little prayer. Afterward it was still early—at least by Taylor time. These days he never went to bed before midnight. Often later.

Sitting at Taylor's homework table, his lips still purply from grape juice, I said, "Buddy, you know I met with Dr. Whitlock and a couple others at the clinic today, right?"

He nodded.

"I also know you know we are out of medical options for treating the cancer in your body. So, what we talked about is how to help you now. At some point, prob'ly soon, maybe after we get the results of tomorrow's CaT, all of us would like your thoughts about some stuff, okay?"

Taylor's face spoke volumes of grief, dismay, belief, and disbelief. Clearly he had done a lot of thinking about this "stuff."

Stray tears streaked down one cheek, then the other, as if taking turns. Cupping his face in the palm of one hand, I wiped away each tear with a thumb or index finger. At last he broke the silence.

"Okay!" he protested. "I just don't want to talk about it right now!"

"That's fine," I agreed. "But we'll prob'ly need to talk about it later on this week, all right?"

Silently he nodded his consent.

Moments later we stood up from our chairs beside the table. As I stretched and yawned, Taylor lunged. It was a surprise attack, tickling underneath my arms and on my unprotected ribs, scoring solid hits. With a wounded cry I jumped with involuntary shock then returned a volley of my own. We laughed and paused to catch our breath.

Then, without an explanation, he grabbed both my hands with his. Without revealing his intent, he plunged downward to the floor, trusting me to break his fall, to keep him from hitting bottom—no small amount of faith considering his weight . . . and especially the Little Mutha in his rear.

Picking up his solitary leg, Taylor tried to swing himself back and forth between my two spread legs. It's something that we often did when he was young, when he was my golden-haired, gleaming-eyed, healthy, pure-joy boy—but also smaller and much lighter.

At least I didn't drop him.

"Whoa, buddy!" I strained to hold his weight. "You have gotten big! Don't think we can do that one anymore. But how 'bout this?"

We danced—something else we did a lot many years ago. First to my left, then to my right, he hopped as we swirled in a circle. Then, without a warning, I held a hand up high and made him do a twirl. While everyone inside the house was sound asleep and outside it was dark and cold, we danced a private waltz. As we hopped and twirled, I sang . . .

> *dan-cing, dan-cing,*
> *dancing-with my-Tay-lor-man*
> *dan-cing, dan-cing,*
> *dancing-with my-Tay-lor-man*
> *dancing-dancing, dan-cing, dan-cing . . .*
> *danc-ing-with-my-Tay-lor-man!*

Full of nostalgic joy, we laughed out loud as again we paused to catch our breath. It was a happiness that erupted up from deep inside, far below, from places in our hearts and souls we ourselves can only barely know.

At last, plunging to rest on his bed, we watched *Zorro* on TV then went to sleep in separate rooms.

Next day came the CaT.

Getting the report took longer than expected. When the phone call finally came, I was at the office. The pelvic tumor, Taylor's doctor said, "has grown a *little*." But nonetheless, grown.

Tumors in the lungs have grown "quite a bit."

Because the attending radiologist had not yet written the report, we didn't know specific measurements. But I really did not need them. The medical conclusions were clear. Radiation to the Little Mutha may have slowed its growth a bit. But it had not stopped. Instead, it grew. And in the absence of treatment to the lungs, tumors there grew even more.

(Here, however, is a mystery . . . Taylor did not have a single pain attack in ten days, not one since our whirlwind trip to see Mahesh in Charlotte, North Carolina.)

From my office I called Debbie with the news. She, in turn, called upon the army of our friends and family. She also told Taylor. When he heard, he wept.

Arriving home, Debbie told me, "Taylor's in his room, reading his Bible. He wants to be alone."

Pleased with his focus, I stuck my head in his bedroom door. Sitting upright against the cushions of his sofa bed, Bible open on his lap, he looked up with a frown, unhappy with the interruption.

"Sorry, buddy. Just wanted to suggest you take a look at Psalm 23. Whenever you wanna talk, just let me know." Blowing him a kiss, I softly shut the door.

After a dinner of meatballs and potatoes, after watching *Wheel of Fortune* on TV, Taylor was ready to talk. Sitting on his bed, we faced each other. His leg and toes stretched toward me and all of mine stretched toward him. With an almost disconcerting calm, I went first.

"Well, buddy, this is hard to believe, isn't it? Looks like God is telling us to get ready for your journey Home. Still, who knows? If he wants, at any time he still might intervene and say, 'Not yet.' But that possibility doesn't let us off the hook to do right now what must be done . . . get ready."

As we talked, Taylor's eyes were leaking. Just like Monday night, however, there were no sobs. And my eyes, by some grace perhaps, were dry as sun-baked bone. This was serious stuff. But there were no hysterics.

I did my best to explain issues like hospice care, DNR (do not resuscitate) orders, and the choice, in time, of staying at home instead of going into the hospital.

"But what I want to know is *how* it's gonna happen," he protested. "*How* am I gonna die?"

I tried to explain what I'd been told three days before.

"It's possible the tumor in your pelvis might squeeze shut or even cut your rectum. But even if it did, we probably could solve that problem with a colostomy."

"Yeah, I thought about that," he said.

"So, as bad as it hurts, the pelvic tumor probably won't kill you. It's the tumors in your lungs that threaten most. If they keep on growing, eventually they'll take up too much space so that your lungs won't work. *But* . . . with the use of oxygen and morphine, along with other drugs, your doctors promise me you *won't* have pain. Well, there may be *some* discomfort, but it won't even come close to the kind of pain attacks you had for several months. In fact, it looks like God has stopped the pain attacks ever since our trip to see Mahesh, don't you think?"

With no more than a second of sober contemplation, he nodded his agreement.

"Tell you what, buddy, that alone's a miracle, something only God could do. So. Of everything I've told you, here are the most important things. God is in control. Cancer isn't. If he chooses to, God still might intervene. But even if he doesn't . . . *You*—are—safe. And you—will—*never*—be—alone. Got it?"

"Yeah, Dad. I got it."

Pointing toward the ceiling, I also reminded him about promises we have received. On this side, death is like going to sleep. But on that Side it's the instant, awesome sight of waking up! Of coming Home! All at once everything works—two legs, two arms, everything!

And the things we'll see! Such beauty! Such love! Most surprisingly, perhaps, it's so touchable, so real, it will be like waking from a dream. It's life on this side that is ghostly, not There—just the opposite of how most people think. But life on this side isn't something we'll forget, like we do most dreams. It's something we'll remember well, but for the first time see in a whole new light.

"Taylorman, all these things are promises God can keep because his Son, Y'shua, paid the way, dying in our place. And you will get to meet him—I think right away. But our pictures are all wrong. Nobody here knows his face. So how will you recognize him? Look for deep wounds or bright red scars like yours. Except, of course, his will be on his upper wrists. And if his feet are bare, you'll see them down there too.

"And, buddy? If you beat me there, remind him that your dad is still out on the dam road in the storm. Don't forget! Tell him that I love him, that I really need his help. Yeah, I know he can hear me say those things. But maybe if you tell him too, he'll let you look in on me and pray . . . okay?"

"Sure, Dad."

After a prayer for help up here on the dam road in the middle of the storm, I began to rearrange Taylor's bed so he could go to sleep.

With my back against the wall, tucking in the corner of a cover sheet, Taylor pounced like Hobbs, Calvin's comic tiger. Cornered, I was trapped with no way to escape. He tickled with such force and so effectively (he *knows* my vulnerabilities), I could not defend myself.

When I finally cried out "Uncle!" he relented with an impish grin, self-satisfied and smug.

"Gotcha!"

That night I wrote our e-mail friends:

Friday, March 17th, 2000

If you are a person who prays, please pray for at least two things, not one.

Yes, pray for a miracle of healing this side of heaven. Taylor wants this even more than we.

But also pray for the miracle of life *today*—laughter, wisdom, joy *right now*—and these latter three whether or not the first request is given to receive.

Gratefully yours . . .

Brian

Husband to Debbie; Dad to Taylor, 11.78; also Dad to Christopher, 14.33, and Jonathan, 6.59—all growing up too fast. Too fast.

SNEAK PEAK AT TAYLOR'S E-MAIL

March 17th, 2000
From: Taylorman
To: Online Prayer Ministry
Subject: Bad News

Hello,

My name is Taylor S. I'm 11, soon to be 12. Well anyway, I have had cancer for over a year and a half.

Well today I just got the most recent reports of a cat-scan and they weren't the greatest. You see, ever since the cancer started, the doctors couldn't find a way to shrink the tumors.

(By the way, I have a very, very rare type of tumors. They are called Osteo Sarcomas—bone cancer.)

I have lost one leg and part of two lungs. And now I have 4 tumors in both lungs. One of them is pretty big. And 1 super-big one in my left hip—that's where the first tumor was.

And well, I really need you to pray for me.

In Christ,

Taylor S.

37 COOL!

A TAYLOR AND FAMILY REPORT

Thursday, March 30th, 2000

Since our trip to North Carolina on March 7th, Taylor hasn't had a single pain attack like those that tortured almost every night for at least three months. He still has moans and groans from aches and queasiness. But part of this, we're relieved to learn, is from a stomach virus.

Apart from this discomfort, the most obvious symptoms of cancer are these: Taylor tires easily and sleeps a little longer. He also has frequent skirmishes with anxiety and boredom. For the most part, however, he's calmly walking toward the river, painfully bloodied but wonderfully cocky too.

With grins and jokes and lots of laughs, we work hard to keep on mocking the bloated, purply, impotent face of Death. What a loser. Especially to us.

Brian

Husband to Debbie; Dad to Taylor, 11.82; also Dad to Christopher, 14.37, and Jonathan, 6.62—and still unlucky heir to Dempsey's air.

"You know, buddy, there were a *lot* of people downstairs in our living room tonight. While you were up here playing with your cousins, we had quite a prayer meeting. In fact, while we prayed *everyone* agreed God told them something about you. Do you know what it is?"

It was a Monday night, April 3rd, sometime around eleven. The house was finally quiet. Our recent visitors along with Taylor's triplet cousins and their parents had gone home. Christopher, Jonathan, and Debbie were in bed. Dempsey was percussing from both ends in the outer hall.

Taylor and I sat at the homework table in his room. We were about to do our juice-and-cracker thing when I asked, "Do you know what it is?"

Seventeen hours earlier the two of us had signed in at Vanderbilt's pediatric surgical center. Taylor was there for removal of his Hickman catheter. Not a morning person, he was a very sleepy kid but excited too. At last he was getting rid of the two-year-old nuisance in his chest! Extraction of the catheter was quick and easy. Taylor kept the tubes as a souvenir. (Both of us agreed it was really cool, in part because it was also kinda gross. We just hoped Mom wouldn't throw the thing away . . .)

All the doctors, all the nurses, smiled. With buoyant happy tones, each one expressed vicarious excitement about our impending escape to the Land of Big Mouse! Dream-Makers, Inc., with the help of an unknown host of givers, was sending our entire family on Taylor's "dream" vacation to Disney World.

We smiled back and said, "Yes, we're excited too." But behind our socially correct response, we knew. While words were kind, we knew that every cheerful mask was a noble effort to hide a grieving heart. Everyone we saw was convinced, and with good reason, Taylor's trip to Disney was his Last Hurrah.

After the procedure, while Taylor caught up on his sleep, I ran up two floors to the Clinic. There I met with Taylor's primary physician and a social worker. They wanted to make sure I *voluntarily* signed two DNR orders—instructions to paramedics and doctors not to attempt resuscitation in the event of Taylor's death.

One document was valid in the state of Tennessee, the other one in Florida—just in case we needed it during Taylor's Disney trip.

Tim and Wendy were the pros with whom I met. Sometime in the last few months Taylor's doctors got informal. In the past I always heard, "Hello, *Mister* Schrauger? This is *Doctor* Dreighboldt." All attempts to use first names had been futile. Then one day I received a call, "Hello, Brian? This is Tim." Shocked, then pleased, in turn, the switch in salutations soon made my heart feel sick.

In any case, Tim and Wendy, the social worker, also expressed best wishes for the trip. But in Taylor's absence I noticed eyes were sad and smiles wan. These voices sang their words with notes of sorrow, a dirge in minor key I know all too well.

It was a bittersweet morning.

With a heavy heart I dreaded Taylor's Last Hurrah to the Happy Land of Make-Believe—a place full of silent Mickey-Minnies pantomiming dreams come true while underneath the costumes are sweaty little actors performing for a paycheck. And each one, according to strict orders, trying to hide-deny-deodorize the sickly sweet smell of mortality and death.

It is a complex, costly myth, eagerly embraced by a countless throng of tourists every year. But the underlying truth beneath the masks and costumes is also why Stephen King sells millions of his novels.

That same day, at seven in the evening, people were knocking on our door. They were friends we invited to pray with us before we leave on Thursday morning. From a list of eleven, ten showed up. Not bad, I thought.

No less than everyone at Vanderbilt earlier that day, each member of our evening group was a professional and a parent. Each one highly regarded in his or her community—and some well beyond. By any standard, this was a credible crowd investing valuable time on our behalf.

But unlike encounters earlier, these people were effortlessly comfortable—with themselves, each other, us. Smiles were warm, laughter easy. The unmasked love was almost tangible.

Even so, in our crowded, cozy living room, I sat on the floor, up against a wall, hoping my low profile might dodge attention; cheerful conversation give-and-take, more easily directed back and forth by people sitting up above on the chairs and sofa. I didn't want to spoil their joy—or pretend, like an actor inside Goofy, that I was delighted.

Upstairs Taylor and his brothers played rowdy games with their triplet cousins. They competed in video games, engaged in pillow warfare, and collapsed together on Taylor's bed, watching TV—either Nickelodeon or the Disney channel.

Meanwhile, in our living room downstairs, men and women turned their attention to a different dimension: the Realm of the Spirit. Their voices were quiet, not loud. Intense, but not desperate. Confident, but not cocky.

They felt like children. And like warriors too. It wasn't spooky. But it was awesome.

They were spontaneous but also very focused. Their singular objective was to summon a special presence of no one less than God himself. The only One invited was the one true God, the God of gods, sole Creator and Sustainer of all things, the intensely personal God of Abraham, Isaac, Moses. The One who calls himself, "I Am," "Yahweh," "Elohim." This God was invited in the name of his wounded sacrificial Son. He was invoked by the Name, Y'shua.

And Someone showed up. Boy, oh boy, did he ever show up.

Sitting on the floor up against the wall, my eyes were squeezed shut hard. But it didn't matter. I didn't go *to* a burning bush. Instead, shoes already off, I was *taken* inside the Flame. Debbie too.

And there we stayed for almost two hours.

In the presence of credible witnesses, the One who showed up also spoke. Among other things, he said . . .

Taylor will live. This cancer will not kill him. He will grow up and bear children. By doing this, I will honor and glorify my Son, Y'shua.

Then, just before the Presence left, he got down on the floor, awkward though it seemed, and took me in his arms. And in his arms, I sobbed. From the bottom of my soul, my eyes and nose erupted, soaking his shoulder and his neck. Unrepulsed, he only hugged me closer, repeating over and over, *I love you, Brian. I am pleased with you. I know what you are going through. I know it very well. And I am proud to be your Abba God.*

Then, gently, the Presence withdrew. Soon, with hugs and smiles, our friends did too.

Taylor wasn't present. He didn't listen in. That's why, after one and all had gone to bed, I said, "*Everybody* who prayed tonight agreed God told them something. Do you know what it is?"

Nonchalant and matter of fact, he replied. "Yeah. I'm gonna be healed."

Fascinated, and with some anxiety, I probed. "So . . . how do you feel about that?"

"Cool!"

Is it possible? Did God actually show up in my living room? Did he really speak?

The next day, like General Gideon, I tested with a kind of fleece. "Debbie, I want you to call every single person who was in our home last night. Ask them if they are willing to be named as public witnesses. If, and only if, they all agree, I will write an e-mail, reporting to the world what happened here."

And so she did.

I felt certain some would not be reachable, out of town someplace, and others would, at least, express some hesitation to be named.

Instead she reached them all. And without a single pause, everyone agreed. All were willing to be named. And so, below, they are.

Whoever this Person is, he came publicly in power and in affirmation, endorsing Y'shua as his crucified and resurrected Son, the Only Way to the heart of Yahweh, to the very same and very personal

God of Abraham, Isaac, and Moses. It was as if he said the words I merely thought while sitting on a plane several months ago, the time when a nervous stranger, with tears in his eyes, made an awkward effort to offer us himself. It was as if the Presence said,

Anyone who loves my wounded Son, loves me, and is a friend forever.

Wednesday, April 5th, 2000

So. Did God show up? Did he speak? Did he hold me? Did he really promise, "Taylor will live, grow up, become a dad"?

I say . . . Yes.

But, hey, believe what you want. It's not as if this is a private affair. Everyone is welcome to watch. Grab a seat. I don't think there's a bad one on the planet. And admission's free!

It's Taylor's life that's on the line. Not that he minds. He's gladly hopped up on the sacrificial altar. In spite of heroic efforts by the medical community to stay his execution, Death's hand is raised, poised to strike a blow that seems unavoidable.

But will it? Or has Death's strong arm been gripped by the stronger hand of God, who whispers, "Not this time. My Son already died for this one. Because of Y'shua, I Am staying this execution"?

All the evidence says Taylor will die, probably in three to six months. But the Voice inside my living room said he will grow up and have children.

Which should I believe? Physical evidence or an invisible promise? The clear opinion of brilliant doctors or the unambiguous voice of God confirmed by witnesses?

I choose the invisible promise from the unambiguous Voice.

We shall see. Take whatever positions you please. For now. But by all means, surrender to and follow the One who wins. He and he alone is the one true God.

Cool.

Brian

Husband to Debbie; Dad to Taylor, 11.84; also Dad to Christopher, 14.38, and Jonathan, 6.64—and coheir to all creation.

The Witness List
Chandler, John and Kim

Finto, Don

Garrett, Glenn and Kathy

Jordan, Mary

Schrauger, Brian and Debbie

Schrauger, Larry and Su

Smith, Debbie and Michael W.

Spirit, Holy

38 CONSTIPATION AND THE MOUSE

TOWARD THE END OF OUR TEN-DAY DREAM-MAKERS' trip to the land and seas of Disney, Taylor's blocked-up plumbing became a big, big deal.

This trip, a fabulous gift to Taylor and his family, came about thanks to generous contributions from countless unknown friends of Taylor (FOTs). They gave us everything: the trip plus spending money, frequent-flier miles, and hotel rooms. By faith these friends quenched the emotional thirst of our heroic but often anxious, bored, and lonely son. Even though we don't know who they are, they are not unknown. My prayer is that their reward will be spectacular.

Upon arrival in Orlando, Taylor was invited by the pilot to sit in the cockpit seat with the captain's hat atop his beaming head. Then for three days we lived in Disney World, where we went full speed, rampaging three main parks: the Magic Kingdom, Epcot, and MGM Studios. One night, with a special pass, Christopher, Taylor, and I played in the Magic Kingdom from 9 P.M. till midnight. We raced from ride to ride, all of which had shorter lines than during day-time hours.

That was the night I folded. For years Taylor had pined for a lava lamp. Two things kept him from getting one: They're ugly, and they're expensive.

"Taylor," I responded to his pleas throughout the years, "why do you want a sixty- to one-hundred-dollar lamp that has glowing purple blobs of ooey-gooey slime?"

But at a shop inside Disney's Magic Kingdom was the perfect lava lamp. No ooey-gooey globs. Instead a lamp of fluid, solid red, in which at least a thousand gleaming stars of tiny silver pieces glittered in the hot and scarlet light. On its top and bottom were a crown and base of metal colored midnight black, punched with tiny holes shaped like crescent moons and stars.

So we bought the thing, then for nine days carried it o'er land and sea and high through deep blue skies until, at last, it came to rest, unharmed and lit, inside Taylor's room. There, every day when the sun went down, it shed its soft, enchanting light under which, many hours later, Taylor finally fell asleep.

Early on the fourth morning of our Disney adventure we all climbed, sleepy-eyed, onto a large, lush bus. It drove us to the coast, right next to Cape Canaveral. There we met Captain Mickey, dutifully posed for pictures, then boarded the incredible *Disney Wonder*. The *Wonder* is a luxurious, enormous, eleven-story-high, brand-spankin'-new ship. There we lived in the nice (but fickle) lap of luxury for the next four days, traveling to the Bahamas and back. On the seas Taylor started to get tired. But still, he pushed. Hard.

He snorkeled, kayaked, swam in crystal ocean water; he ate free ice cream, went to shows aboard the ship, and shopped with pure delight, buying things for others as well as for himself. It was at night, usually during supper, when he could not bear to sit. Insisting he must leave, he retreated to his room. In part he was just weary. But I also knew, just like many other tourists, he'd not made a solid contribution to any flushing throne since home.

Still, he always rallied.

When the cruise was done, we weren't. Instead we went back to Orlando's Mouseville kingdom where we hit the parks again for two full days.

Along with the rest of us, Taylor did almost everything. Far and away, however, his favorite activity was playing in the water anywhere swimming was an option. He was 100 percent thrilled, delighted, to go in and out of water on a whim. After two years of tedious torture putting on and taking off tacky safety patches, the inanimate symbiote inside his chest, the cursed Hickman catheter, was *gone!* He was *FREE!*

Taylor's favorite day was the second to last, when we went to Typhoon Lagoon, one of Disney's water parks. One attraction there was a lazy river, a wide but shallow waterway circling the park. On and off all day, Taylor insisted that I join him in it. We hopped in separate tubes, holding one crutch each. With the silicon-padded handle protruding from each forearm prop, we hooked each other's tube then twirled and swirled in the currents, bumping into other tubes, splashing, even singing as we floated round and round and round.

Neither of us said so, but we knew. This was very special. It was the close connection of two happy aching hearts remembering an idyllic past, rejoicing in a glorious now. And mourning when someday our two tubes would float apart.

That same day at Typhoon Lagoon, Taylor rode some mild slides (mindful of his bottom) and played in the giant wave pool while I watched from out of sight. Since we did not have the camera, my eyes took pictures, freezing them inside my mind: a bushy blond-haired, one-leg'd boy standing in the shallow wake of a giant wave, alone but uninhibited, lost in total joy.

He also snorkeled with some sharks. It's true!

There is a place inside Typhoon Lagoon where swimmers who are willing can paddle on the surface of a pond. With goggles and a breathing tube, they look straight down at unshielded sharks who, mingling with stingrays, meander to and fro only several feet below.

Late that afternoon, wet but very happy, we three guys rode a jampacked bus back to our resort. We sat on a special bench near the back. Across the aisle toward the front, there was a boy, maybe eight years old, hiding in the shadows. Underneath the wide brim of his sun hat, two shy eyes peeked out. Wide with wonder, they were fixed on Taylor.

Taylor didn't see him, but I did. "Hey, Taylor!" I leaned over, whispering in his ear. "Don't look now, but there's a boy across the aisle who sees you but can't believe his eyes!"

Taylor didn't say a thing. But I saw his wheels turn. All he did at first was smile his impish, Mona Lisa grin. But when the boy stood up to get off the bus, several stops before our own, Taylor paralyzed him with these words . . .

"Hey! Guess what?" The boy stopped and looked into Taylor's eyes as he continued. "Y'know that place in the park today where we could swim with sharks?"

The boy nodded. Taylor lifted the empty left leg of his swimsuit.

"Well," he deadpanned, flapping the cloth up and down, "*that's* what happened to me!"

Eyes wide as silver dollars, the boy was rendered mute. He never said a word. His dad and I exchanged a knowing look and shared a silent laugh. And when the boy got off the bus we watched him meet and tell his mom, with emphatic gestures, the incredible shark story the one-leg'd kid just told him!

Every day throughout the trip, on land and sea, we ate Mouse food and drank Mouse drinks. And that made Taylor a bloated Mouseketeer. Which brings us to the pleasant subject of constipation. Crass as it may sound, constipation was a big deal, especially with respect to Taylor. Because of the large tumor in his central-left *puh-toosh* (as Taylor called it), right next to his rectum, we were constantly concerned about this exit at the rear.

In spite of valiant efforts using everything but Draino, eight days into Mouseville nothing had, or could, come out. The mounting pressure was so great Taylor had his first pain attack since visiting Mahesh six weeks before.

It was about a level five on the PITA scale. Not as bad as some he'd had, but a level five that lasted two hours was no fun—for Taylor or his family. In our hotel room Taylor held a pillow to his face to muffle moans, unbearable to Christopher and Jonathan. While lying at his side, I rubbed Taylor's upper back and shoulders. Eventually the suffering retreated.

Next day Taylor went full speed with Mom, ferocious in his zeal, hitting stores in Downtown Disney for last-minute acquisitions of Mouse gear to bring home. But when the sun went down on both Friday there and Saturday at home, the pain came back along with its companion, high anxiety. At last on Sunday afternoon, with the prayer-assisted aid of enough emollient to blast an adult into outer space, Taylor's "back door" finally came unblocked. Although Handel never intended it for this, we sang his "Hallelujah Chorus." We also prayed that Taylor, like the Energizer Bunny, would keep going and going and going and going and going . . .

39 BENNY AND THE CAT

A TAYLOR AND FAMILY REPORT

Wednesday, May 3rd, 2000

Thirteen days ago, Debbie, Taylor, and I joined at least ten thousand other people, including our good friends Barry and his wife, Sheila, at the Gaylord Entertainment Center in downtown Nashville for a long night of worship and *praise*. The whole meeting was conducted by one of *those* guys. For many years I've heard rumors about and caught glimpses of him while surfing channels on TV. His swoop of hair is perfect but must be harder than a helmet. His silky suits are immaculate, his articulation skills well honed. He offers everyone a "miracle from God," which, he claims, God is eager to endow on anyone who will "just believe it."

And the miracle that's offered? Healing from physical diseases.

My response to this man on TV, this one who in Y'shua's name claims a "ministry" of healing, has always been to gawk, roll my eyes, and groan, then quickly change the channel.

Yikes. My harsh heart is exposed. Lately I have heard an interesting axiom: "God will often offend the mind in order to reveal the heart." Must God fit only in *my* box? God forbid. If I've learned nothing else these past two years, I've learned, much to my dismay, that he does *not*.

So, thanks to Barry and Sheila, there we were, front and center, sitting on the second row surrounded by ten thousand, maybe more. We were there to learn and to receive whatever God would give us. This did not mean, however, that we unhitched our minds.

When Taylor wasn't in pain, he thought various parts of the four-hour(!) service were either boring, fascinating, or fun. His main problem that night came from periodic pain attacks. But even when he hurt, he usually stayed involved. Hence, while thousands round us sang, "Hallelujah, Hallelujah," Taylor tugged at my sleeve and sang into my ear, "*Ooow*-lelujah, *Ooow*-lelujah . . ."

Ironically, his worst bout with tumor pain began and ended with the show's dramatic declarations of healing. In between the waves of his attack Taylor pulled me down to whisper-shout in my ear, "Boy, oh boy, Dad, healing *hurts!*"

I laughed but also thought, *He prob'ly doesn't know it, but he's right.*

Armed with lots of liquid morphine, the pain did, at last, recede. As it did, hundreds of people came to the platform right in front of us, claiming they had just been healed. Then, without exception, each one was "slain in the Spirit." Cushioned by men who stood behind them ("catchers"), they fell flat on their backs and *spazzed* with jerks and wobbling body parts as if epileptic. It was quite a scene.

In any public meeting that's long or loud, Taylor usually has pain. When he does, he always insists we take him home. But not that night. He endured the pain until it passed and never asked to leave. So we stayed. We even got to meet the preacher backstage at almost midnight.

The TV-preacher-healer-man could not have been kinder. He quietly listened to a brief summary of Taylor's condition, shaking his head with sorrow. Then, asking two others to join him, he made the time to softly pray for Taylor's healing.

Whoa! I thought. *This guy's all right. No less flawed than the rest of us. But, perhaps, no more so either. Within the complexity of all he is, here is a truly compassionate man.*

Later I remembered my response to the man on the plane several months ago: *Anyone who loves my wounded son, loves me, and is a friend forever.*

So too is this TV-preacher-healer-man.

He is my friend forever.

When we finally left that night, walking to the car, Barry said, "So, Taylor. Did you feel anything when he prayed for you?"

"Nooo," Taylor answered. "But can we come again tomorrow?"

"If you wanna come again, we'll come," I replied. "But why don't you sleep on it and let me know how you feel about it after you wake up?"

When he did, he still wanted to go back.

"Y'know, Dad, it is kind of a pain to go again. I mean, I'd much rather do somethin' with one o' my friends—like have him spend the night or play a game on my PlayStation." He paused and frowned, then calmly said, "But . . . on the other hand . . . I guess it is my life that's at stake."

"That's true," I agreed. "And special meetings can be helpful . . . as long as you don't think you *have* to go in order for God to do something special in your life. It's *his* choice. If he's going to heal your body, he'll do it no matter what you do or where you are. He could do it right here in your room.

"Are you with me?"

"Yeah," he pondered with a pause. "But I'd really like to go . . . *if* it's okay with you."

And so, on the evening of Good Friday, we went again. Sixteen thousand filled the place. This time Taylor had a lot less pain—and much more participation. Prompted to "lift up your hands if you want to be healed," Taylor stretched his arms high as they could go. Once again, he leaned on me for balance.

When, after several minutes, his upraised arms got tired, he whispered in my ear, "Dad, would you help me hold up my arms?"

"Sure, buddy. No problem."

After a while it was time to bring 'em down. As he did so, he grinned, leaned over, and said, "Y'know, Dad, you holdin' my arms up like that kinda reminds me of the time when Aaron and Hur held up Moses' tired arms."

"Me too," I choked. "Me too." Then I thought, but didn't say, *Just like you've been holding up mine . . . Just like you've been holding up mine . . .*

That night, after declarations of healing, Taylor turned to me with watery eyes. "Dad? I think, maybe, the bump on my tumor might've shrunk a little bit!"

Just above his bottom, the Mutha is now trying to poke through his skin. The bump looks like a reddish purple misplaced elbow bone.

"So, do ya want to go up front and tell him?"

"Noooo," he answered, wavering.

Later, though, when the stage was swamped with teens, Taylor felt more comfortable and was, in fact, summoned by my new strange friend, the preacher, up onto the stage. I hopped up too, steering Taylor toward some chairs where he would not be hit by falling flopping kids.

If Taylor falls down, I'm gonna be there to catch him. No way I'm gonna let him bump that tumor, I determined to myself.

But when he came to Taylor, the preacher did not yell, "Fire on ya!" like he did to most. Instead, without a word, he embraced Taylor and held him close while his lips moved in soundless prayer.

"Hey, buddy!" I asked him afterward, "what'd he say when he prayed?"

"Dunno," Taylor answered. "I could kinda hear some words, but it was just too loud in there."

"Huh. So did you feel anything when he prayed for you?" I asked again, thinking of the Mutha.

"Yeah," he drolled, "it kinda hurt my nose when he hugged me."

There was brief hope the tumor might have shrunk. But within a day, and ever since, it's clear the tumors have not shrunk or gone away. Prompted by a relentless level four of chronic pelvic pain, yesterday Taylor went to Vanderbilt for a new set of CT scans.

And as I write, THESE RESULTS JUST IN . . .

There are new tumors in both lungs.

The large tumor at the base of Taylor's right lung has grown "significantly," from five to seven centimeters in its largest dimension.

There is a new, small lesion on the dome of Taylor's liver.

The pelvic mass has grown by about 20 percent. It "displaces the bladder to the right and appears intimately associated with the rectum. However there is no evidence of bowel obstruction."

In summary, there is clear "progression of metastatic disease . . ."

A word of truth breaks through. Numb with sorrow and with death on every side, I go home, again, with news . . .

Brian

Husband to Debbie; Dad to Taylor, 11.91; also Dad to Christopher, 14.46, and Jonathan, 6.72.

40 THE MATRIX

AT BEDTIME ON FRIDAY, MAY 3RD, I SAT ON TAYLOR'S bed and said, "Buddy, we need to talk."

"What about, Dad?"

"Well, your doctor called this afternoon then faxed stuff to my office. We've got results from yesterday's CT."

Taylor didn't cry. But his eyes bled intelligent awareness. Agony. Grief.

As for myself, I had dreaded this necessary conversation. But once it finally started, I was stunned by the atmospheric change inside my inner landscape. The terrifying storm on my soul's stony shore, with all its angry drowning waves, was gone. At least for now. It was as if God himself whispered the command:

Peace. Be still.

From this calm, this eerie, sunlit eye, I continued.

"There's good news and bad news. But mostly it's bad. Good news is that the pelvic tumor doesn't look like it's blocking your bowel. Bad news is that all the tumors have grown. And for the first time the cancer has spread to a major organ outside your lungs. There's a small spot, a lesion, on top of your liver.

"*You*, of course, are perfectly safe. But your *body*, already in big trouble, isn't winning this fight. Now, that doesn't mean God can't step in and heal. He can. Maybe he will. But he hasn't yet. And he might not."

Taylor nodded that he understood. For a moment we sat. Then he softly said, "I thought so . . ."

Taking a deep breath I looked him in the eye and saw a man.

Several months ago Taylor surprised me with the news he had, in fact, hit puberty. Since that day I've watched him change. His body has matured. His face has lost that prepubescent look. His blond hair is so thick water rolls right off it. Now with a stylish cut, he often takes twenty minutes in the bathroom, moussing it just right before going out in public.

His almost-teenage manner and his blossoming appearance are pleasing to my eye. They tickle and delight me. Lately I've begun to see the emerging build and features of the man Taylor has already been for a long, long time.

Speaking man to man, I said, "There are some things I'd like to say to you, if that's okay."

When he nodded his consent, I added, "We both know I can talk too much." This evoked a faint, wry grin. "So, if I get to a point where I've said enough, just tell me to shut up, okay?"

He agreed. Smart kid. Best friend. Wise man.

Eye to eye, both pairs dry and somber, I dived in.

"You know there are thousands of people praying for you." He waited for me to continue. "Lots of them sincerely believe you're going to be healed. I hope and pray they're right." Lightly squeezing the wonderfully soft but tensile feel of his strong right leg, I hastened to add, to emphasize . . . "But healing, at least in your body, is not what's going on. We must not pretend, we will not pretend, this bad report is meaningless or unimportant. We will not ignore or try to wish away the truth.

"Here's what's true: The truth is that all cancer's nasty. But the kind of cancer in your body is one of the worst. And it's spreading so fast, you just might be walking on two new legs a lot sooner than we'd like.

"It's also true that God, not cancer, is in control. Cancer has not and cannot go anywhere in your body without his permission. And he might let it go farther. A lot farther. That's sure how it looks right now.

"But no matter where he lets it go, no matter what he lets it do, he will give you nothing less than *his* power, *his* presence, even his dry wit—which in the face of Death is worse than spit!

"God will do this for you because he's already given you a gift *nothing—no one*—can ever take away. He's given you himself. As if it was yesterday, God remembers, God knows, what it's like to suffer an unjust painful death. But the reason he *remembers*, the reason he *knows*, is because he beat it!

"Now he lives inside. Remember the day you invited him to move in? Because you did, the two of you are linked. And nothing, absolutely nothing, can ever break that bond.

"So the *truth* is, no matter what happens here, the two of you have already conquered cancer. This body *will* die." Again I squeezed his leg.

"Our only question is, 'When?' If your body isn't healed and this cancer wins, even then you beat it. Because cancer cannot beat the *two* of you.

"You know all about suffering. You know it very well. But in days and months ahead, you must also remember, remember, *remember,* something else you know: *No* amount of suffering, *no* amount of pain, not even Death itself, can break the link God has forged in his own blood with you.

"And *that's* the Truth. You with me?"

Again he nodded.

"Good. Well, based on the Truth, there are two things I think you've gotta do. Is it okay if I keep talking? Or should I shut up?"

"Go ahead," Taylor said, still sober. "Don't worry, I'll letcha know."

I plowed ahead.

"All right, two things I think you've gotta do . . . First of all, you've gotta pray—on your own, all the time. Just do the best you can. Tell God exactly what you feel, what you want, what you need. This doesn't have to be anything fancy. You don't have to have a lot of words. The important thing is to keep—an—open—line."

I briefly raised my eyebrows. With his eyes, Taylor telepathed he understood.

"That leads to the other thing. You've gotta *listen* to God . . . for—your—self. Keep reading your Bible and listen—hard.

"Then, because you've prayed . . . on—your—own . . . and listened to God . . . for—your—self . . . then, *then,* you'll be able to think for yourself, to make your own decisions.

"The reason this is so important is because it's really easy to let other people do all the praying, all the listening for you. Then before you know it, almost automatically, they're making your decisions too.

"There are two problems with this. First of all, there are decisions coming up that belong only to you. No one else. Just you.

"The other problem is that everybody, and I mean everybody, is at least a little screwed up—and some of us, a lot!

"Think about it . . . Everybody farts. But almost nobody wants to talk about it, let alone admit it. In fact, most people tend to think that suffering and death are somehow less obscene as topics to discuss. These are the ones who when they fart are most likely to pretend they didn't or flat out deny it: 'Wasn't me!' Because they wish they didn't fart, especially in public, they pretend they don't. In fact, lots of people pretend so well, they actually believe it—even when others all around them are choking on fresh methane!

"It's called 'wishful thinking.' But it isn't like a story. Instead it's like a virus that has infected the entire world. And if this virus messes up the way people think about farts, just think how much it messes up their thinking about suffering and death!

"Here's the *bottom* line: It's easy for other people to think they've heard God when they haven't. Or, if they have heard him, to not understand what he meant. I'm not saying you shouldn't listen to other people. You should listen, but to some more than others—like Mom and Dad.

"But once you've listened, take everything—no matter what it is, no matter who said it—take it all to God. Then listen to *him*. After that, take the choices he gives you and, with his help, make your own decisions.

"Now . . . there are gonna be times when you're uncertain and confused. When this happens, still, *still,* make your own decisions. As long as you keep seeking him, God will never let you wander down a road he doesn't want you on. Yes, there will be times when you decide to let someone else make certain choices. But the only reason you do is because they're yours to give away.

"So, buddy, it's time for me to ask you something. I know you know what other people think God has told them about the cancer. But what about you? Have you heard anything from him about what's going to happen?"

Taylor's features reconfigured into agony. Tears flowed. In between sobbing gasps, he protested, "Do we have to talk about it now??? Can't we talk about it later???"

I blew a lengthy sigh and stroked his cheek.

"It stinks, buddy. The whole thing really stinks. But the reason it really stinks is because it's really there. Sooo . . . yeah, we've gotta talk about it now. *And* later."

We sat in silence, a momentary pause broken by an answer full of fear. Not fear for himself. Fear for me.

"I'm pretty sure I'm gonna die."

The statement sat there during several breaths, truth no longer hidden. Then in utter agony Taylor protested with a desperate wail, "But I'm not ready to die yet!"

I kissed him on the forehead. "It's okay, buddy. It's okay. Just please remember it's not your job to carry stuff that belongs to Mom, your brothers, me. It's God's job to take care of us, not yours.

"As for not feeling ready, I'm not ready either. On the other hand, whether in three months or seventy years, when the time comes *God* will make you ready for your journey Home."

"Y'know, Dad," he responded, calmer now. "Over the past coupla months I knew God could heal me, even that he might . . . But I don't think it's gonna happen that way."

"Me either, buddy." My voice was soft, sandwiched on both sides by the high-pitched whine of modern silence. "I hate it. But I also think your body's gonna die from this damnable cancer.

"But remember this. No matter what we think or how we feel, God's going to do what he wants to do. So, we're gonna keep on asking that he heal you. Still, our *first* request is that he'll make the *real* you grow and prosper no matter what the stupid cancer does.

"And if God does bring you Home? One thing's for sure—it will be fabulous beyond your wildest dreams! Yes, I'll be sad. But I'll be jealous too. Very jealous. Just remember, if you get There first—and if God lets you—be sure to keep on prayin' for your old dad!

"Why would God let this happen? I think there are two reasons. One reason is to rescue you from something worse you would go through if you kept on living here. The other is because you are God's prophet. He sent you to show the rest of us that, with his help, we too can endure any kind of suffering, any kind of death, with humor and with grace.

"When that happens, people who remember you, those who turn to Y'shua because they saw him in you, all of them will become your sons and daughters. *That's* how God will make you the daddy you've always wanted to be. But unlike most dads, you're going to have hundreds, prob'ly thousands of children! Cool, huh?!"

Taylor grinned then politely said, "Hey, Dad? 'Member what you said about me tellin' you something?"

I laughed. "Time to shut up, huh?"

"Yeah." Taylor smiled. "Let's see what's on TV before we go to bed."

Turns out *The Matrix* was on HBO, a fun movie with a great premise: *Reality isn't anything like the way it seems.*

"Did you catch that, Taylor?"

"Yeah. Cool!"

Then we went to bed, sleeping long and well. And that night Taylor had no pain.

41 THE EYES HAVE IT

USUALLY DEBBIE TOOK TAYLOR TO HIS APPOINTMENTS at the clinic. But on Monday, May 15th, I did. Mainly because I wanted

Taylor's doctor, an authority he respects, to make it very clear, as he had to me, that new experimental treatments would not be worth the effort. In light of our conversation, Taylor needed to hear this for himself then make his own decision.

Instead, much to my surprise, his physician hemmed and hawed, using words I knew Taylor couldn't understand. "You could do this, or that, or that, or that," was the essence of his advice.

With frequent interruptions in order to interpret for Taylor's ears, I finally said, "Doctor, I'd really like you to tell Taylor about the odds, just as I was told several weeks ago."

That's when he really got nervous.

"I'm not saying you *have* to do any of these things," he almost pleaded, talking more to me than Taylor. "But, you know me," he continued, eyes darting all around, his voice a little shaky. "I'm an eternal optimist. No matter what the odds, I like to think there's always hope."

Instead of gentle clarity, what Taylor heard was anxious ambiguity. Not because his doctor didn't care. Just the opposite. He loved Taylor so much, it was simply too hard to calmly face this boy, his patient, and in essence say, "We've lost. The cancer's going to win. Live it up. Have all the fun you can. And I'll make sure you don't have any pain." Still, Taylor saw something I missed, something more than his doctor's complicated words. Afterward he told me, "Know what, Dad? There were a coupla times I thought he was gonna *cry*."

As we drove away Taylor made it clear he wanted to look into some of the studies. He wanted to fight, not quit. Inside myself I groaned. Looking at my watch I said, "Hey, buddy, remember Vanderbilt's groundbreaking ceremony this afternoon? It starts in about an hour. Mom said you were invited as a special guest. How 'bout we stick around? Are you up to it? There'll prob'ly be free food!"

"Yeah, I'm okay. Let's go."

And so, not knowing what it would be like, we did.

The event was the groundbreaking ceremony for the new Monroe Carell Jr. Vanderbilt Children's Hospital. Taylor and I arrived thirty minutes early. Almost right away, we were accosted by a photographer who shot a lot of pictures. On his heels other smiling people came up to say, "Hi, Taylor!" The general consensus was . . . "You've changed! Look at all that hair! Why, I hardly recognize you! My, but you look handsome!"

Taylor beamed. Before we left the house he had spent a lot of time moussing his hair just right, especially the front, which he made to stand up straight, like the edge of a well-trimmed hedge.

"Taylor!" the event's administrator said, "I didn't think you'd be able to come today. But I am thrilled you're here. We have a place for you to sit, up on stage, with three other children. Would you like to join them?"

"Do it, buddy!" I whispered in his ear. "You'll get to be on the news!"

Delighted but feigning an aw-shucks look, Taylor let himself be ushered to a front-row seat, not only in front of the cameras, but also smack-dab next to the podium.

Still early, I stood behind the couple hundred chairs, admiring the view of heroic wounded children, especially my striking son: handsome and polite, agile and persistent. A man.

My reverie was interrupted by a nervous, anxious-looking doctor. He was the same one with whom Taylor and I met about an hour earlier. This time I saw for myself the extra moisture in his eyes. "Brian, I just want you to know that I'm not trying to push you toward any of the options we discussed. If you choose not to pursue any of them, I just want you to know that I will support that." His tone was almost desperate.

"I understand. And thank you . . . By the way, after we left your office, Taylor said he wants to be at Camp Horizon the same week you'll be there, just like the last two summers."

His eyes turned down. "That would be great," he said, then quickly shook my hand and walked away.

Rattled by his manner, especially by his eyes, I looked for a place where I could stand away from the growing crowd, someplace where I could clearly see Taylor but not be obvious to others. I saw the perfect spot. It was just behind the TV cameras toward the front and side, stage left. Someone else was there. Still, I went.

"Dr. Pietsch!" I said, sticking out my hand. "Mind if I join you?" He agreed.

John Pietsch had operated on Taylor four times. He put in the Hickman then, almost two years later, took it out. He also did two thoracotomies, removing tumors along with pieces of both lungs. Pietsch is quiet, maybe just a little shy. But he exudes intelligence. Determination. His eyes are quick to twinkle or to flash. His smile is real but minimal. His wit is dry but razor sharp. I'd often thought he was a man like Taylor—and like Taylor someday would be.

"Dr. Pietsch, I know you're not an oncologist. But I also know you are a pro and you've seen Taylor's latest CT pictures. Do you mind if I ask you a question?"

"Not at all," he answered, smiling with kind eyes.

"Well, here's the deal." I did not look at his face while I spoke.

"Taylor and I just met with his doctor earlier this afternoon. He laid out a number of possible experimental treatment plans we might consider. I'm not a doctor, but my strong inclination is not to pursue any of them. Taylor would have to go out of town, away from friends and familiar surroundings. Most treatments would make him feel worse. And all this sacrifice, all this added discomfort, for therapies that cannot save his life.

"I don't think any of them are worth it. Do you? What do you think?" I asked, turning my face back toward his.

His eyes were still kind but no longer smiled. They seemed to have more water than they needed. "I agree with you," he said.

I quickly looked away, fighting for composure. Not quite succeeding, my voice wobbled. But I charged ahead and said, "My inclination is to do everything possible to make Taylor comfortable, to enjoy life all we can, but to stick with the course of palliative care . . . As a doctor, but especially as a dad, do you agree with me on this?"

I took a chance and looked him in the eye again. This time I saw sadness, grief for Taylor . . . and for me. "I agree," he said again, eyes almost overflowing.

I turned away but stood beside him. My throat ached with swallowed sobs. Hot tears rolled down both cheeks before plunging to the pavement like divers doing suicidal cannonballs. They splashed and then evaporated—out of eyes, out of sight, disappearing in thin air.

"I'm sorry," I choked out sideways to a fellow dad, apologizing for loss of control. I didn't want to embarrass him, make him feel uncomfortable.

"That's okay," he said. "That's okay."

I knew he meant it.

We watched while dark suits spoke, introducing dignitaries and celebrities, everyone on stage except the four heroic children until, at the end, as an apparent afterthought, the moderator stuttered through their names.

People clapped politely. Maybe I did too. But throughout the ceremony, all I saw was Taylor, posture perfect, leg curled on the seat, face intent and focused on each (mostly boring) speaker. He was a living sculpture of pure beauty, utterly oblivious to his radiant self (as true beauty always is).

Afterward, while looking for him, I ran into a number of other doctors, including Ian Burr. Like all the others, he shook my hand, looked me in the eye, and said how good it was to have Taylor there. I looked back and thanked him only to see red lines around his retinas, cracks in a leaking dam of sorrowful conviction. Afraid my own might burst again, I quickly moved away.

Like bright residual spots from a camera's flash, Taylor's vision remained suffused with the happiness of the event—even though he felt some pain as, out of the spotlight, we headed home alone inside our darkened van. The only things suffusing me, like high-resolution photographs, crystal clear, were eyes. Eyes I saw at the groundbreaking. Especially the doctors'.

Although no one ever said so, if medical professionals could foresee the outcome of Taylor's fight . . .

The eyes had it.

Inside the van, driving down the freeway, focusing on traffic, I speak.
"Hey, Taylor?"

"Yeah, Dad?"

"While you were being famous, I saw Dr. Pietsch."

"Really? I wondered where you were. I tried to look around and find you but couldn't."

"Actually I was pretty close but over on your left, behind the TV cameras. Anyway, I told him about our meeting earlier today, about different treatments you might, or might not, choose."

"So, what does he think?"

"That's what I asked him, both as a doctor and a dad."

"And?"

"Well, he doesn't think they're worth it."

"Really . . ."

"Yeah. And you need to know, I agree."

"Will you still call and see about 'em?"

"Sure, if that's what you want," I lied.

"Well, yeah . . . if you don't mind."

"Nah, I don't mind. Love you, buddy."

"Love you too, Dad. I wonder what's for supper."

 ## 42 UNCOMMON SCENTS

BY MID-MAY, TAYLOR'S ONLY COMFORTABLE POSTURE for sleep was kneeling—single knee on the floor, his torso on the bed. Any other nighttime posture was just too painful. Every time he went to sleep it was on his red and swollen knee, padded with a pillow.

Debbie and I continued to put our hands on Taylor and pray. We asked God for spiritual vitality, courage, freedom from pain, and healing. In response, God continued to grant the first two requests but denied the latter.

Grateful for the gift of Taylor's awesome spirit, we still asked . . . Why??? Why the refusals???

Medication helped control the complex pain—still that unusual mixture of phantom pain, related to the amputation, along with conventional pain from the growing pelvic tumor. So far Taylor had not felt more than mild discomfort from the growing tumors in his lungs. Slowly but surely, however, he faced an increased shortage of breath. Some of his episodes with respiratory distress were triggered by anxiety. But increasingly all it took to get winded was an effort as simple as going upstairs to his room. As his spirit grew stronger, his body grew weaker.

"You know, Dad, more and more it's like my body can't keep up with *me!*" Always said with a mixture of surprise, irritation, and curiosity, implying, *Weird! How can this be?*

One evening I spent the night in Taylor's room. Just before we did communion, Taylor stood and scooted to turn off the TV. As he punched the remote, he turned and looked at me. His face was serious, surprised. Then he struck with unexpected words . . .

"Dad? Remember what you told me? . . . *If* God takes me Home to Heaven, it'll partly be because he's rescuing me from something worse?"

"Yeah, I remember."

Twelve days had passed since that conversation. Since then, however, nothing had been said about these subjects. Now, out of the blue, Taylor zeroed in on one small part of what we discussed.

"Know what?" Taylor continued. "That makes me feel kinda *good.*" His tone and face reflected astonished bewilderment. How could he actually feel *good* about this? And yet, he did!

"Cool, buddy!" But what I felt was shock. There had been no warning this was coming. Mind racing, I breathed a silent prayer and continued.

"Remember how I told you to listen to God for yourself? Well, guess what? You heard him! *That* is how he often does it . . . He takes something that you've read or heard and focuses your heart on it. And when the message is from him, something special just for you, he fills you with his peace—even joy!"

"So, Dad, do you think that means I'm gonna die?"

I thought so. He thought so. This too had been discussed. But this time I chickened out. Avoiding his eyes I answered . . .

"Well . . . maybe. But technic'ly it sounds like God only told you the reason why—*if* he decides to bring you Home." Both of us knew what I pretended not to know. "And keep in mind," I hurried on, "because of Y'shua, it's only our bodies that die, not *us*."

Later on, going to sleep and staying asleep was a night-long battle. Whenever pain woke Taylor up, I scrambled to get him a worm. (*Worms* are what we called his squirts of liquid morphine, so named because whenever Taylor needed them, he tilted back his head and opened up his mouth like a baby bird, desperate to be fed.)

The rest of the night, when pain only haunted Taylor's body and his dreams but didn't wake him up, I scooted over on the bed and whispered in his ear, "It's okay. You are all right. You're safe. I'm here."

I prayed a lot of silent prayers. Often too I buried my face in his bristly blond hair and inhaled.

Friday, May 19th, 2000

Cancer stinks.

But when I see Taylor I see Light, not Darkness. When I inhale his scent, I smell Life, not Death.

Even at the brink in unspeakable grief, whenever I see him, whenever I touch him, when in his absence I think about him, I feel hope, not despair. Companionship and thunderous applause, *not* silent isolation. *Not* nothingness. How can this be???

There must be an awesome symbiotic Someone inside the all-too-mortal vessel of my precious son. And as that vessel breaks, even as it's crushed, more and more of that awesome Someone is revealed . . . with a startling fresh scent of spring-like sweetness, with a glory unmatched by any transcendent vision.

As his body suffers, Taylor's spirit is sometimes wounded, sometimes weary. But in the main it is a growing giant, larger, stronger in every way—in wit, in curiosity, in knowledge. And most of all, in love.

Could there be any greater miracle in his life than this? Eradication of the cancer? Regeneration of a new left leg? Much as I still pray for these things, even if they're granted, c'mon!

None of these prospective miracles could *begin* to compare with the *already* present, *already* visible miracle of Taylor's unstoppable, unquenchable spirit. And so as his body suffers, even in my anger and dismay, I smell the scent of Life, not Death.

And sometimes I catch a glimpse of that Someone inside Taylor. Someone with whom he is closely linked. Someone who, for the sake of Love, will not, could not, ever let him go. Smack-dab in the middle of this horror, inside the very heart of Taylor's suffering, I see Y'shua. And in him I see nothing less than the fullness and the glory of God himself living inside my wounded son.

And I weep such complicated tears . . .

Brian

Husband to Debbie; Dad to Taylor, 11.96; also Dad to Christopher, 14.50, and Jonathan, 6.76.

43   TAYLOR'S CROSS

"SO WHAT DO YOU WANT FOR YOUR BIRTHDAY?" I asked Taylor.

"Wellll . . . maybe a watch," he answered. "But you know what I *really* want."

"Yeah, I know. Wanna look at some?"

"Sure!"

It was Saturday afternoon, the twentieth day of May. After going to the movie *Dinosaur!* the boys and I were killing time at a nearby mall. Suddenly we screeched to a halt in front of a store displaying countless crosses and chains. "Tell you what, buddy," I told Taylor. "You find one you like and I'll get it for you now. It'll be an early birthday present, okay?"

"All right!"

He proceeded to carefully examine almost every tiny cross hanging in each cabinet, settling, at last, on one that wasn't plain but on which there hung the Son. Above his head were the letters, INRI, a Latin acrostic that stands for "Y'shua of Nazareth, King of the Jews."

"Sure you don't want a plain gold cross, Taylor? Some of those are pretty nice."

"No," he firmly said. "I really want one like this."

We made the purchases: a small gold crucifix and a thin gold chain. Thrilled, Taylor wore his present home, often pulling out the cross from underneath his shirt to look at it and gently touch the tortured hanging Man.

"Happy birthday, buddy."

"Thannnk yeeeew, Da-ad!" he answered with playful exaggeration.

The next day was Sunday. Both of us slept in. These days almost every night we stayed up late and fell asleep together. As Taylor wearied of the battle, he really wanted me closer than the other room. No longer comfortable with Dempsey's nighttime company (she tended to bump his pelvic tumor), Taylor often took the risk and asked, "Hey, Dad? . . . Would you . . . *mind* staying here with me tonight?"

"You bet. I'd love to. Just let me brush my teeth and grab my pillow."

Under the soft red light of his sparkly lava lamp, he would fall asleep, knee on the floor, torso on the bed, head on a feather pillow. Scooting over, I placed my hand on his back, then his head, and sometimes softly stroked his cheek. He almost always won the race to dreamland. Usually around 4 or 5 A.M., I woke up, stumbled to my bed, slept in, woke up again, and exercised.

That afternoon about twelve people came to our house to pray for Taylor. When I reminded Taylor they were coming, his eyes, at first, flashed displeasure at the inconvenience.

"Buddy," I explained, "they're coming here because they love you. You're welcome to join them when we pray or, if you want, you can just say hi then hide out in your room."

"I guess I'll prob'ly join ya." This was a first . . .

"That'd be great. But if you do, *remember* what I told you. No matter what other people pray or say, talk with God and listen to him for *yourself.* I promise, he'll make his voice clear to *you.*"

"Okay, Dad," he sighed, adding a clear but silent groan that meant, *I know, I know . . .*

While people prayed, Taylor sat on a cushion. It looked like he was in the middle of a football huddle while athletes gathered round him. Some stood, heads bowed. Others fell to their knees.

As they prayed, I peeked. Taylor's head was bent in earnest contemplation. And in his hand, pulled out again from underneath his shirt, was that golden cross on which hung The Man. With a deep furrow in his brow and eyes shut tight, Taylor gently rubbed his cross.

Then I understood.

What Taylor needed most was not an empty shiny cross. He needed a bloody one with God himself in agonizing pain, nailed, dying, hanging on it.

For Taylor, strength and hope could only come from a God who in his viscera knows pain. Cruel suffering. Death. Who then, but only *after* this, won. And did it all *for Taylor*.

All the prayers that afternoon were passionate, each one begging God to heal. At my request, most remembered to also pray for Taylor's spirit. And there were some tears—by which, more than any words, I was comforted. To me they were precious gifts of love, purest liquid diamonds erupting up and out from deep inside the soul.

After prayers were done I felt compelled to speak, but really did not want to. Nervous, heart pounding, I cleared my throat and said, "Excuse me. I have a message from God to share with you." The looks that shot my way were no less shocked than mine.

"Each of you today, along with thousands more these past two years, came to bring God's healing touch to Taylor. And, in fact, you have. For this we are grateful. But bringing God's touch to Taylor was never the main event.

"The main reason God brought you into our lives as part of Taylor's story was to bring his healing touch to you—*through Taylor*. He wants you to know this. What you do with the information is up to you."

Late that evening, after pizza and TV, the rest of the family was long since in bed. Taylor and I shared communion in his room. That's when I gently probed, "So how are you feeling about all this?" by which I meant the apparently unstoppable cancer—or, more accurately, unstopped by God.

"Okay, I guess," he answered. "I just wish I didn't have so many decisions to make!" His voice was heavy, troubled.

"What decisions?" I asked, although with a sinking heart I knew the answer.

"You know . . . decisions about whether or not to try an experimental treatment. And if I do, which one."

As I had emphasized (overemphasized?), Taylor was thinking for himself. But this was a burden he didn't have to carry.

"Oh . . . I understand. But ya know what, buddy?"

"What?"

"Those decisions simply aren't an option right now. In light of your body's condition, they're just not available. You don't have to worry about that stuff anymore. We're at a point where all decisions about your health are up to God alone. Okay?"

"Okay," he answered, exhaling with a sigh that sounded like relief. As if to say, *Whew! Glad that burden's off my back!*

Once we were positioned on his bed under the glow of the twinkly red light, I leaned over and wearily whispered my half of our litany. "Good night! I love you! See you in the morning!"

On bended knee, cross around his neck, and already almost out, he mumbled back, changing the order as always. "See you in the morning . . . Good night . . . I love you, too."

And then we went to sleep.

44 THIN AIR

A TAYLOR AND FAMILY REPORT

Monday Noon, May 22nd, 2000

This morning's surgical procedure, insertion of an intrathecal catheter at the base of Taylor's spine, was supposed to be short and simple. It was neither.

Debbie called me at the office just after Taylor was rolled away. She told me his left lung is surrounded by fluid. As a result that lung cannot expand or contract. It cannot breathe. In effect it has been suffocated, not drowned. No wonder Taylor's been so short of breath.

When this was discovered prior to surgery, Taylor's thoracic surgeon, Dr. Pietsch, recommended the fluid not be drained right now. Two reasons: The percentage of oxygen in Taylor's bloodstream is 87 percent. It should be 94, but it could be worse. Eighty-seven percent is like living in thin air at the base camp of Mount Everest. The body is forced to acclimate, but its life is not endangered. Taylor's fingertips are slightly blue, but I'm told he is okay. With supplemental oxygen, he doesn't *have* to use his left lung.

So why not drain the fluid anyway? According to Dr. Pietsch, if it was drained, it would refill—probably quite fast. And if a drainage tube stayed in, Taylor would be miserable. He knows what they are like from two surgeries last August—and he *hates* them. Bottom line? There is no reason to add to his discomfort, especially since a drainage tube probably wouldn't help all that much.

Still, Taylor's respiratory limitation presented an anesthetic challenge. This morning's procedure should have taken fifteen to thirty minutes. Instead it took almost two hours.

As I write, Taylor's in recovery. It's been a long time, but once again he's a resident at Vanderbilt. At least for two more days.

Debbie will stay with him from midmorning to midafternoon. I'll be there every night. He'll never be alone.

Separately, I thought you'd like to know . . .

Taylor turns twelve on Sunday, June 4th.

I guess he's kinda burned out on e-mail. But he still loves to open envelopes. If you're so inclined, please send your birthday greetings to our home address.

Much, much thanks for loving our weary warrior son.

God bless . . .

Brian

Husband to Debbie; Dad to Taylor, 11.96; also Dad to Christopher, 14.51, and Jonathan, 6.77 (all growing far too fast). And still reluctant guardian of Dempsey the farting boxer.

PART IV
WALKING TAYLOR HOME

45 MIND AWAKE

A TAYLOR AND FAMILY REPORT

Thursday, May 25th, 2000

"Guess what, Dad?" Taylor hoarsely whispered last Monday afternoon. He was awake for the first time since minor surgery earlier that day. His raspy voice sounded like an adolescent version of Marlon Brando's *Godfather*. The only thing missing was cotton balls stuffed up both cheeks.

"This time when they took me into surgery, I remembered more than ever before!" Intense, competitive, curious, Taylor's tried for two years to maintain conscious awareness all the way down the slide into anesthetic sleep.

"When the doctor put on the gas mask, I said, 'So long!' And then . . . you know what it's like to see red squares swimming in black when you shut your eyes? Well, that's what I saw next. It felt like I was spinning round and round and round." As he spoke he lightly spun his head.

"When that happened, I knew I was still able to talk. So I said, 'Almost gone! Bye!'"

Enormously proud of this accomplishment, he qualified a bit, admitting, "Maybe I just thought I said that last part . . ."

Later I asked the doctor if, in fact, Taylor'd said out loud, "Almost gone! Bye!"

Grinning, he confirmed it. "In fact, when all of us on the [surgical] team heard the words, our first reaction was to look around at each other, wondering who said it. Then we realized it was *Taylor!* What a kid!"

Monday night started well. We talked and watched a movie. But then it turned bad. Really bad.

Taylor felt the need to urinate but couldn't. Winded and weary he ruefully protested, "I've forgotten how to pee!"

Then came spasms in his colon. A simple tablet of Imodium finally won that battle. But I had to go to war with, and almost draw blood from, a childish medical intern in order to get the Imodium. *(Arrrgggggghhhhhh!)* Once Taylor took it, sleep finally came at about eleven-thirty.

But it didn't last for long.

By three in the morning Taylor had been out of surgery for fifteen hours and still had not urinated—an important postsurgical function. Concern led to a decision. A Foley catheter had to be inserted. I cringed in empathetic agony. It didn't work.

Frustrated and worried, it was pulled out. (Just writing about it makes me wince.)

Then, ten minutes after the failed attempt, much to everyone's relief (so to speak), Taylor was able to go—a lot! Holding him steady as he stood by the bed, I cheered.

Then, almost immediately, celebration ceased.

In the process of getting out of bed and standing up, the new threadlike tube in Taylor's back came out of its socket, an opening no bigger than a needle's eye. A puddle of liquid morphine dripped onto the floor.

At five-thirty Tuesday morning Taylor's doctor came by, hooked it back up, then secured it with Super glue. By this time I was ready to sniff the stuff.

Finally, thankfully, Taylor went to sleep for at least eight hours.

When he woke up, however, he was atop a slippery slide of misery.

In the hours that followed, slowly but surely he descended into what seemed to be an endless, inescapable canyon of sheer anguish.

The problem was, no matter how he positioned himself he hurt. Really hurt. But the new, unusual focus of discomfort was his chest, not bottom. He couldn't lie on his back. He couldn't lie on his stomach. He couldn't lie in any convoluted position without chest pain. The growing pressure of anxiety and pain was overwhelming. It finally exploded in a hot torrent of angry, screaming tears, subsiding at last to helpless weary sobs.

At one point he tried standing up. But even then he hurt. With this dismal discovery he turned around toward me. Grabbing my arms he made me put them around his torso. When I did, he drew close and hugged me tight. Squeezing with his pale arms, he buried his face in my chest and wept . . . a tortured little boy holding, being held, by his helpless daddy.

Taylor knew there was nothing I could do. But he hugged me anyway. And I hugged him back, baptizing his bushy head with hot and helpless tears of speechless love and sorrow.

I don't know how long we stood there. The pace of time was, and remains, very strange. But there we stood, holding one another, broken hearts spilling love, until that position also was simply too uncomfortable for my wounded warrior son.

It didn't feel like help from God when his help arrived. But looking back, his help is exactly what we got.

At 9 P.M. on Tuesday it was time to give Taylor his evening meds. That's when it dawned on me. Since insertion of the spinal catheter, we had stopped all morphine by mouth. But this new pathway of medication was primarily addressing Taylor's *pelvic* pain, not the rest of his body.

Suddenly I realized that, for some time, doses of oral morphine had controlled a kind of pain of which we were unaware . . . *chest* pain from the pressure on his lungs.

Now that oral doses were withdrawn, the chest pain was unmasked.

That was the revelation (I know it didn't come from me). With it, the answer was simple. All we had to do was reinstate a regimen of oral morphine at half the previous dose. So we did.

Forty-five minutes later Taylor was peacefully asleep—another victory won because of many prayers.

When he woke up Wednesday, he stayed up all day. He watched movies and played video games with Christopher. Then, at last, we all went home late that afternoon.

Which was, of course, yesterday.

Four days ago he was tubeless, free. Now he's tethered to two tubes, one for oxygen, the other for a morphine drip.

Still, last night he came downstairs where, with Christopher, we watched the season finale of *Star Trek Voyager*. Then he hopped back upstairs where we talked, took communion, watched a little Letterman. As it grew late, Taylor faded fast. Head plopped down, his eyes were barely open.

"Buddy, you look tired. Let's turn off the TV and go to bed."

"No, Dad! I'm not tired. My mind is wide awake. It's my stupid body that's tired." The frustration in his voice was also curious, perplexed.

Finally we went to sleep, Taylor still doing so on bended knee.

From now on he's never left alone. Mostly we stroke his swollen leg, his soft head, his strong back, whispering, "I love you! I'm proud of you!"

And when he has the strength, we talk.

"Taylor?" My voice is calm, matter-of-fact. "You have loved me better than anyone in all my life. I've told you that, haven't I?"

"Yeah, Dad, you have."

"Okay. Just wanted to be sure . . ."

Mind awake and eyes wide open Taylor walks toward Home, bursting with curiosity, mystery, and a fountain of dry wit. Now that he knows what it's like to consciously go under anesthesia, and with a gleeful quip, it seems he's no less determined to consciously cross over, *waking up* in that place that really is his Home.

His birthday is on Sunday, June 4th. He will have a party. But perhaps not here. Perhaps, instead, he'll party with

> his cousin Camille
> his Aunt Cindy
> his Grandma Belon

and with

> Hope Guthrie
> Matthew Tait
> Lizzy Lemky
> Valerie Grace Wheeler
> Brianna Cadman
> Robert Gross . . .

And with thousands, thousands more. But best of all, with Y'shua. And with two strong legs. And maybe, just maybe, he'll get that go-cart he's always wanted. But with capabilities beyond his wildest dreams, able to ride screaming between the stars, totally free, as long as he wants . . . to the deafening cheers of a countless brilliant host, a sound drowned out by just two hands . . . the singular applause of One.

Whether here or There, but especially There, you too are invited to celebrate Taylor's birthday . . . Taylor's life . . . Taylor's God.

You might not be in Heaven on June 4th. But you *are* invited. The only thing you have to do, if not already done, is RSVP to God's invitation just to you in and through his Son . . .

Brian

Husband to Debbie; Dad to Taylor, 11.97; also Dad to Christopher, 14.52, and Jonathan, 6.78. And still reluctant guardian of Dempsey the farting boxer.

4 6   SECRET MISSIONS?

ON THURSDAY NIGHT, MAY 25TH, I WALKED INTO Taylor's room and kissed him on the forehead.

"Hey, Dad, where've you been?"

"Hey there, sweet thang. Sorry I'm late. Thought I'd better write an e-mail to all the people prayin' for you. Took longer than I thought. Give me a few minutes to change and zap some o' Mom's cold supper. Maybe you can come downstairs with Christopher and me while I eat? Watch something with us?"

"Yeah, prob'ly. But hurry, all right?"

"Will do. Have you had anything to eat?"

"A little."

"Hungry?"

"Nah, not right now."

"Have you been able to go to the bathroom?"

"Number one, not two."

"When did you take your last dose of Lactulose?"

"I dunno. Coupla hours ago, I guess."

"How 'bout another hit?"

"Yeah . . . I guess."

"Know what, Taylor? I just love watching the expression on your face when you swallow this stuff! Could I get you to do that look again?" He did. I laughed.

"Ha, ha," Taylor flatly said but with a smile too.

While I ate he came downstairs (with help), plopped down on Christopher's giant stuffed dog, and watched the Discovery Channel for about an hour. Snaking behind him, all the way from his room upstairs, was a tube with supplemental oxygen. And beside him was a small "smart" pump controlling the flow of morphine to, and in, his back.

Good news was, his pelvic tumor didn't hurt. But his right leg was getting swollen, numb, hard to control—partly from the morphine, partly from being on his knee almost around the clock.

Still, at nine that night, he slowly plodded back upstairs. We kept a careful eye on his plastic leashes, trying not to tangle, trip, or pull them out. I wondered if we'd even try another trip outside his room.

With Jonathan in bed and Christopher still one floor below, Taylor and I knelt side by side next to his bed. Switching off *I Love Lucy*, I turned my face toward his and said, "Taylorman? Mom said something to me last night. And I put it in today's e-mail."

"What?" he asked with a slightly slurry voice. With all the morphine going into his system, through his back and by mouth, he was starting to talk and act as if he was a little smashed. Although his words were understandable, his head tended to wobble when he turned to look me in the face. Sometimes, tired from the effort, he flopped his face down on a pillow even as I spoke. Was he cognizant? I wondered.

"We don't know for sure, but your mom and I think there's a chance you're going to get a go-cart for your birthday. That's because it's starting to look like you might have your party in Heaven, not here. And just think about the kind of stuff a go-cart There can do!"

"Huh!" Taylor grunted, face still in the pillow. As I spoke, Debbie walked into the room. She caught the gist of my remarks. For more than a year whenever anyone's asked Taylor, "Anything I can get for you?" he's always, always quipped, "Yeah—a million dollars and a go-cart."

It was hard for her, but Debbie had, at last, accepted that probably soon Taylor would be going Home. She spoke up . . .

"That's right, Taylor honey. And if you have your party in Heaven, you won't need a million dollars. You can just tell God to send it to us!"

Instantly Taylor's head snapped up from the pillow, though still a little wobbly.

"*Tell* God?!" he quipped, pretending to sound shocked. "Mo-om! You don't *tell* God anything!"

We roared. Not only was his reaction quick and unexpected, it was also right on target.

"You're right, smart guy!" I laughed. "But you could *ask* him, okay?"

He nodded. Gratified, he grinned. He yanked our chains right well! No doubt his mind was razor sharp and wide awake in spite of all the morphine in his system.

Later in the evening he asked, "Dad? Today's Thursday, right?"

"Yup."

"Good! Cuz Friday is my favorite day!"

"How come?"

"I dunno. Prob'ly cuz school gets out and it's your last day at the office. It's when the weekend starts!"

"I agree, buddy. Fridays are great. But, listen, I won't be going to the office for a while, at least for a week."

"Really?!"

"I promise."

Taylor's eyes were lively with anticipation.

"Do ya think I could have some friends over tomorrow? Like maybe Trey and Ashton?"

"If you have time before your nurse gets here, sure. But you'll have to get up before noon."

"Oh, yeah . . . okay." Now that his Hickman catheter was gone, he had to be poked with a needle, a prospect he didn't relish.

"But, Dad, don't forget! I've *gotta* see *MI-2* this weekend, okay?" (The movie *Mission Impossible 2,* remember?)

"Whenever you feel up to it," I promised, "we'll go."

"Yes!"

As the night grew late and his body weary, Taylor did not want to turn in. Around 12:45 in the morning his head was slumped on a pillow as he knelt toward the end of his bed.

"Hey, buddy?" I prodded. "How 'bout we hit the sack?"

Head still on the pillow, he opened his eyes and said, "Dad, are my tubes outta the way so I could get up and move?"

Perplexed by his response, I checked and said, "Yup, you're clear. But where do you wanna go?"

"Just over there a little ways," he replied without an answer.

Knowing any move would be a major effort, I persisted with a hint of irritation. "We can do it, but it'll take some work. What do you want to do? Can't you at least tell me what you want to do?"

"Trust me, Dad! I *promise* you're gonna like it." Tired, sad, and just a little grouchy, I surrendered. Putting one hand underneath each arm, I bent my legs and lifted. As I held up almost all his body weight, he made four hops around the corner of the bed to its base, opposite the head.

Lifting up both arms, he reached and locked them round my neck. Then, drawing close, he hugged me tight, pressing himself against me. With his face on my chest he softly trumped, "Toldja you would like it."

He caught me unaware. Once again, in spite of weary grumpiness and grief, repulsive bulging tumors in my spirit that have been there all his life, he shocked me with his unaffected love, his pure delight in *me*. My throat ached as I swallowed fewer than half my helpless sobs while large and hot and unwiped tears rolled down my stubbly face.

"Well, buddy, you sure were right about that," I whisper-cried as I hugged him back. "You've always been the best hugger in the world."

Moments passed.

"Know what?" I said. "This reminds me of what we often did when you were a boy. When you hugged me, I carried you to our bed and sat down. All at once I rolled on my back, then up again—back and forth, back and forth. Sometimes, out of breath, we rested for a minute while I lightly tickled you. And sometimes, usually in my chair, you put your arms around me and fell asleep. Sure wish we could still do that."

"Well, why not? Let's try it," Taylor answered.

And so, we did. It took a couple tries, but soon we found a position that was comfortable for Taylor. He nestled his head in the notch between my upper chest and arm. His face turned in toward mine underneath my chin. I thanked God for the moment but thought it wouldn't last, that soon Taylor would have to rearrange himself and move away.

Instead he said, "Hey, Dad? Are there gonna be *ranks* in heaven? You know, like generals or something like that?"

All at once my tears dried up, pulse picked up, head began to spin. My brain felt like a hard drive whirling at top speed while arms raced back and forth across the surface desperate to retrieve old data. In my heart I whispered the prayer God's heard from me the most, *Uh, Lord . . . help!*

"Good question, buddy!" I stalled for time. "The Bible says God's gonna give rewards to members of his family. But his rewards will be for trusting him when we do stuff, for expressing his love to other people. And I tell you what, sweet boy, you've got a *bunch* of rewards comin' your way. Till I met you, I'd only read about people with your kind of faith, your kind of stubborn love."

"Yeah, Dad, but what about *ranks?*"

"Okay. As I understand it, God's also gonna give us different levels of responsibility as part of his rewards. I really don't know what these things'll be. But I do know that heaven will be a community with structure. Maybe like angels have right now.

"So, yeah, sounds to me like there will be ranks. And I'm sure yours'll be a high one. But I don't know what they'll be called. Generals, majors, lieutenants, and privates? Princes, dukes, knights, and squires? . . ."

"Okay," Taylor said with a hint of exasperation, ready to move on. "I guess my real question is this: Do ya think God ever lets people come back to earth on secret missions? You know, like double-o-seven, but with a license to . . ."

Both minds raced to find the best pun.

"How 'bout, 'like double-o-seven, but with a license to *heal*'?" I suggested with a tone that also told him, *Beat-cha!*

He grinned. "Yeah, like that? Do ya think he does?"

Back to groping mode. "We're not told either way," I said. "Angels are sent on secret missions like that all the time. I think we often see them and just don't know it, especially when we're around strangers—like in the mall.

"But the Bible makes it clear that angels are a different race than humans . . . I do think all human history will be in God's master library, any part of which we'll be able to visit and study. And there are hints in the Bible that people in heaven are able to see what's going on down here. But actual visits like angels do, entering into the flow of history? I don't know. I guess I kinda doubt it. Still, that only means I don't know."

"Huh," Taylor sighed.

"Sorry I can't give you a better answer, buddy. I love your questions, but I don't know most of the answers. Mainly because the Bible doesn't give us a lot of details about what heaven's like."

"How come, though?" Taylor asked. "Why doesn't God tell us more about it?"

"Now *that* I can answer," I chuckled. "If we knew, if we could see what it's really like, we'd do one of two things. We'd become obnoxious braggers or suicidal. Some of us would be like mean children, sneering in a singsong voice, 'God likes me better than you-oo . . . I know somethin' that you don't!' Others, like me, would be very tempted to jump off buildings or shoot themselves in the head! I think there're a lot of us who just couldn't put up with all the stuff in this life if we saw what's There.

"In fact one writer of the Bible *had* a vision of heaven. He later wrote a letter. In it he thought out loud whether or not he should go ahead and die, which he knew would be lots better, or stick around for a while, helping people come to know and follow God in the middle of all the smelly stuff of life. Just like you're teaching people by your example."

"Okay," Taylor yawned. Then, lying on my chest, he fell asleep, his position comfortable. It was a special moment, a priceless gift of love from Taylor—and from God through Taylor—to such a grump as I.

We lay there for two hours. I held my head up, no pillow for a prop. Stroking Taylor's back, I inhaled his heady scent through bristly blond hair. His strong and pounding heart pumped right next to mine. I watched him breathe in painless peace, his spirit warming me and mine warming his. For a time his wounded body was my blanket from the cold and my old body his.

And once again I marveled at the miracle, the privilege given me. From billions of men who've been, who are, who ever shall be, I alone held, and hold, the never-ending honor of being Taylor's dad. I knew then as I know now: Anything this world might favorably bestow, anything at all, would be nothing, worthless next to this.

Still, I am so dense.

Only later did it dawn on me what really worried Taylor. He didn't care about ranks or secret missions out of simple curiosity. For him the issues were personal. Very, very personal. He was desperately worried how much he'd miss me, how much he'd miss his mom and brothers. And he knew how much I would suffer if, in fact, he went Home ahead of me—as we both believed he would.

What Taylor *really* wanted to know was if God might give him a sufficient rank to let him go on secret missions so that he could visit us. So that he could see me. And maybe bring some comfort. When this awareness hit, like a revelation, I marveled. And I wept.

47   WELL HE QUIPPED

FRIDAY, MAY 26TH, 2000

Cords and tubes were strewn across the bedroom floor. Plus a new addition—a shiny stainless steel IV pole. Sandra, our competent and cheerful home healthcare nurse, brought it in when she arrived. It was about 12:30 in the afternoon.

After Taylor said good-bye to friends Trey and Ashton, he made his way to a place where he could endure insertion of an IV port into his arm. Though tired, pale, anxious, he deftly maneuvered around the pole, over cords. And all the while watching out for trailing tubes to which he was already leashed. There were two of them. Soon there would be three.

Looking at the pole and all the cords, he quipped, "Looks like picture day at school!"

Insertion of the port was difficult. Although it hurt, Taylor was too tired to complain. Once the procedure was done, a bag was hung. Exhausted, Taylor conked out as his thirsty body drank purified water through a thin blue vein in his too-white arm.

Earlier that day Debbie brought Taylor his morning meds, taken at 6:30. Usually he woke up just enough to pop and swallow, then in a wink fell back to sleep. But this morning, though only half-awake, Taylor remembered it was his favorite day: Friday.

"Mom? Be sure to wake me up at ten." He was insistent. "I want to have time for my friends to come over before Sandra gets here!"

Although it was at least two hours earlier than normal wake-up time, Debbie gently stirred him at the hour he requested. Promptly he was up and dressed, entertaining both friends in his room, playing games on his computer.

After his port was in place, Taylor slept late into the afternoon. Concerned he might be awake all night, I nudged him from his slumber. "Tay-lor," I softly sang with a tantalizing tease. "Guess what I have?"

"Mmmnrrrr . . . what?" he mumbled with his eyes still shut.

"Birthday cards—lots of birthday cards! If you don't get up pretty soon, I won't be able to help myself. I'll have to open 'em. And if that's what I have to do, I get to keep half the money anybody sends you!"

"Oh, no you don't!" That woke him up, at least up on his knee against the bed so he could spread out and open the cards. He was up but fought to keep his eyes open. He also looked a little puffy, and his speech was slurred.

But his mind was wide awake and razor sharp. The first thing he did with each card was shake to see if checks or bills fell out. If they didn't, he witted a dismissive, "What? No money!" then tossed the unread card aside. Once he provoked the response he wanted from me ("Tay-lor!"), he took each one back and read it.

"Get well," he read from many. "Yeah," he cracked, "get well *poorly!*"

Laughing at his offhand commentary, I said, "Taylor, all that morphine's makin' you a little drunk—and I think you're enjoyin' it!"

All he did was wryly grin.

"This one says, 'Get well,'" he read from another. "Hey! What happened to '*soon*'?"

Most greetings came from people Taylor'd never met, including a basketful from children in the state of Washington. Inside a homemade card one boy kindly wrote, "I'd sure like to be your friend someday."

"Someday!" Taylor retorted. "Why not *now?*"

"Good point," I chuckled. "No one ever becomes a friend *some*day, cuz *some*day never comes. It's either now or never. Are ya with me?"

He grunted that he was, but didn't stop his hunt for hidden treasure in the mail. Every time something floated out we said, "Yahoo!"

"Tell you what, Taylor . . . I'll just keep this for you, okay?"

"Oh, no you don't!" he protested, grabbing paper money and putting it out of my reach.

As usual, Taylor stayed up late on Friday night. Just before one in the morning (Saturday), it looked like he was out. Face down, his eyes were shut; his breathing was relaxed. Before repositioning ourselves for a full night's sleep, I flipped the TV channel.

There he was, the preacher-healer-man! The same one we had gone to see a month ago along with several thousand others at the Gaylord Entertainment Center here in Nashville.

I watched, bemused, but remembered the man's gentle kindnesses to Taylor.

Suddenly Taylor's head popped up an inch. With a tiny squint, he barely opened tired, swollen eyes. Instantly perceiving who it was, he drolled in slurry monotone, "Been there. Done that. Didn't work." Then he plopped his head back down, eyes shut.

I laughed so hard it hurt. His body might be tired, but if anything, his mind was more awake than ever. There was no malice or complaint in what he said. He was just having fun—with me.

Saturday, May 27th, 2000

When Taylor roused himself on Saturday I almost didn't recognize him.

"Whoa, buddy!"

"What?" he slurred. As I helped him move, we both looked at his swollen leg.

"We need to call reporters," I said. "Looks like we've discovered Big Foot!"

"No fair," he protested. "That was my line!"

Soon after, I offered other news. "Don't know how to tell you this, bu-ut, your face is lookin' like a water balloon!"

"Really? Let me see." I showed him. "Weird!" he concurred, curious but without concern.

Taylor's kidneys were not processing fluids going into his body through the IV port. His neck was so swollen, the oxygen tube made a bruise. And one eyelid bulged so badly it could hardly open up. After giving it some thought I said, "Know what, buddy? This IV thing's not workin' for you. Fluids are goin' in, but they're not comin' out. My guess is, your kidneys are gettin' tired. They can't work fast enough. I think we should turn the thing off. You can have anything you want to drink, but I don't see any reason why you should look like you're getting ready to float down the street in Macy's Thanksgiving Day parade. And this way you'll have one less tube to worry about. What do you think?"

"Fine with me." He shrugged.

So I clamped it off and disconnected it. Six hours and one large dark draft of urine later, most of the swelling was gone. Taylor looked better, but his pallor was paler and his strength was clearly waning. Even so, he remembered the movie he could hardly wait to see. "Can we go see *MI-2* tonight?" he asked.

"Wel-l-l-l, why don't we wait till you're just a little stronger? We can always catch a late show—or go sometime tomorrow."

"All right," he conceded. "But I *want* to see that movie! I've *gotta* see it."

"Don't worry, I won't forget."

Although he was too weak to go out to the movies, he rallied well enough for a night of munchies, small talk, and critiques of TV shows. Our favorite snack was corn chips along with several drops of olive oil and an extra dash of salt—delicious and nutritious!

Debbie came in the room to take a picture. We agreed to pose on one condition: her first shot had to be of see-food. She grudgingly agreed. In unison we opened up our mouths, exposing to the camera lens unswallowed corn-chip mush—*see-food*—as the flash went off.

"Now, that's what I call a picture!" Taylor quipped. Then we posed politely, placating a mildly piqued parent who'd lost her appetite.

When bedtime finally rolled around we did communion next to Taylor's bed. Traveling to and from his homework table across the room was too much of an effort. If grape juice stained the sheets or rug, so what? First of all we prayed. Then I read out loud the Bible's explanation of the bread, or cracker, after which we ate it. As I started to continue with the grape juice (in lieu of wine), Taylor interrupted.

"Dad?" he asked. His head lightly wobbled and, as always now, his speech was both breathy and blurred. "How many apostles were there at the Last Supper?"

"Twelve," I answered. "Why?"

"Well," he said, tilting back his head and putting a finger in his mouth, "I think I've got a coupla the apostles stuck in my teeth."

Trying not to laugh, but failing, I said, "Well, don't worry about it. I'm sure you'll wash 'em down with the grape juice." After which we prayed and read and went to bed.

Sunday, May 28th, 2000

Sunday morning Taylor's uncle Cliff, one of my two brothers, and his sixteen-year-old son, David, showed up by surprise. They had driven through the night all the way from northern Michigan.

While I slept in (in my own bed to which I'd crept at five o'clock that morning), Cliff tiptoed into Taylor's room. When he whispered his hello, Taylor woke up thrilled. It was early, but Uncle Cliff was here—and Uncle Cliff is *fun*.

While David and Christopher talked in another room, Cliff and Taylor had some time alone.

"Taylor," Cliff asked, "do you mind if I ask you somethin' kinda serious?"

"Sure! I mean, no! Go ahead!"

"You know that I'm a pastor, right?"

Taylor nodded.

"Well, lots of times I've told people they can have joy even when they're suffering. But I've never known anyone who's been through as much as you. So I guess my question is, is it true? Can you really have joy at the same time you're really, really hurting?"

Taylor looked at Cliff with eyes that seemed to say, *You really don't know?* But what he said, with animated emphasis was this: "Well, *yeah!* There've been *lots* of times I've come out of surgery with *horrible* pain, and Dad has made me *laugh!*"

What Taylor didn't say, and maybe didn't see, was that during those same times he was the one who, in the midst of pain, often made me laugh.

All Cliff said was, "Thank you, Taylor," as he marveled, wordless.

Later that same morning, with help, Taylor insisted on showing us maneuvers he developed in a war game. Sitting at his computer, he was plagued by a headache, could barely keep his eyes open, and had to lean on Uncle Cliff in order to keep from falling off his chair. But as soon as the game began, he was a four-star general, commanding an entire army. Commander Taylor's job was to prepare and lead his soldiers against an unseen equal force.

Preparation meant mining natural resources to underwrite the cost of fighter bombers, power plants, production facilities, fortresses, runways, and training of special troops. But preparation also meant denying intelligence to the enemy while at the same time obtaining intelligence about the enemy. Where is he? How well is he armed? How are his troops deployed? What is he developing? Unless he obtained this vital information, Commander Taylor could never lead his troops in victory.

On the screen all the land is black until it has been scouted out by plane or by troops—or even by a single soldier. Only then can the commander see the lay of the land and learn vital information. The sooner this information is obtained, the better the commander's odds of defeating the enemy along with all of his strong forces.

While Cliff watched, he saw Commander Taylor send out a solitary spy. The scout's only mission was to gather information about the enemy. Deeper and deeper he traveled, all alone, into blackness. As he moved ahead, land was illuminated, enemy positions were revealed. But the soldier had no backup. The farther he went, the more obvious it became: He'd never make it back alive.

Unable to contain concern and wondering, in part, if Taylor was aware of danger to his man, Uncle Cliff exclaimed, "Hey, Taylor! That scout you sent out? He's a dead guy!" Cliff's unspoken questions were obvious. Are you aware of this? Do you know what you're doing to this guy?

"Yeah, I know," Commander Taylor shrugged, ho-hum. "It's a suicide mission. After all, ya can't beat the enemy if ya don't know where he is."

When encouraged to take a break and finish the battle later, the exhausted commander rallied with a shout, fiercely barking, "NO! Once you're in a war, you don't ever, *ever* quit!" Moments later, when the enemy attacked, Commander Taylor and his troops stayed the course and won. The enemy retreated.

Cliff was stunned as the full impact of Taylor's words struck their intended target . . . Enlightenment. Understanding. Taylor's game was more than role-play. More than preparation. More than practice. More than showing off. It was an explanation. Without words he said, *I too am on a mission. I don't especially like it, but it's okay. At least in part I know the reason why.*

After a nap, Taylor woke again on Sunday afternoon. He was stubborn as a mule. "This is still Sunday, right? Well, I. Wanna. See. *M. I. 2!*"

Nothing would dissuade him.

"Mo-om! My body's only gonna get weaker. I've gotta see it *now*."

We helped him dress, combed his hair, and wondered.

He just might die in the theater, Cliff thought. *But, if he does, he does. Let's go!*

I too endorsed the effort but felt that by the time Taylor reached the stairs outside his room, he'd find out for himself that this mission was, in fact, impossible. I was wrong. He made the discovery several inches past the foot of his bed. His mind was wide awake, but his leg was almost useless, virtually dead weight, and his body simply didn't have the strength.

Awareness, understanding, hit him hard. Falling to his swollen knee, he softly cried a one-word expletive, then dropped his head and wept. Dropping to my knees and hands, I joined him, propping his forehead up against my own. Then head to head, skin to skin, we cried, two falling streams of runny noses and hot tears, the lava of our grief.

"I'm sorry, buddy. I was afraid this would happen. And you're right. It really, really stinks."

Five minutes later, lesson learned and awareness intact, Taylor swiveled on his knee, propped his arms up on the bed, and said, "Okay, let's watch a movie here!"

Cliff ran to the store and bought a recent comedy everyone wanted to see—an ingenious spoof of *Star Trek* called *Galaxy Quest.* When he returned Taylor took the movie in his hands and whispered, "Dad, c'mere! I've gotta ask ya something . . . in *private.*"

After others politely left the room, we knelt shoulder to shoulder. As he spoke, Taylor's tune was conspiratorial.

"So, Dad," he slyly said, "does this movie belong to *us* or to Uncle Cliff?!"

I laughed—as he knew I would. "Well, since Uncle Cliff doesn't have a DVD player and you do, my guess is that it's yours." (Sheila Walsh and her son, Christian, gave the player to Taylor.)

"Okay," Taylor said. Without breaking character he pulled the movie close and clutched it tight. "But I still better hang on to it, so he doesn't *steal* it!"

When, as Taylor intended, I immediately told Cliff, we both roared.

Again, I was amazed. Even with a fresh understanding of what he soon would face, Taylor chose to focus on life. And with his help we all did the same, laughing in the face of Death. This too, he knew, was part of his mission—his mission impossible too—*accomplished*.

While Taylor rested from his efforts, several of us lingered in his room. Christopher and David played a video game; Cliff checked e-mail; I read a book. Still at the foot of his bed, Taylor knelt beside it, head on his hands and pillow. He was exhausted and, it seemed to all of us, unconscious. When he raised his head an inch or two and slurred, "Dad, would you c'mere a second? I wanna tell you something," I hastened to his side. Concerned, I said, "Sure, buddy. What is it?"

"Ooooooh," he moaned, "I'm *sorry*, Dad . . . I *forgot!*" Then he plopped his head back down.

"That's okay, sweetie, that's *o*-kay." I stroked his head, reassured him, then went back to my chair and book. Several minutes later, the same thing happened. My heart was heavy with the belief that Taylor's mind was getting murky. Still contemplating this with sorrow, Taylor asked me once again, "Dad, would you c'mere a second? I wanna tell you something." For a third time I hastened to his side.

"Ooooooh," he moaned, he paused, then turned his head and brightly said, "Am I buggin' you yet?!" As I gasped with laughter he continued ruefully, "Shoot! Betcha if I'd done it a few more times, I woulda bugged ya!"

Everybody howled, especially Cliff. "That was a perfect setup," he complimented Taylor, who grinned with satisfaction.

After eating pizza for supper, Taylor said, "My leg aches." Unable to hold up his torso by himself, Cliff held him steady while I rubbed ointment on his leg. Taylor sighed with contentment—it really did feel good—and said to Cliff and me, again with drunken speech, "Know what? I've . . . got . . . the . . . two . . . of . . . you . . . wrapped . . . around . . . my . . . little . . . pinkie!"

We chuckled with sweet sorrow and heartily agreed.

That night when he was in position to go to sleep, Cliff was there to say good night.

"Uncle Cliff," Taylor mumbled, "I want you to tell me some stories about Dad when he was a kid."

Uncle Cliff complied with a couple zingers, things I don't remember well, if at all, but things that are still fresh in my younger brother's memory.

Thinking he was asleep, Cliff began to say good night.

"No, you can't leave yet," Taylor teased, eyes shut. "You've gotta stay until you've told me at least a hundred stories!"

Cliff complied with several more, then left to go to bed.

"I just love those stories about you, Dad!" he muttered before we prayed.

"I know you do, hot dog," I teased. "You just like knowin' how I misbehaved."

"Yup," he agreed. But what he really enjoyed was seeing me as I used to be, as a kid like him, who struggled with brothers, who pulled pranks and almost always got away with them.

Monday, May 29th, 2000

Taylor was up early Monday morning, at least by ten o'clock, insistent that his friends be invited for a visit. Upon arrival everyone agreed to watch Taylor's new movie, *Galaxy Quest.*

Trey and Ashton, Taylor's friends, along with Christopher and cousin David sat on the bed and chairs. They watched and laughed while Taylor, perched on swollen knee, struggled to hold up his head. About halfway through the movie, Taylor simply could not stay awake. As we turned it off, he muttered good-byes to friends as I helped him reposition for a nap.

"Know what, Dad? Every time the last two days when I've said good-bye to friends, my heart has started pounding hard!"

"Hmm," I answered with a kiss. "Just like you, I understand. I understand."

When he woke again I held a brand-new batch of birthday cards. Too weak to open them himself, I did the task and read them to him, celebrating when a dollar bill fell out.

"Hey, Dad, listen to this!" he interrupted, then took two breaths, in and out, in and out. "My breathing sounds cool. Kinda sad, but cool. It sounds like soldiers bein' shot by arrows. Can you hear it?"

I put my ear next to his mouth while again he inhaled. Faint but clear, his exhalation carried with it an involuntary rasp, a small chorus of wet sighs.

"Yup, you're right. I hear it."

"Pretty cool, huh? Boy, I sure am killin' a lot of bad guys!"

"That you are," I agreed. "That you are."

He put his head down and slept while I stood guard beside him. Time went by. Eyes closed, head down, he mumbled something.

I put my ear next to his lips and said, "Did you say somethin', honey? Cuz if you did, I didn't catch it."

"Yeah, Dad?" he rasped. "Y'know how the History Channel sometimes does programs on the history of guns?"

Perplexed and suspicious of delirium, I said, "Yeah . . ."

"Well, y'know, I was thinkin' . . . they really oughtta do a program about the history of knives, don'tcha think?"

"Ooookay," I replied. My tone was kind but mixed with worry too.

"Well . . . ," he continued slowly, "y'see, there're all kinds of knives— curved ones, straight ones, long, short. I just think it'd really be interesting." Then he paused. I didn't say a word.

"In fact," he said with perfect timing, "did you know there are special knives made just to . . . *cut the cheese?*"

Hook, line, sinker, he snagged and reeled me in. Still flopping with surprise, he cut the line and dropped me in his bucket where, with laughter, I gasped for air. And he did it with his eyes shut. I figured it was payback for stealing his Big Foot line several days before.

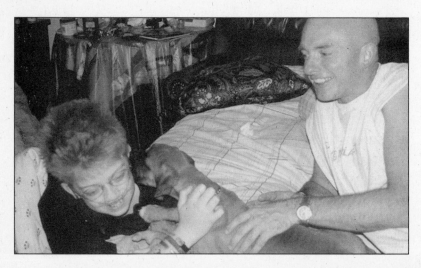

Still, Taylor's decline was dramatic. His face was pasty white; his body strength was minimal. But he rallied in the afternoon when a friend from our congregation brought by a special visitor: a boxer puppy girl. She climbed up on the bed and with stubby tail wiggling with furious happiness, licked Taylor's face, his hands, his arms, his lips. Delighted, Taylor grinned and did his best to pet her.

"She's yours if you want her," the owner offered. Debbie and I were hesitant.

"But I've never had a dog from the time she was a puppy," Taylor protested. He pled to keep her. We agreed.

"So what're ya gonna name her?" we asked. Taylor's other dog, the animal love of his life, is Dempsey, our ten-year-old, matronly boxer. She was named, as Taylor knew, after a famous boxer from the ring, Jack Dempsey, a man who lived and fought and died long before Taylor's life and battle.

Like Dempsey, his new puppy was a girl.

"I think I'll call her Jackie."

Debbie took pictures as Jackie joined our family, adopted by Taylor. Apparently pleased, Jackie again kissed Taylor on his cheeks and lips.

"Hey, buddy!" I whispered in his ear. "Look at this. Jackie's doin' what all the girls would *love* to do. She's kissin' you on the lips!"

"Da-ad," he growled, "if I felt any better, you'd be in big trouble!"

"Okay," I said, contrite but smiling too. "I won't tease you anymore."

"Better not," he muttered, thrilled with Jackie, with her warmth, her touch, her enthusiastic love. Although he took her for himself, he also took her for his family, a gift received then given as a comfort and a balm.

During these days Taylor's body plummeted to helplessness, losing its war against the evil Mutha and her nasty brood. There was a final battle coming, and he knew it.

As human hope and inhibitions dropped away, Taylor partied hearty, free. But what I saw underneath the worn-out cloak of his dying, crippled body was something quite amazing. It wasn't bitter, hopeless, mean, or weak. Quite the opposite.

Instead there stood an awesome man, a soldier dressed in dazzling armor. With a helmet crystal clear, his mind was bright and mighty. Its immortal beauty almost blinded all who saw it, illuminated by intense refracted Light.

His chest was covered with a pure and gleaming vest. Around his waist and loins there was a plain but special belt, itself a kind of weapon. Powerful as Truth, it held the armor tight so that it wouldn't slip. (I also noticed that it protected private parts—the ultimate athletic cup!) On his single foot there was an awesome shoe that gripped the ground beneath. *If only he had two,* I thought, *it would almost be impossible for him to stumble to the ground . . .*

In his right hand was a weapon, a sword bigger than Goliath's and sharper than a surgeon's blade. It hummed with power stronger than the stars. Not only could it slice through dragon hide like butter, it could, like a dragon only better, fire endless rounds of *super* fire bolts.

Beneath the soldier's left hand, holding him up as a crutch, was the perfect shield, light but impenetrable. In its center on the front was the golden face of a roaring Lion emerging, it seemed, from the bloody wounded side of a white and gentle Lamb. Behind the Lamb four corners of a midnight cross were etched in living gold.

And between the folds of armor, peeking through almost translucent mortal skin, was a pure and blazing cloak, an undergarment if you will, of silky purest white. Had all of it been visible, unveiled and unfettered, I am convinced it would have sizzled human retinas into crusty, sightless orbs.

The wounded warrior's face was, at once, irresistible and frightening. His eyes twinkled with merriment, and his laugh was real. But just below the shine of gaiety was the steely glint of determination. And underneath the laugh was the soulish growl of a mighty gladiator ready to fight to the death.

Raising his sword toward the King, he cried, *"Moriturite salutamus! We who are about to die salute you!"*

But this man, the one revealed underneath the boy, was no god, no flawless saint. He was a mighty warrior, but badly wounded too. He was a soldier, but a child. He was a man. And he was my son.

He only has one leg! I cried. *How can he fight? How will he keep from falling down? How will he hold up that shield we both know he'll have to use?*

Even as I asked the questions, I heard, I knew the answers.

"This time, my son, Taylor's not alone in the storm of battle, high up on the

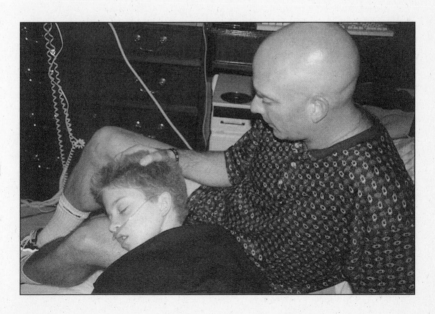

dam road. This time you are with him, by his side, all the way across. You're right—he is a knight. And you shall be, as you've been, his squire, his assistant.

"Yes, the battle will be fierce. Yes, your son is crippled and could easily fall down. That is why I'm sending you to hold him up, to help him keep his balance, to help him lift the shield of faith, to fight along beside him. With my weapons, gifts from me he cannot lose, still he can and will be wounded. But in the end, because of me, he'll win.

"You shall hand him safely off to no one less than I as I greet him on the Other Side. And, for him, his arrival Here will be greeted by at least a million cheers.

"In return for this service on my behalf, you too shall be an amputee, crippled and dependent. This is your reward. Be grateful. Learn from it and use it well, my son. Learn from it and use it well. Someday soon, when your last fight comes—as, indeed, it shall—if you've studied well my gift, you'll know you're not alone. And you too shall win the Prize.

"So be it."

Taylor was ready. How very well he quipped! How very well equipped!

48 BRAVEHEART

MONDAY NIGHT, MAY 29TH, 2000

"Hey, Dad? What are some of Satan's other names?"

"Well, let's see . . . the Bible has quite a few. He's called Liar and the Father of Lies. Other names include a Roaring Lion on the hunt,

Deceiver, and shape-shifter who can make himself look like an angel from God, a snake, and a dragon. He's also called Prince of Darkness, Ruler of This World, Prince and Power of the Air, Evil One, Tempter, a Murderer, the Enemy, and the Accuser of God's people.

"Good question. Why do you ask?"

"Oh, I dunno," Taylor slowly slurred. "Just wondered."

"Okay, buddy. But keep in mind that God's Spirit lives in you. That's why the Bible also says. 'Greater is he who's in you than he who's in the world.'"

"Okay, Dad."

It was about ten o'clock at night. Debbie had just helped Taylor change out of "movie clothes" into his favorite sleepwear—an oversized T-shirt with a huge majestic portrait of a bald eagle emblazoned on the front. It was time for Eagleman to go to bed. His skin was pasty white, his breathing shallow, his eyes too heavy to lift. Still, he resisted.

"Before I go to bed," he said, "would you mind reading something from my Bible?"

"Sure!" This was the first time in his life he'd *asked* me to read it to him. "So what do ya want me to read?"

"Phuh!" he huffed. "Somethin' about Heaven, I guess."

"You got it." I scrambled to grab his *Kids' Study Bible, the New International Reader's Version.* It's a Christmas present I gave him in 1997 when he was nine and a half years old. It's easy to read. I don't think it has a sentence longer than fifteen words. It's also delightfully blunt.

A memory hit. It was a day, shortly after Christmas '97, when Taylor said to Christopher (then eleven), "C'mere!" Side by side they sat on the sofa. Taylor pointed to a verse and said, "Read this!" When he did, both boys gasped and giggled.

"What're you two laughin' about?" I asked. They were too shy to say, so made me come and look. In Genesis 4:1 Taylor's Bible reads, "Adam had sex with his wife, Eve."

"What a great translation," I said, laughing with them, "because what it says is true! Keep reading!"

It took awhile, but for the last two months or so, Taylor had been reading it almost every day.

But now, unable to read for himself, Taylor wanted to hear something about the Place in which he soon would live. The Place just around the corner. The Place at the end of the dam road. The Place where real life begins and where it never ends. The Place called Home.

At last I found a passage. *Oh, God!* I cried out in my mind. *This is so hard. Help me!*

"Okay, buddy. Here's a part that tells about God's throne and what will happen there." I read . . .

I saw a Lamb that looked as if he had been put to death. He stood in the center of the area around the throne. The Lamb was surrounded by the four living creatures and the elders.

. . . The Lamb came and took the scroll from the right hand of the One sitting on the throne. Then the four living creatures and the 24 elders fell down in front of the Lamb. Each one had a harp. They were holding golden bowls full of incense, which stand for the prayers of God's people.

Here is the new song they sang . . .

"Wait a second!" Taylor interrupted. "Read that again." He was having trouble staying conscious. Shaking his head, trying to make it obey, he fought to stay alert. After hearing it again, he mumbled, "Cool! Kinda sounds like King Arthur and the round table."

"You're right! It does! I never thought of it that way . . . Wanna hear what they sang to the Lamb around the throne? Or are you too tired?"

"No! Keep reading!"

"All right. Here's the song . . ."

You are worthy to take the scroll
    and break open its seals.
You are worthy because you were put to death.
    With your blood you bought people for God.
    They come from every tribe, language, people and nation.
You have made them members of a royal family.
    You have made them priests to serve our God.
    They will rule on the earth.
Then I looked and heard the voice of millions and millions of angels.
They surrounded the throne. They surrounded the living creatures and the
elders. In a loud voice they sang,
    "The Lamb, who was put to death, is worthy!
    He is worthy to receive power and wealth and wisdom and strength!
    He is worthy to receive honor and glory and praise!"
    All creatures in heaven, on earth, under the earth, and on the sea, and
all that is in them, were singing. I heard them say,
    "May praise and honor for ever and ever
        be given to the One who sits on the throne
        and to the Lamb!
Give them glory and power forever and ever!"

As I finished the passage, Taylor's head was slumped down on a pillow.

"Pretty awesome, huh?"

Taylor mumbled something in his pillow.

"Ready for bed, sweetie?"

Furious with his rebellious bones, he emphatically replied, "No! I wanna hear some more. Keep reading!"

While I looked for another passage, he again propped himself up on his arms and shook his drooping head.

"Okay," I said. "Here's one that describes the City we're gonna live in, the place that is our Home. You and I have talked about this a lot, remember?"

He nodded yes as I began to read . . .

I saw a new heaven and a new earth. The first heaven and the first earth were completely gone. There was no longer any sea.

It was the Holy City, the new Jerusalem. It was coming down out of heaven from God. It was prepared like a bride beautifully dressed for her husband.

I heard a loud voice from the throne. It said, "Now God makes his home with human beings. He will live with them. They will be his people. And God himself will be with them and be their God. He will wipe away every tear from their eyes. There will be no more death or sadness. There will be no more crying or pain. Things are no longer the way they used to be."

He who was sitting on the throne said, "I am making everything new!" Then he said, "Write this down. You can trust these words. They are true."

He said to me, "It is done. I am the Alpha and the Omega, the First and the Last. I am the Beginning and the End. Anyone who is thirsty may drink from the spring of the water of life. It doesn't cost anything! Those who overcome will receive all this from me. I will be their God, and they will be my children."

As I read, Taylor constantly interrupted. "Wait a second, Dad. Read that part again."

We went through the passage at least four times until he was satisfied he got it.

"Know what?" he asked. "That City reminds me of the Tabernacle."

Dumbfounded by the clarity of his mind even as his brain and body teetered on the brink of death, I agreed.

"You're right! God designed the Tabernacle and the Temple, in part, to be like pictures of the City. And just think . . . the City itself will be fourteen hundred miles, *cubed!* I mean, it's just awesome to think about. My guess is that it'll be a city in space orbiting the earth like an extrashiny moon. And we'll be able to beam up and down, in and out, anytime we want. Awesome, awesome, awesome!"

Taylor's head was slumped.

"Buddy, I know you're fighting it, but I really think you should go to bed, okay?"

"Okay," he reluctantly relented.

Actually, he didn't go to bed. As he had for several days, he slept propped up on Christopher's stuffed dog—big as a Saint Bernard. Surrounding the stuffed animal, right next to Taylor's bed, were at least twenty different pillows to further cushion and to prop.

When, at last, Taylor's head plopped down atop the Saint Bernard's, I leaned over, whispered a prayer in his ear, then said, "Good night! I love you! See you in the morning!"

"See . . . you . . . morning," he barely muttered back, utterly exhausted. "Good . . . night. Love . . . you . . . too."

Up on his bed I turned off the yellow light but left the lava lamp turned on. Lying on my side up on Taylor's bed, I reached over and stroked his head while he slept beneath the shallow waves of morphine and wet breathing.

Debbie joined me on the queen-sized bed. We both felt sure the end was near.

Tuesday, May 30th, 2000

About two o'clock that morning, Taylor moaned. Really moaned. I propped him up, injected extra morphine through the port in his arm, then called his home healthcare nurse, Sandra. She arrived at three.

Listening to his lungs, she searched to find his heart. It had moved. Fluid on the left side of his body not only stopped that lung, it also rudely shoved his heart over to the right. Pounding hard, it squeezed against the remaining portion of his small right lung. There it hammered at a frantic pace 130 times a minute. And his breath was extra wet.

"This is it," she said and upped the dose of morphine. Higher doses were supposed to calm the body down so that it didn't feel distress, especially from declining lung capacity.

Determined Taylor would not walk this walk, fight this fight alone, I got down on the floor, propped him up against my chest, put my arms around him. Dressed in a sleeveless shirt and running shorts, and Taylor in his eagle shirt, we were ready for a crossing I begged God would make easy.

At first it seemed he might. With enough morphine in his blood to kill a Belgian horse, Taylor's rapid pulse grew weaker as I felt it chest to chest. Throughout the night I whispered love things in his ear.

By noon, ten hours later, his breathing was interrupted by long pauses. Christopher, Debbie, and I (and by then two nurses) took turns, kissing Taylor, saying many times, "I love you! Anytime you're ready, go ahead. We will see you soon in Heaven."

Suddenly, at three that afternoon, Taylor insisted he sit up, even get up on one knee and lean atop his bed.

"Where am I?" he mumbled, confused. "Did I just come out of surgery?" He recognized that fuzzy feeling, one he always fought to escape, preferring clarity of thought.

"No, buddy," I replied. "Today is Tuesday. It's three o'clock in the afternoon. The reason you feel so groggy is because you've got a lot of morphine in your body to take away the pain. Don't worry. You're safe. I'm right here. So are Mom and Christopher. Sandra too."

"Huh." He plopped his head down, trying hard to process what he'd heard. He also got another dose of morphine. But refusing to lie down, he was determined to sit up, balancing with help.

Thirty minutes passed.

Suddenly he spoke, offended and alarmed.

"Wait a second," he commanded. "Am I dying?! I don't wanna die! Why does everyone want me to die?"

His clarity, his words, his understanding rocked every person in the room. Taylor was awake! He understood! He knew! He knew very, very well! And he was not a happy man. Instead the angry warrior roared. Up to this point for about twelve hours he'd heard a cacophony of voices. Many times they gently said, "I love you. You can go Home anytime you want. We will see you soon."

His mind was wide awake. It was his stupid body that wouldn't work the way he wanted. Still, on his own he figured out what was going on. But he didn't want to go! Why then was everyone telling him to leave?

"No one wants you to die, honey. No one. I don't want you to. But remember all we talked about? This is something that must happen. But you, *you,* are safe."

He muttered discontentedly, letting truth sink in, fighting hard to see, to comprehend, through the heavy haze of morphine.

And fight he did. With understanding came fierce anger and determination not to quit. Once again his heart started pounding hard. He would not give up the fight. He would never, *ever* quit.

Moments later Taylor turned to me with heavy-lidded eyes and said with horror, "Dad! I see hell!"

That's when my spirit roared, *ARRRRRRGH! God! NOOOOO!*

But what I said to Taylor in a soft but urgent voice was this: "Don't be fooled, my warrior-man. Don't be fooled. That. Is. *Not*. For. You! You know that God himself has gone there for you. You know he loves you. You know he's going to bring you safely Home. Do you hear me? Do you understand? Talk to me, buddy. Talk to me!"

"Yeah . . . but, Dad?" he wailed. "I feel like I'm falling! I'm scared! I don't know what to do! What'm I supposed to do? *Help me!*"

Again I spoke with urgency and passion. I poked his mind, his spirit. I made him think, helped him to remember. "Taylorman, I am here and I will not go away. I'm holding you right now. Can you feel my arms?" I lightly squeezed.

"Yeaaah," he said, hesitating, wondering what was next.

"Taylor, sweetheart, you are perfectly *safe*. I'm right here. So are Mom and Christopher. Best of all, Jesus is here too. *None* of us are going *anywhere*. And because we're here, *nothing* bad can happen to you. We simply will not let it. Do you hear me?"

"Uh-huh," he grunted through the grogginess.

"Now listen! Remember! *You* are *not* going to die. Jesus already did that for you. And because he did, all that lies ahead of you is life. *Life* and *life* alone!

"Can you hear me? Do you remember?"

"Um-hmmm," he hmmmed, as if trying to tune in but not getting a clear signal.

"Look, there're only two things you've got to do. The most important is to remember: You—are—loved. Then all you've got to do is go to sleep. Just go to sleep. After all, you can't wake up until you've gone to sleep!"

As he moaned in an apparent swoon, I summoned others in the house.

"From now on," I said, "Taylor hears one voice. Mine. The mixture of our different voices is scary and confusing inside his morphine haze. From here on out he hears just me. At least most of the time.

"If you have something you think Taylor needs to hear, tell me and I'll tell him. Or if you feel compelled to say something directly, you must get my permission. I will prob'ly say okay. But you've got to clear it first.

"This is the way it's gonna be," I growled. "Any questions?" Apparently there weren't.

Then I pulled Debbie aside and said, "Get on the phone—right now! Call all the people you know who are praying for Taylor. Tell them to *stop* praying for healing *here*. It's not gonna happen. God has made that clear.

"Stubborn prayers against God's plan for Taylor have left him open to attack. The only reason Taylor said he can see hell is because wrong-minded prayers have left him unprotected.

"It's his *spirit* that needs protection, strength, and help. *This* is what must be prayed for. Pass the word. Tell others to do the same. No exceptions. Got it?"

She agreed and hit the phone. And I went back to work.

For many, many hours Taylor fought with fear, repeating several times his questions, sometimes shouting out, "Where am I? What'm I supposed to do? Help me! Help me, now!"

Over and over I whispered in his ear, repeating answers that he knew. I coached and cheered him on.

"Taylorman, I love you. Mom loves you. Christopher and Jonathan love you. You know that, right?"

In a small and slightly doubtful voice, he answered, "Yes."

"And Jesus loves you. You know that too, don't you?"

In a different kind of tone, somewhat exasperated, Taylor whispered back, "Well, yeah!"—as if to say, *C'mon, Dad! Duh! Of course I know that!*

"Well then," I replied with a grin in my voice, "when you remember that you're loved, it's impossible to stay scared."

It took a while, but fear finally lost its grip. Still, he fought and fought and fought.

After the sun went down, Taylor began to thrash. While sitting, he threw his torso forward, face down and with incredible momentum. Or, lying at an angle on my chest, he sometimes flung his head toward the steel frame of the bed beside him.

Taylor never needed a firm scolding. All his soft heart ever needed was a gentle dose, two parts admonishment-correction mixed with ten parts love. As he thrashed, however, I used my firmest voice and barked, "Taylor, be still! BE STILL!"

Somehow that seemed to penetrate the haze and for a time he slumped in peace as I whispered with soft praise, "That's it. That's it. I love you, sweet boy. I love you . . ."

Then, after a time, he thrashed again. Once again I sang with two opposing tones, a *forte* verse and then a *piano* chorus, but still a single song. How odd.

"I've never seen anything like this," whispered Carol, a family friend and hospice nurse by profession. She came to relieve our weary friend, Sandra, taking a shift while Sandra went home to rest.

"Anyone else would have died hours ago," Carol continued. "But he is such a fighter!"

"That's my son," I bragged with tears. "That's my son!"

"This is where I really have a problem with *why,*" she continued. "Why does God allow this? Perhaps because it's easier to finally let them go? But I don't know. This is when I doubt."

"Hmmph," I hmmphed. "I'm way past doubt. Way, way past that."

For in my mind I screamed with horror, *Why! Why, God, why??? Has he not suffered enough?! Isn't it enough that he now must die??? Why must he suffer more? Why must this too be so horrific? Why? Why?? WHY???*

Sitting with my son, sweaty-smelly-unshaven-sore, I saw him fighting Hell itself on his way to Heaven. Pride and horror danced on the platform of my soul. How could this be? How could these two waltz as one?

Auschwitz. Bergen-Belsen. Dachau. Nazi prison camps flashed through my mind. And in my mind I swore, *Never again! Never again will I condemn a man or woman angry with God. I understand these people. They are my friends! I love them.*

Job's crushed and brokenhearted wife, mother of dead children, came to mind as well. Vilified for thousands of years, I cursed all who have condemned her. "Hypocrites! Arrogant fools! Would any of you have done differently? Can none of you understand? Are you blind? Or deaf? Or heartless? Or all of the above? I *understand* Job's wife! She is my *friend!* I *love* her!"

And Lord, I yelled with angry, silent words, *I too would curse you and die—right now. The only reason I refrain is for Taylor's sake. But when he's gone, what then? How can I go through this and still put my trust in you??? It would be one thing if you let this happen to me . . . But to do this to my son! . . .*

As I held Taylor close, his heart beating next to mine, my body both his bed and blanket, I grappled with God. As I wrestled endlessly, Taylor's terrifying questions, repeated many times, echoed in my soul . . .

What's happening to me?

Am I dying?

I don't want to die!

I'm falling! Help! Help! Help me quick, right now!

I see hell!

Why does everyone want me to die?

I'm scared. I'm so, so scared.

These questions, these terrifying fears, were not new. They were well known. They were, in fact, my own.

Could it be all the times I had screamed these things, *God* was holding *me*, shouting through the haze of my despair, "BE STILL! That's it. I love you. I'm here. Now, be still"? Just like I was doing with my precious son?

Late Tuesday night, close to Wednesday morning, Taylor was calm, resting on top of me as I lay back on Christopher's stuffed dog. Debbie slept on Taylor's bed beside me. Carol rested on the floor. Christopher, with Uncle Cliff and David, lounged on a couch and chairs downstairs. Jonathan was in his bed with Dempsey as companion.

Reading lights were off. All that bathed the room was the soft and twinkling red glow of Taylor's lava lamp—and some yellow light leaking through the bedroom door from the hallway just beyond it. Wide awake, acclimated to the darkened room, I watched.

Stairs creaked. Christopher appeared, quiet but very much awake.

He tiptoed into the room, looking puzzled. Putting his ear next to Taylor's CD speakers, he frowned. It was turned off. He walked back out into the hall, looked around, and tilted his head, perplexed.

Not wanting to wake Taylor, I caught his eyes and waved him over.

"What's wrong, buddy?" I whispered.

"Can't you hear it?" he asked.

"Hear what? I don't hear anything."

He hesitated, doubtful, maybe fearful too. "Angels, Dad! I hear angels singing!"

With hot and blurry eyes and through swallowed gasps, I whispered, "You do? What's it sound like, buddy? What's it sound like?"

"It's . . . *beautiful*," he said, his face transmitting awe.

While others slept, I watched while he listened. He heard what I could not. But what he heard was true, was real. It was a tiny glimpse of Taylor's fight from Heaven's point of view. It was a golden shaft of Light piercing through the horror.

My oldest son, just fourteen, also was a man. He was my companion through most of Taylor's battle. Fully engaged, he too embraced and faced head-on the ghastly sight of his brother's slow and agonizing death. He never looked away. He never ran. Bursting with grateful pride, I still worried this event might kill his spirit just like it might murder mine.

"Christopher," I whispered after time had passed, "always remember this. Always. This is a gift from God for you to carry and to help you all your life. And because you were brave enough to tell me, it was a gift from God to me as well."

Wednesday, May 31ˢᵗ, 2000

"Hey, Taylor," I whispered in his ear shortly after midnight, "it's Wednesday warrior-man! I love you! And I'm so proud of you!"

Hours passed. The cycle slowed but didn't quit.

Taylor sometimes thrashed. I commanded, "BE STILL!" He always slumped, obedient. And I always whispered the chorus, "That's it, sweetie. I love you. I love you!"

At 4 A.M., while all around me slept, I kept watch, holding Taylor, wide awake. Suddenly I heard a voice, crystal clear, not slurry—young and healthy, not worn out at all. It said, "Taylor."

The voice was Taylor's own. And I knew that intonation. It was the way he shyly answered when a kindly grownup asked, "Hey there, soldier. What's your name?"

Oh, Jesus! I cried out from my spirit, *let it be you or your angel— however you do this. Please go ahead and take him Home. Oh God, please!*

Then, in the same clear voice, I heard Taylor say, "Bye!" This time the song of his voice added a regretful "Okay!" as if responding to the words, "All right, Taylor. Hang in there. I'll be back soon."

No! Don't go! I begged with unsaid words.

Was Taylor delusional?

Moments later he thrashed again, almost hitting his head on the metal bed frame only inches away.

"BE STILL!" I once again commanded. As he slumped, he spoke, once again with clarity.

"I'm sorry, Dad!" he clearly spoke with mystified regret. "I don't know what's wrong with me. I just can't help myself."

"Oh, buddy, buddy, buddy. It's okay. Do you hear me? It's okay. I love you. I just don't want you to hurt your head. But I love you, I love you. And I'm proud of you. So very, very proud."

He fell asleep without an answer.

About an hour later Taylor spoke again, pleading, insisting, "I've gotta sit up, Dad! I've gotta sit up!"

"I know you do, buddy. Let's do it."

Sitting on a pillow, his torso stayed upright as, from behind him, I held him steady with my left arm draped across his chest. In my right hand was the telephone. Sandra was preparing to return for another shift, relieving Carol. I whispered in the phone the kinds of meds we needed, rejecting some I knew from past experience did not work for Taylor. All of us were prepared for more battle. Taylor's pulse and respirations were no less alarming than fifty-two hours before. But no more disturbing either.

After hanging up the phone, I added my right arm to the left, holding on to Taylor as he sat. I made a decision. But before I could speak, I heard Taylor say, "Hi!"

His voice was cheerful, clear, and young.

"Hey, buddy!" I responded from habit, then realized he spoke with the same voice I'd heard about an hour earlier when he said his name followed with a "Bye!" Was Taylor, once again, talking with someone only he could hear and see?

This time, however, I didn't dwell on it. Instead I whispered in his ear, "Listen, buddy. I'm gonna get up for a few minutes, shave, and take a shower. Mom is right here, and Carol will hold you up, okay?"

"Mmm-hmm . . ."

After ruffling his hair, slowly, stiffly, I stood up. Carol softly held Taylor's head against her breast.

"Thank you, Carol. I'll be right back."

Walking into our master bedroom I pulled off my smelly sleeveless shirt then in slow motion moved toward the bathroom sink. Looking in the mirror, I saw a hairy, gray, and scrubby stranger. His bloodshot eyes looked straight back, drunk with grief and anger and despair. But determination too. I might abandon God after this was over, but I would *never* abandon my son.

(. . . *Just like I will* never *abandon you* . . .)

Debbie rushed into the room. "Carol says to come! Right now! Hurry!"

"Get Christopher," I told her and softly shouted for him down the stairs. "He made me promise we would call him too." Shirtless, I fled back to Taylor's side.

He had, at last, been summoned. Taylorman was going Home. His breathing was peaceful. Gentle. Halting. Slow.

Debbie, Christopher, and I crouched round him in a semicircle. We whispered enthusiastic cheers.

"I love you, Taylorman! I am so proud of you! Well done! Well done! Well done, indeed! We will see you soon! I love you! I love you! Well done! Well done! Well done!"

As we spoke, one last time Taylor broke through the haze. His eyes lit up with a twinkle. His mouth curved upward in his famous Mona Lisa smile. Then, with mischievous joy etched upon his face, he exhaled his broken body's final breath.

As he did, sunlight broke the eastern sky. And the bulb inside his sparkling lava lamp burned out.

The battle was over.

The cancer was dead.

But the dragon was defeated.

And my wounded warrior son had *won*.

No longer on the dam road, he was safely Home.

And free.

49   TAYLOR GOES HOME

THE MORNING TAYLOR DIED I PICKED UP THE VACANT body and put it on his bed, the echo of his smile still etched upon its face. For the first time since the pelvic tumor had returned, I placed my open palm underneath, fingers wide, and felt the dead invader.

Hard as a rock, the obscene growth filled up my hand. I knew it had expanded but had no idea it had grown so large, so hard, as if exposed to Medusa's very face.

"Oh, buddy, buddy, buddy. How much you suffered! How much more than I ever knew . . ."

I finally shaved and showered. There were miles to go before I slept. There was work to do.

A couple hours later two men drove up in their boxy limousine. Dark, ill-fitting suits hung awkwardly from mortal frames crowned by tired, mournful faces. When they saw our steep stairway, they worried. How would they secure the body on the pallet so that it would not fall?

Seeing their predicament I said, "Please, let me."

And so, underneath Taylor's broken, precious frame, I put one arm beneath his leg, the other below his neck and shoulder. Bending my knees, I picked up the blond-haired, smiling corpse and carried it down-stairs, out the door, down more steps, then placed it on the stretcher in our driveway. Before the sheet, the shroud, was made to cover up the face, I once again inhaled deep the still-sweet scent of Taylor through his hair. I slowly kissed the forehead of where he used to live, then let the body go.

Determined to pass the news to our vast e-mail family, I drove to the office and wrote . . .

A TAYLOR AND FAMILY REPORT

Wednesday, May 31st, 2000

So much has happened in the past six days, I could write a book just about this short part of Taylor's battle.

For now, I can only tell you that as his body declined, his spirit shined brighter and brighter. It was so brilliant, everyone who saw it was stunned, amazed—and this is *not* hyperbole.

At 5:15 this morning, it appeared Taylor's Last Battle could easily continue many hours. I went to take a break but within a minute was called back.

Thankfully, thankfully, Taylor was, at last, going Home.

Since then, I've wondered . . . when I finally left his side in utter weariness-despair, was Taylor in some way released to come and fetch me? Even as he himself laid hold of life that is life indeed, an event that occurred at about 5:30 this morning?

As I write these few words, Taylor is in Heaven. And he's learning the turf on two strong legs in a brand-new body, radically healed.

He's with family, friends, and unknown thousands, even millions, of heavenly fans.

Because of his faith, more precious than life, his reward is immense.

And now he knows the answers to his many, many questions about Heaven. (At the very least, he is now the pro compared to my desperate status as a wannabe.)

But best of all, he's in the loving presence of Y'shua, the Author and Finisher of Taylor's faith. In Y'shua's embrace and compared with his praise, even the glories of Heaven are pale.

For now, however, let me shut up and give you information about the funeral. . . .

Last of all . . .

Please consider singing "Happy Birthday" to Taylor this coming Sunday, June 4th. That's when he turns twelve. His celebration there, I am convinced, will be an awesome bash, thoroughly organized, I think, by his thrilled aunt Cindy and grandma Belon. And without a single absentee from his many, many peers who have, themselves, valiantly preceded him.

One more thing, I guess . . .

On this Sunday, June 4th, do *something* special to honor Taylor's God. For apart from him, Taylor's life, and the glory of his life, would have been impossible.

And so for me, and for Debbie too, we are . . .

> blessed with a wound that will not,
> blessed with a wound that *must not* ever heal; and
> blessed with the eternal privilege of being
> Taylor's dad and mom.

Well done, our hero son. Well done, indeed.
If God makes a way, I will write your story.
But right now I really need a nap . . .

Dad (Brian)

Husband to Debbie; Dad to Taylor, 11.99; also Dad to Christopher, 14.54, and Jonathan, 6.79. And still reluctant guardian of Dempsey the grieving boxer.

Hey, buddy! God made a way! He let me tell your story.

O God! Let this book be the seed that Taylor never had. Let it be a mighty seed planted in the fertile womb of your living Spirit. Let it multiply and grow and bear him countless children as you yourself have promised.

THE END

Hey! Wait a second, Dad! That's not the end! You've gotta tell the rest!

But, buddy, while I know the vision is true, I also know it's not perfect.

So what?! It is so, so close, you've gotta tell it. Pleeeeeease, sweet wonderful Daddy, best Daddy in the whole entire world?!

Ha! How can I say no to that?!

Okay . . . here it comes . . . Sir Taylor and the King . . .

Yabba-dabba-dooooo!

EPILOGUE

SIR TAYLOR AND THE KING

THIS IS A TRUE STORY. EVEN THOUGH IT STARTS LIKE this . . .

Once upon a time . . .

There was a preteen boy who fought a huge and evil fire-breathing dragon, including the dragon's army horde. Although it often seemed the preteen boy fought all alone, he really did have Help. Help that was, at first, invisible. But while he couldn't see it, Help was always there. And Help was very, very strong.

It was the dragon who started the fight. He attacked the boy with a secret weapon—the Mutha and her ugly, ruthless litter. The Mutha and her juvenile delinquents were an especially wicked kind of cancer. Over time, the boy was bloodied and disfigured. He even lost a leg and hip.

But he never, ever quit the fight. In just two years, the boy became a man. And more! Still imperfect, flawed and mortal, just like you and I, he became a mighty warrior. After fighting the dragon again and again, there grew a furrow in his brow. It came from pain and red-hot anger. It came from thoughts like this:

How dare this evil thing attack my body! How dare it try to eat my soul! It cannot win! It will not!

In times like these, from his eyes and mouth, and even from his many wounds, an almost blinding light broke through. For behind the banged-up armor, beneath the wounded skin, there was a growing spirit the dragon could not conquer.

It was the kind of spirit that no cancer, even with an army, and no dragon, no matter how strong, could ever kill. The boy's spirit could be wounded. It could be hurt. But it could not ever die. And it would not ever quit.

The enemy attacked. Again. Again. Again. Over and over again. Impotent with rage, the dragon and his horde surrounded the boy-knight. They roared and roared and roared! Horrible sounds! Terrible smells! Frightening cries!

And in the middle of it all, almost all alone, the boy-knight stood on just one leg, not even twelve years old. But still he stood and fought and fought and fought. Although he wobbled and he hopped (in order to keep his balance), the boy stood firm and never, ever quit. Even though it seemed he fought alone, he really did have Help. But at the time it didn't seem like much.

Cheering him on, trying to help him stand—and understand—was the boy-knight's squire-dad. If he could have, he would have stepped right in and taken the boy's place. But it was not allowed . . . because, in the truest sense, Someone Else had already done that very thing.

Still, because of love, forged in the heat of many, many battles, the squire-dad was allowed to stand beside his son while he fought and fought and fought. With scalding burns, ugly whiskers, smelly breath and armpits, the squire-dad could only do three things. He coached and coaxed his boy-knight warrior. He also prayed and prayed and prayed.

The boy's last battle was, indeed, horrific. But it was awesome too! After three long days of rage that never stopped—all of a sudden, the dragon horde saw they couldn't win. The Mutha and her killing bully brood were losing! The knight by his fight was destroying them!

And so the dragon horde, not wanting to be captured but enraged at their defeat, gave up and ran away. As he saw the dragon run and cancer dying at his feet, the boy-knight was still standing. But now he did so on two legs!

The bloody, fiery battleground on which he had been fighting turned into an arena. It was at least a mile high and brighter than ten suns. And as he stood, unmoving, the appalling sounds of battle turned into thunderous applause and cheers. On every side were countless witnesses gleaming in the light, millions who stood and stomped and roared in unison, "Tay-lor! Tay-lor! Tay-lor!"

At first the boy was stunned, confused. He squeezed his eyes shut tight.

I'm on two legs and feel great! he thought in disbelief. *Is the battle over? Am I still alive?*

At last he bowed his head and took a peek. At his feet he saw an almost ghostly thing. It was a shell, a husk—like a hologram. It looked sad. But it was real. It was the boy's old body, the cocoon where he had lived. Until today. He was moving out. The boy-knight took a rich, deep breath in the Place he stood and noticed that it made the shell below take a tiny gasp.

Cool! he thought and tried again. Just barely, he still could make the old shell move.

Then he noticed something else. All around the husk, the place he now was leaving, were Dad and Mom and Christopher, and Jonathan close by. Like a distant echo, faint but clear, the boy heard each one say through tears, "I love you, Taylorman! I'm proud of you! See you soon!"

Heart touched by their grief, the boy cupped his mouth and

shouted, "I'm okay! I love you, Mom! I love you, Christopher! I love you, Jonathan!"

Then to his squire-dad (with whom he had a special bond) he cried again, "I love you, Dad, me-mad-me-fi-fo-fad!"

His dad responded! Could he hear?

"Well done, buddy! Well done, my warrior son! Well done, well done, indeed!"

Desperate now to comfort those he loved, the boy-knight raised his eyes for help. As he did the stadium grew silent, breathless, as the mighty King himself strolled, step by step, step by step, toward the new boy-man.

"Hey, Dad!" the boy-knight shouted, looking down at him again. "It's the King! I know it's he—I can see his hands and feet! Here he comes! Look! Look!! Look!!!"

Silently, the King reached out and took the boy-knight in his arms. The boy-knight hugged him back in silent wonderment. *I know that hug, those tears!* he thought. *I know that hand stroking my head! They're just like Dad's . . . only better . . . even better!*

Then, at last, the King spoke:

Behold, My knight
wounded no more!
By faith he fought!
By faith he stands!
By faith he wins the Prize!

My family and My friends,
it is My honor to present
no longer a boy-knight

but now, a man among men,
a prince in My Kingdom!

Holding up his hand, the crowd held back its cheers while the King turned and looked Prince Taylor in the eye. Seeing Taylor's soul, knowing Taylor's heart, the King composed and then performed one last mighty sober verse.

As for Our prince's squire-Dad,
now himself an amputee,
wounded like My Father
with worse wars yet to come,
he is hereby be-knighted,
now squired by the love and prayers
by this, his princely son.

Glancing at Prince Taylor then turning to the crowd again, the King cried out with joy,

Welcome, Prince Taylor!
Now all . . . Welcome Taylor Home!

And there erupted such a cheer, such a shout of happiness and joy, all Heaven shook with its jubilant vibration. When at last his smile erupted, dazzling with delight, there was an echo of it in the shell below. Then, stepping forward, chrysalis gone, came Prince Taylorman!

Perfect face. Perfect form. Perfect balance too. Clothed in light with golden hair, his eyes were laser blue—though with those perfect eyes he could not see his head or face. (Of course not—there wasn't any mirror.)

Accepting the King's invitation, Prince Taylor jumped up on a skateboard-ski tied behind the King's own chariot. Hitched at the front there stood a large white horse, quivering with awesome strength, wild and untamable to all except the King.

Suddenly, without a warning, off they went! Not straight, not flat, but up and to the right. Spinning off the stadium's top edge with a double twist, Prince Taylor caught a cosmic wave created by the pull.

"That's one horsepower?" Taylor teased.

"Yes," the King laughed, "and I am it!" as Prince Taylor flipped and twirled and swirled. He bounced off stars, spun up and through black holes, caught "air" off mogul galaxies. Sometimes he skirted outside the wake then jumped back in, cutting to and from tiny slices of countless dimensions, places full of mysteries to solve and time enough to solve them, wild frontier lands someday to explore and perhaps to tame.

Prince Taylor whooped it up with his Friend, with the King of kings. They shouted and they laughed. They smiled and they played.

Together forever, there wasn't any rush. Instead, enjoying the ride, they took their time . . . and rode the long way Home.

So, is that better?

Yes! Thank—you—Da-ad!

You're welcome, buddy . . . Good night! I love you! See you in the morning!

See you in the morning! Good night! I love you too!

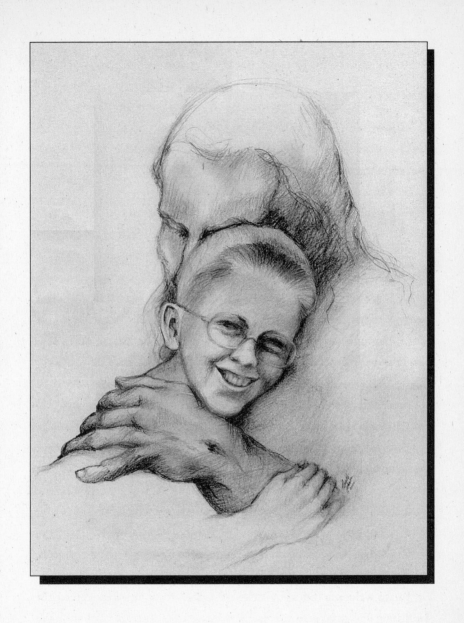

SIR TAYLOR AND THE KING

THE AUTHOR
PROPOSES A TOAST

FIRST OF ALL, DEAR READER, I LIFT MY GLASS AND propose a toast to us. The very fact you're reading this means I am not alone: through agony and ecstacy, through joy and sorrow deep, you too have made the trip with me, walking Taylor Home. By his faith, Taylor's safe. By faith, that is, in God's wounded warrior Son who died for him . . . for you . . . for me. By his death he paid the debt we owe. And by his resurrection he is alive today, in the flesh, as God the wounded warrior King of kings, His Majesty, Y'shua. May you and I embrace by faith this priceless gift, just as Taylor did, so that we too may know, even here high up on the dam road in the middle of the storm, we belong to God. And that no matter what, he will bring us safely Home just as he did Taylor.

Together now we raise our glasses high to all who fought beside us during Taylor's two-year war. To medical professionals, countless troops of doctors, nurses, aides, housekeepers, and volunteers; to Vanderbilt Children's Hospital and the National Cancer Institute, to all who make these institutions work from the bottom to the top; to untold thousands here in Middle Tennessee who selflessly embraced our family as their own; to an unknown host of people all around the world who read e-mail reports and responded with their priceless gifts of love; especially to children who poured out their hearts in letters, cards, gifts, and prayers; especially to Taylor's best friends—to Trey, Ashton, Matthew, Perry, Chris, Tyler, Matt . . .

To each of you, may you know, know in your heart of hearts these things: you are known and loved by name; you are precious to our family. Your prayers, your treatments, and your love did not lead to loss. Instead through them God himself touched Taylor, making him a mighty man who simply grew too grand to fit here anymore. Because of all God did through you, Taylor did not lose. He won. When his body died the cancer was defeated. But Taylor, Taylor stood, and stands today, on two strong legs, very much alive. May you always know God's healing touch brought to you through Taylor.

A special toast to W Publishing Group, to all the people there, to editors, executives, support staff, and typesetters, to everyone in marketing from artists to each mighty sales soldier, all of whom took the chance to forever stand with humble pride for publishing this work. May your risky faith be vindicated one thousandfold and more.

To friends from God who have stood close since Taylor left for Home: Bonnie, Sheila, Terry, Cliff, and Larry; and to all who staked their names and reputations on endorsing this true story: may you know ten thousandfold God's comfort and encouragement—as he through you has given me.

Last of all, by name, to Yahweh, to Y'shua, to the Father and the Son: I pledge to you eternal thanks and praise for letting me take part in the holy horror of your loving heart by choosing me to be the dad of one of heaven's heroes. So be it.